INVENTORY OF THE COUNTY ARCHIVES OF TEXAS

No. 181 Orange County (Orange)

WPA Records

Prepared by
The Texas Historical Records Survey
Division of Community Service Programs
Work Projects Administration

The University of Texas, Official Sponsor

Bureau of Research in the Social Sciences
The University of Texas, State-wide Co-Sponsor

Heritage Books
2024

HERITAGE BOOKS

AN IMPRINT OF HERITAGE BOOKS, INC.

Books, CDs, and more—Worldwide

For our listing of thousands of titles see our website
at
www.HeritageBooks.com

A Facsimile Reprint
Published 2024 by
HERITAGE BOOKS, INC.
Publishing Division
5810 Ruatan Street
Berwyn Heights, MD 20740

San Antonio, Texas
Texas Historical Records Survey
December 1941

International Standard Book Number
Paperbound: 978-0-7884-7758-4

To bring together the records of the past and to house them
in buildings where they will be preserved for the use of men
living in the future, a nation must believe in three things.
It must believe in the past. It must believe in the future.
It must, above all, believe in the capacity of its people so
to learn from the past that they can gain in judgment for the
creation of the future.

                                        Franklin Delano Roosevelt

FOREWORD

The Inventory of the County Archives of Texas is one of a number of guides to historical materials prepared throughout the United States by workers on Historical Records Survey projects of the Work Projects Administration. The publication herewith presented, an inventory of the archives of Orange County, is number 181 of the Texas series.

The Historical Records Survey program was undertaken in the winter of 1935-36 for the purpose of providing useful employment to needy unemployed historians, lawyers, teachers, and research and clerical workers. In carrying out this objective, the project was organized to compile inventories of historical materials, particularly the unpublished government documents and records which are basic in the administration of local governments, and which provide invaluable data for students of political, economic, and social history. The archival guide herewith presented is intended to meet the requirements of day-to-day administration by the officials of the county, and also the needs of lawyers, businessmen, and other citizens who require facts from the public records for the proper conduct of their affairs. The volume is so designed that it can be used by the historian in his research in unprinted sources in the same way he uses the library card catalog for printed sources.

The inventories produced by the Historical Records Survey projects attempt to do more than give merely a list of records - they attempt further to sketch in the historical background of the county or other unit of government, and to describe precisely and in detail the organization and functions of the government agencies whose records they list. The county, town, and other local inventories for the entire country will, when completed, constitute an encyclopedia of local government as well as a bibliography of local archives. Up to the present time approximately 1,400 publications have been issued by the Survey in the country as a whole.

The successful conclusion of the work of the Historical Records Survey projects, even in a single county, would not be possible without the support of public officials, historical and legal specialists, and many other groups in the community. Their cooperation is gratefully acknowledged.

The Survey program was organized by Luther H. Evans, who served as Director until March 1, 1940, when he was succeeded by Sargent B. Child. The Survey operates as a Nation-wide series of locally sponsored projects in the Division of Community Service Programs, of which Mrs. Florence Kerr, Assistant Commissioner, is in charge.

HOWARD O. HUNTER
Commissioner of
Work Projects

PREFACE

The Texas Historical Records Survey is a unit of the State-wide Records Indexing and Inventory Program, co-sponsored by the Bureau of Research in the Social Sciences of The University of Texas. This program is a part of the State-wide Clerical Research and Records Project, sponsored by The University of Texas, which operates under the Reasearch and Records Programs Section of the Division of Community Service Programs of the Work Projects Administration.

The objective of the Survey in Texas is the preparation of complete inventories of the archives of each county, municipality, and other local governmental unit.

This publication, an inventory of the archives of Orange County, includes, in addition to descriptive entries for each extant records series, a historical sketch of the county and a map of its past and present boundaries; an essay on the present governmental organization, accompanied by a structural chart; a discussion of the conditions under which the records are preserved, accompanied by floor plans of the courthouse; and a brief statement of the legal status of each office and agency, prefatory to the listing of its records.

The Survey is now engaged in preparing a comprehensive statement of the general law regulating county government, to be entitled "County Government in Texas." It is expected that this book will serve as a handbook on the organization, structure, and evolution of county government and records in Texas, and will make it unnecessary to repeat in each inventory information applicable to all counties in the State. The office essays in this inventory are, therefore, limited to the creation of the office and its present status, the manner in which it is filled, the term, and special legislation affecting Orange County. Pending issuance of the volume on county government in Texas, it is suggested that the reader consult the Inventory of the County Archives of Texas, No. 94, Guadalupe County for more detailed essays than those found in the present inventory.

The Inventory of the County Archives of Texas will, when completed, consist of a separate volume for each county of the State. Each unit of the series is numbered according to the particular county's respective position in the alphabetical list of the 254 counties. Thus, the volume for Orange County, herewith presented, is number 181. Units of the inventory are issued in mimeographed form for free distribution to State and local public officials, public libraries in Texas, and to a limited number of libraries and governmental agencies outside the State. <u>See</u> page 177, this inventory, for a list of the publications of the Texas Historical Records Survey Project.

The records of Orange County were inventoried during 1936-37, and after the move to the new courthouse the inventory forms were rechecked in 1939. A complete verification check was made in the summer of 1940. The volume was compiled and edited in the State office of the project.

The courteous cooperation of the Orange County officials, for whom this work was done, is acknowledged.

December 29, 1941   The Editors

ABBREVIATIONS, SYMBOLS, AND EXPLANATORY NOTES

Abbreviations and Symbols

alph. . . . . alphabetical(ly)
approx. . . . . approximate(ly)
arr. . . . . arranged, arrangement
art(s). article(s)
aver. . . . . average
bsmt. . . . . basement
c.c. county clerk
CCP . . . . Code of Criminal Procedure
C. E. . . . . Civil Engineer
ch(s). chapter(s)
chron. . . . . chronological(ly)
comp. . . . . compiler
Const. . . . . Constitution of Texas
C.S. . . . . called session
dbl. . . . . double
d.c. . . . . district clerk
ed. . . . . editor
_et al._ . . . . _et alii_, _et aliae_ (and others)
et seq. _et sequentes_, _et sequentia_, (and the following)
f.b. file box(es)
f.d. . . . . file drawer(s)
fl. . . . . floor
fm. . . . . form(s)
Gam. Laws . . . . _Gammel's Laws of Texas_
H.B. House Bill
hd. . . . . head, headings
hdw. . . . . handwritten
HRS . . . . Historical Records Survey
ibid. . . . . _ibidem_, in the same place
j.p. . . . . justice of peace
Leg. . . . . Texas Legislature
n.d. . . . . no date
no(s). number(s)
numer. . . . . numerical(ly)
off. . . . . office
passim . . . . here and there
p(p). . . . . page(s)
PC . . . . Penal Code
pr. . . . . printed
pt(s). . . . . part(s)
PWA . . . . Public Works Administration
RCS . . . . Revised Civil Statutes
rm. . . . . room

sec(s).	section(s)
ser.	series
shff.	sheriff
sic.	thus; it is so
s.s.	county school superintendent
sub(s).	subdivision(s)
SW	Southwestern Reporter
t.a.c.	tax assessor-collector
Tex.	Texas Supreme Court Reports
treas.	county treasurer
v.	versus
va.	vault
Vernon's Texas St. 1936	Vernon's Texas Statutes, Centennial Edition, 1936
Vernon's Texas St. 1939 Supp.	Vernon's Texas Statutes, Centennial Edition, 1939 Supplement
vol(s).	volume(s)
WPA	Work Projects Administration
x.	by
--	placed after date means from that year on
&	and
&c	and so forth

Explanatory Notes

Titles of Records. Exact titles of records are written in solid capitals without parentheses (as in entry 2). In the absence of titles, descriptive titles have been assigned, which are written in solid capitals and enclosed in parentheses (as in entry 3). If a record title is not descriptive of the contents of the record, an assigned explanatory title (or explanatory words), written with initial capitals and enclosed in parentheses, has been added (as in entry 16). The current or most recent title of a record is used as the entry title, and title variation is indicated (as in entry 1).

Dates. All dates used are inclusive. Missing records are indicated by broken dates.

Quantity. When two or more types of containers are considered in a single entry, the quantity is shown in chronological order, insofar as possible.

Labeling. Figures or letters in parentheses, following the number of volumes, file boxes, or other type of containers, indicate the labeling. If no labeling is indicated, it may be assumed that there is none.

Discontinuance. Where no statement is made that the record was discontinued at the last date shown in the entry, it could not be definitely established that such was the case. Where no comment is made on the absence of prior, subsequent, or intermediate records, no definite information could be obtained.

Description of Records. The description of the contents of a record applies only to the current or most recent record unless change in contents is actually shown in a record entry.

Indexing. All indexes to records, unless otherwise stated, are self-contained.

Condition of Records. Records are in good condition unless otherwise indicated.

Dimensions. Dimensions are always given in inches, unless otherwise indicated, and, therefore, the symbol for inches (") is omitted.

Location of Records. All records are in the county courthouse unless otherwise noted in the entries. When all or the majority of the records of an office have a common location, the location is indicated in the last sentence of the office essay instead of in each individual entry.

Cross References. Title-line cross references are used to show the continuity of a record series which has been kept separately for a period of time and with other records for different periods of time. An example is that in entry 411: "1939-- in Outstanding Bonds Sinking Fund Bonds Sinking Fund Cash, entry 425." They are also used in all artificial entries - those set up to cover records which must be shown separately under their proper office even though they are kept in files or records described elsewhere in the inventory, as in entry 109, or in those set up for a record which is never kept separately but is found in two or more records of miscellaneous content, such as entry 13. In both instances, the description of the master entry (entry of miscellaneous content) shows the title and entry number of the record from which the cross reference is made, as, for example, these words in entry 3 do: "Also contains: Public school land applications, 1916-27, entry 109." Dates shown in the description of the master entry are only for the part or parts of the record contained therein, and are shown only when they vary from those of the master entry.

TABLE OF CONTENTS

General

County Offices and Their Records

Table of Contents

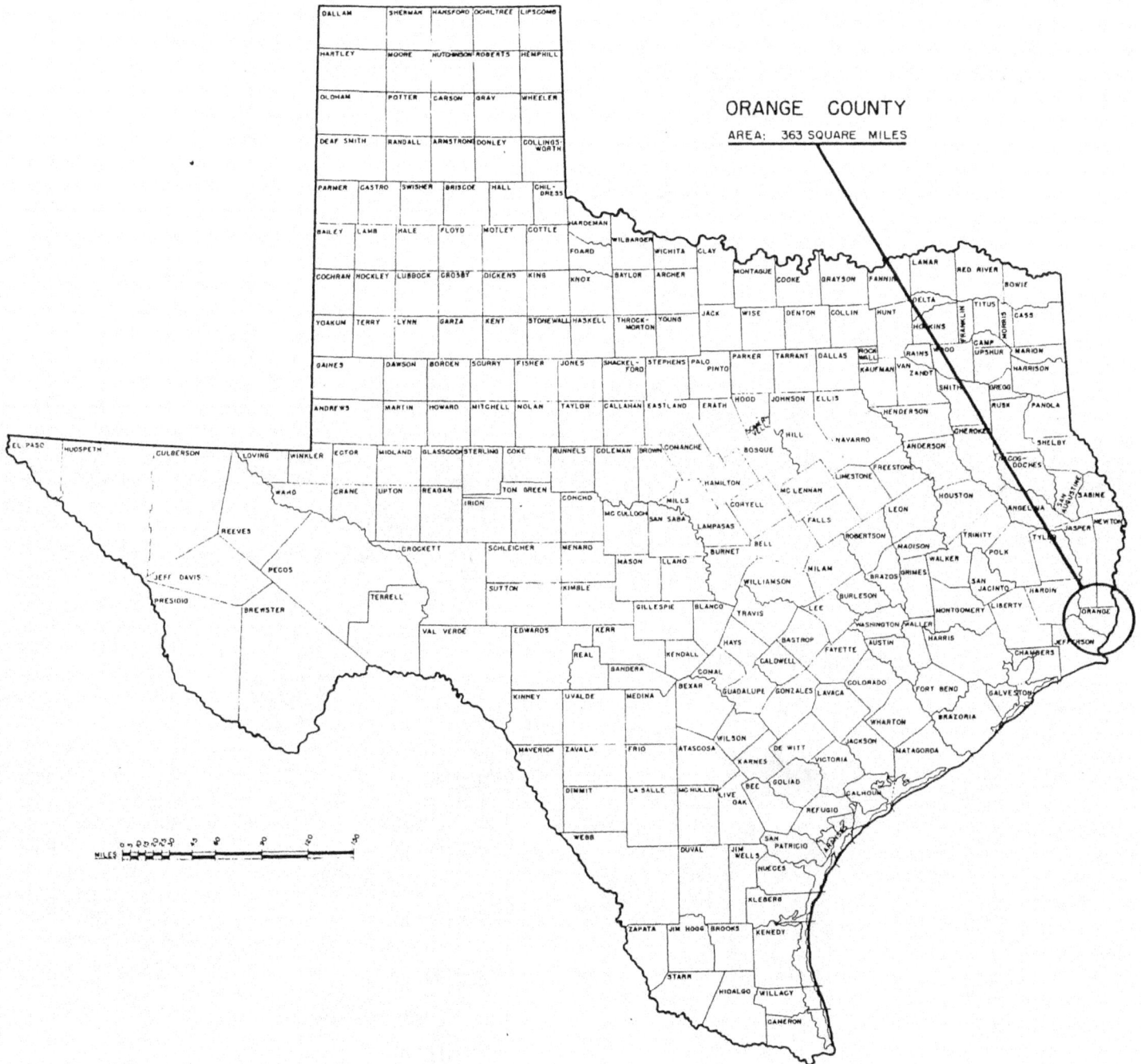

ORANGE COUNTY

AREA: 363 SQUARE MILES

TYLER

JASPER NEWTON

HARDIN

KOUNTZE

SILSBEE

EVADALE

BUNA

DEWEYVILLE

HARTBURG

SABINE RIVER

PINE ISLAND BAYOU

NECHES

WEST FORK

GRAYBURG

TEXLA LEMONVILLE

MAURICEVILLE

Cow Bayou
Settlement
(Patillo's P.O.)

VIDOR

Niblett's
Bluff

Ballew's
Ferry

GRATIS

ORANGE

COW BAYOU

BEAUMONT

TERRY

GILLA

Duncan's
Woods

ORANGE
(Madison)

Green's
Bluff

AMELIA

CHINA

HOME

LIBERTY

RIVER

PORT NECHES

FANNETT

JEFFERSON

TAYLOR BAYOU

BAYOU

PORT
ARTHUR

SABINE LAKE

WINNIE

STOWELL

SABINE PASS

CHAMBERS

SALT BAYOU

SABINE PASS

SABINE PASS

SABINE

LOUISIANA

INTRACOASTAL CANAL

HIGH
ISLAND

EAST BAY

PENINSULA

BOLIVAR

GULF OF MEXICO

N

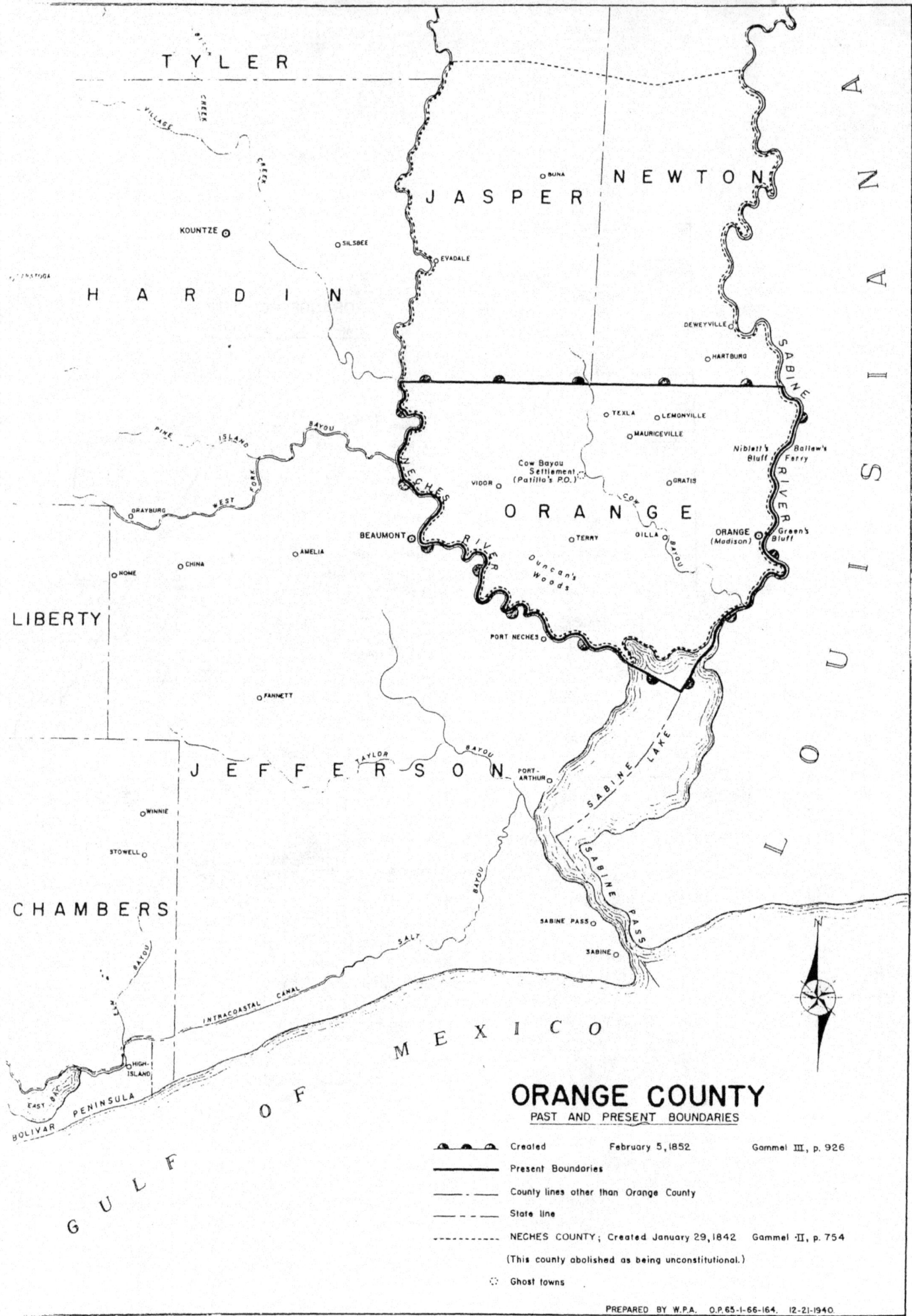

ORANGE COUNTY
PAST AND PRESENT BOUNDARIES

Created   February 5, 1852   Gammel III, p. 926

Present Boundaries

County lines other than Orange County

State line

NECHES COUNTY; Created January 29, 1842   Gammel II, p. 754

(This county abolished as being unconstitutional.)

Ghost towns

PREPARED BY W.P.A.   O.P. 65-1-66-164.   12-21-1940.

1. HISTORICAL SKETCH

Physical Characteristics

The history of Orange County is essentially the story of the utilization and development of the natural resources of the region. For more than a century agriculture, lumbering, and shipping have been the chief occupations of the inhabitants. The county lies on the fertile coastal prairies of southeast Texas, where alluvial and sandy soils produce abundant crops. It is heavily timbered with long- and short-leaf pine, cypress, oak, gum, ash, magnolia, and hickory trees. The Sabine River on the east and the Neches on the southwest provide waterways on two sides.

Historical Background

Long before French and Spanish explorers first entered this country, the cannibal Attacapa Indians inhabited the region of present Orange County. Their village was on the east bank of the Neches. While the men hunted and fished, women of the tribe cultivated fields of maize.[1]

The first white settlers in the region were probably French traders and trappers, who moved into the Attacapa country after the establishment of New Orleans in 1718. Contraband goods were bartered for horses, hides, furs, and corn.[2] About the time Louisiana came under the active rule of Spain, Acadian exiles were sent to make their homes among the Attacapa, and it is possible that some settled in the lower Neches-Sabine region.[3]

Following the Louisiana Purchase in 1803, Spain and the United States recognized a narrow buffer strip east of the Sabine as neutral ground.[4] But it was not until after Mexico won her independence from Spain in 1821 that Anglo-Americans began to hew their cabin clearings in the big woods of present Orange County. In the early 1820's a boatman named Green was navigating the Sabine River, and using a landing called Green's Bluff, at the present site of the city of Orange. About 1824 Bob Johnson and his wife moved across the Sabine from Louisiana and settled near the

---

1. Frederick Webb Hodge, Handbook of American Indians North of Mexico, pt. I, p. 114; Herbert Eugene Bolton, Texas in the Middle Eighteenth Century, p. 334, and map opposite p. 350.
2. Herbert Eugene Bolton, Athanase de Mezieres and the Louisiana-Texas Frontier, 1768-1780, I, 30, 31.
3. France ceded Louisiana to Spain by the secret treaty of Fontainebleau in 1762, but the cession was not announced in Louisiana until October 1764, and the Spanish Governor did not arrive until 1765. Alcee Fortier, A History of Louisiana, I, 142-144, 148, 153, 159.
4. The Texas Almanac for 1936, p. 84.

landing.[5] At the same time, James, Absolm, John, and Jane Jett settled
in the low country a short distance west of the Sabine.[6]

David and Jacob Garner settled at Green's Bluff in 1825. In October
1830 John Harmon, his wife Elizabeth, and their children came down the
Sabine on a great raft to Green's Bluff. Harmon went ashore with his
rifle and shot a turkey and a fat deer. The family then debarked and
settled.[7] About 12 miles due west of Green's Bluff, on the bank of Cow
Bayou, in the vicinity of the present town of Terry, another community
grew up.[8] Its leading citizen was George A. Pattillo, who arrived in
1830, with James Pattillo, David Cole, W. H. Hodges; and Benjamin, Sarah,
and Stephen Jett.[9]

The woods were at first considered enemies by these early settlers,
who toiled to clear small farms on which to raise grain. Before long,
however, many discovered that the virgin woodlands afforded more lucrative employment than livestock raising and farming. With crosscut saw,
froe, and mallet they set to work cutting shingles to be transported to
Galveston. This was the beginning of a great lumber industry.[10]

Other settlers in the meanwhile pushed westward to the Neches. In
the early 1820's Gilbert Stephenson, with "gun, shot pouch, powder horn,
and piece of punk" had made his camp on that stream. He soon crossed the
river to settle in present Jefferson County,[11] but others of his family -
William, John, John, Jr., James, Warren, Elijah, Louise, and Eva - settled
on the east bank. They were closely followed by David Burrell, John Cole,
Isaac and Bradley Garner, Jr., David Harmon, Joshua Cole, O. H. Deleno,
Jeramiah Day, and William, James, and Jessie Dyson.[12]

In 1829 the Mexican Government authorized Don Lorenzo de Zavala to
introduce 500 families into a vast East Texas area embracing, as a small

---

5. A. F. Burns, "Bob Johnson Family, Which Furnished 2 Sheriff's (sic)
    for Orange County, Came Here in Early '20's of 18th (sic) Century,"
    Orange (Tex.) Leader, May 29, 1936.
6. "Names of Persons Living in Orange County Area in 1836 Are Found in
    Various Land Transaction Records," Orange (Tex.) Leader, May 29, 1936,
    hereinafter cited as "Names of Persons," Leader.
7. "John Harmon Is First White Man to Obtain Land Grant in County,"
    Orange (Tex.) Leader, Aug. 30, 1940.
8. Frank W. Johnson and Eugene C. Barker, A History of Texas and Texans,
    II, 696, hereinafter cited as Johnson and Barker, Texas and Texans.
9. "Names of Persons," Leader, May 29, 1936.
10. R. E. Russell, "History of Orange Written in 1911 Tells of Early
    Days," Orange (Tex.) Leader, Aug. 30, 1940, hereinafter cited as
    Russell, "History of Orange," Leader.
11. WPA Writers' Program, comp., Beaumont, p. 37.
12. "Names of Persons," Leader, May 29, 1936.

part, all of present Orange County. But he was unsuccessful, and present-
ly transferred his contract to the Galveston Bay and Texas Land Company,
an ambitious enterprise with headquarters in New York City. Cholera,
misunderstandings with the Mexican Government, and other factors retarded
colonization by this company,[13] but the influx of other settlers did not
abate. Colonists from Stephen F. Austin's settlements were overflowing
his grant and pushing eastward toward the Sabine.[14] A claim was being
advanced in the United States that the Neches River, not the Sabine, was
that nation's western boundary, a claim which probably encouraged Louisi-
anians to enter the Orange region.[15]

The Cow Bayou settlement, which was the principal one between
Louisiana and the town of Liberty, on the Trinity River, was attached as
a precinct to the Mexican municipality of Liberty in 1832.[16] Another
community, Duncan's Woods, had its beginning in 1834, when John Bland
moved there from Louisiana with his family - Mary, Joseph, Oliver, and
Peyton.[17] Groups of log houses now dotted the banks of the rivers and
bayous.[18] In 1834 the Mexican Government extended the time on Zavala's
contract and recognized the Galveston Bay and Texas Land Company as his
legal agent. Colonization from that source began anew. Late in 1834 a
land commissioner, George A. Nixon, was sent to issue titles.[19] The
first title to land in present Orange County was issued to Wm. Stephenson
on January 29, 1835, for a tract on the east bank of the Neches. Twenty-
five more titles were issued in present Orange County that year.[20]

---

13. Mary Virginia Henderson, "Minor Empresario Contracts for the Coloni-
    zation of Texas, 1825-1834," Southwestern Historical Quarterly, XXXI
    (1927-28), 304-315, hereinafter cited as Henderson, "Minor Empresario
    Contracts," Quarterly.
14. WPA Writers' Program, comp., Beaumont, p. 36.
15. "Boundary - United States and Mexico," Register of Debates in Con-
    gress, vol. XIV (1837), pt. 2, p. 128.
16. Johnson and Barker, Texas and Texans, II, 696.
17. "Names of Persons," Leader, May 29, 1936; see also A. F. Burns, "Mr.
    and Mrs. J. C. Turner Believed To Be Oldest Native Born Couple Now
    Residing in Orange County," Orange (Tex.) Leader, May 29, 1936.
18. WPA Writers' Program, comp., Beaumont, p. 36.
19. Henderson, "Minor Empresario Contracts," Quarterly, XXXI (1927-28), 313.
20. Texas General Land Office, Map of Orange County, November 1921, which
    shows other titles issued in 1835 to Thos. H. Breece, Nancy Davis,
    Pinkney Lout, and Martin Palmer, on the Neches; Sam'l Davis, Wm. Davis,
    Jas. Dyson, Wm. Dyson, Susan Fraisier, Jno. M. Henrie, Geo. A. Patillo,
    in the Cow Bayou region; Wesley Dykes, Jno. Harmon, Anthony Harris,
    Jno. Jett, Stephen Jett, Joseph Richey, Vel Richey, and C. Stevens,
    inland from the Sabine River and Sabine Lake in the southeastern
    section of the present county; Theron Strong and Claibourne West,
    slightly east of the center of the present county; Jno. Allen,
    Richard Ballew, and Chas. Morgan, just west of the Sabine Narrows in
    the northeast section, and Wm. Clark, also in the northeast.

The settlers, predominantly Anglo-American, chafed increasingly under Mexican rule; and in few sections of Texas did the growing demand for a more representative government find as sympathetic response as in this region. As a result of a number of meetings and conventions, the Mexican Government created the municipality of Jefferson on December 9, 1835.[21] The boundaries of this new governmental unit were the same as those of the present county of Orange; they included no part of present Jefferson County territory. The settlements west of the Neches remained under the jurisdiction of the municipality of Liberty. A site on the east bank of Cow Bayou was selected as the seat of justice of the new municipality, and it too was called Jefferson.[22]

During the Texas Revolution, most of the able-bodied men of the area left their fields untilled and their cabins unprotected to join the Texan Army. In the spring of 1836 only boys in their teens were to be found in the more settled sections. In April, according to G. W. Hargraves, a young man of the lower Sabine-Neches region:

> . . . Sam Houston wrote to me that Santa Anna was coming to
> Sabine water, and he wanted me to help stop him. I beat up
> for volunteers to go and help Houston and got twenty-one men.
> . . . When we went to start, I furnished the ammunition and
> supplies; I spent $42 for ammunition, $6 for flour and $10
> for meat for the trip. . . .[23]

After Texas won its independence in 1836., Jefferson became one of the original counties of the Republic. On December 21, 1837, its boundaries were extended to include not only all of present Orange, but also all of present Jefferson and parts of present Chambers, Hardin, and Galveston Counties.[24] Tevis Bluff, on the west side of the Neches was renamed Beaumont and became the county seat.[25]

Early minutes of the Jefferson County commissioners court indicate that the old municipality was the dominant section of the new county. The principal business of the commissioners, aside from levying taxes, dealt with roads, bridges, and ferries, and three of the first four road precincts were east of the Neches. The first road undertaken was from Beaumont to Ballew's Ferry on the Sabine. George A. Pattillo was the sponsor of more motions than any other member of the court. His first proposal was for a toll bridge over Cow Bayou.[26]

---

21. Gam. Laws; I, 955.
22. Johnson and Barker, _Texas and Texans_, II, 696.
23. WPA Writers' Program, comp., _Beaumont_, p. 41.
24. Gam. Laws, I, 1452.
25. WPA Writers' Program, comp., _Beaumont_, pp. 42, 43.
26. Jefferson County, County Clerk's office, Minutes Commissioners
    Court, vol. A-2, pp. 1-50, _passim_.

Ferries were being operated in 1838 by Richard A. Ballew on the Sabine and W. C. Beard on Cow Bayou. William Ashworth operated a ferry across the bay and another up the Neches to Beaumont. R. E. Booth was bonded and licensed to operate a toll bridge across Adams Bayou. On November 6, 1838, a bridge was recommended for the "east bayou of the two bayous called Bunches Bayou,"[27] but the fragmentary condition of the early records makes it impossible to determine whether the bridge was built then.

Among the outstanding residents of the early county was Sheriff David Garner, of whom it has been said:

> The law on the Neches began with him . . . His jurisdiction extended all the way to the Sabine, over a region still under the influence of the lawless spirit of the Neutral Ground. . . . The valiant sheriff was also county tax collector - a position as hazardous as that of peace officer. . . . His duties extended over a portion of Texas in which land titles were - in the confusion of the first years of the Republic of Texas - either in dispute, unmarked or vague. The tax assessor and his colleague, the sheriff and tax collector, journeyed into the wilds of the Neches-Sabine area, over roads that in wet weather became impassable even to horseback riders. These two men and their successors became the instruments of progress. . . .[28]

On January 29, 1842, the Congress of the Republic of Texas attempted to create a new county called Neches, carving it from a portion of Jasper County and that part of Jefferson that constitutes present Orange. The new county was to exist "for judicial and other purposes . . . except that of separate representation in Congress, which shall be as heretofore."[29] Before the year was out, however, the Supreme Court of the Republic ruled this attempt and others to create "judicial" counties unconstitutional.[30] The only traceable effect of this brief and nominal countyhood was the new name of "Madison" for Green's Bluff, the Congress having so designated the intended county seat of Neches.[31]

The victory of the United States in the war with Mexico brought the region a sense of governmental stability it had never known, and gradually within the next few years its two major industries developed. Prior to the Mexican War the settlers were as yet herdsmen, cultivating a little cotton on the river banks but usually devoting most of their cropland to

---

27. Jefferson County, County Clerk's office, Minutes Commissioners Court, vol. A-2, pp. 4-39, passim.
28. WPA Writers' Program, comp., Beaumont, pp. 48, 49.
29. Gam. Laws, II, 754; see map, facing p. 1.
30. James Wilmer Dallam, comp., Opinions of the Supreme Court of Texas from 1840 to 1844 Inclusive, p. 473.
31. Gam. Laws, II, 754.

corn and cane. Some shingles were also made, but now commercial production of lumber - the first in Texas - began; and about 1859 Louisiana
emigrants tried growing rice without irrigation, planting their seed in
marshy spots and even in dry ponds and depending upon rains to bring them
to maturity. This system, called the "providence plan," characterized
Texas rice growing until recent years. For some time rice was grown
chiefly for home consumption, but the region's other products found a
commercial outlet through the Galveston market. By 1852 steamboats and
sailing vessels were regularly plying the Neches. The Sabine also float-
ed a large volume of lumber, logs, grain, and other products to market.[32]

Creation and Organization

Orange County was created on February 5, 1852. The boundaries set
forth at that time have remained unchanged and are as follows:

> Beginning at the mouth of Big Alabama creek, from thence
> east with the line of Jefferson and Jasper counties to the
> Sabine river, thence down said river with its meanders to
> Sabine Lake, thence west to the mouth of the Neches river;
> thence up said river with its meanders to the place of
> beginning.[33]

The act of creation commissioned W. B. Ellis, C. S. Hunt, and A. H.
Reading to organize the county, and specified that "the town of Madison,
alias Green's Bluff, be, and it is hereby made the Seat of Justice of
said county and shall be styled 'Madison'."[34] The origin of the county's
name is uncertain. It has been said that it was named for the fruit,
which, since the earliest settlement near the mouth of the Sabine, had
been grown for domestic purposes;[35] but local tradition has it that A. H.
Reading came to Texas from Orange, New Jersey, and hence the name of the
county.[36]

The first recorded meeting of the commissioners court, on May 7,
1852, was attended by George A. Pattillo, chief justice; Nathaniel Bonner,
Charles H. Saxon, George H. Guptill, and James H. Pattillo, commissioners;
Harrison Barnes, sheriff; and W. W. Wadsworth, clerk. The court noted
92 men available for jury service, arranged for the registration of stock
brands, and then turned to the building of roads. Road precincts were
defined; construction work was ordered on a route northward from Madison

---

32. Johnson and Barker, _Texas and Texans_, II, 695-699.
33. Gam. Laws, III, 926.
34. _Ibid._
35. Z. T. Fulmore, _The History and Geography of Texas as Told in County Names_, p. 276.
36. Information obtained from former County Judge Bland, August 1940, by Perry Davis, HRS Supervisor.

to the county line to facilitate travel to Burkeville, Newton County; and
the court established a county road leading from Turner's Ferry on the
Sabine, via Cow Bayou bridge, to the ferry "kept by Tivis" on the Neches.
The commissioners then adopted the first county tax, and divided the
county east and west of Cow Bayou into election precincts 1 and 2, re-
spectively.[37]

On August 16, 1852, the first police force was organized, with John
Merriman, captain; Abraham Merriman, Asa L. Stark, Charles Milatz,
Pleasant Davis, and George C. Taylor, privates. In August and November
ferry licenses were granted to Alexander McLain, Adams Bayou; E. B.
Thomas, mouth of the Neches; and Ursan Guidry, at Ballew's Crossing.
Guidry's tax, $25, was higher than that required of the other ferrymen,
indicating the continued importance of this old Sabine ferry. He was
ordered to keep good pens on the east bank for swimming horses and cattle,
and was permitted to charge the following tolls: Man and horse, 25¢;
lead horse, 12½¢; light one-horse pleasure carriage, 50¢; two-horse carriage, 75¢; ox wagon or cart, $1; swimming stock, 3¢ per head; for long
ferriage to Birch Landing, tolls ranging from $1 to $3.[38]

The years of early countyhood were lean ones. On November 15, 1852,
the treasurer reported that only $6 had been received into county funds
since the August term of court.[39] An inventory of all merchandise in the
county in 1856 came to only $10,700; and in that year only $633 was collected in property taxes, $72 in poll taxes.[40] A traveler found the
county thinly settled; many abandoned farms; herds in poor condition; and
a "few hogs, converted by hardship to figures so unnatural that we at first
mistook them for goats." Seeking to buy corn for his horse, he was told
"folks didn't make corn enough to bread them, and if anybody had corn to
give his horse, he carried it in his hat and went out behind somewhere."[41]

Nevertheless, the county seat propered, and on September 1, 1856,
with a population of 600,[42] it was incorporated.[43] Early in February
1858 Madison was reincorporated with a new name - Orange - and under the
new charter its limits were extended.[44]

---

37. Comr's. Ct. (1852-60), vol. A, pp. 1-14, in Commissioners Court Min-
    utes, see entry 1.
38. Ibid., pp. 14-20.
39. Ibid., p. 20.
40. The Texas Almanac for 1857, pp. 61, 66.
41. Frederick Law Olmsted, A Journey Through Texas, pp. 381, 383.
42. Jacob De Cordova, Texas: Her Resources and her Public Men, p. 280.
43. Gam. Laws, IV, 771.
44. Ibid., pp. 1000, 1275. The present town of Orange was also known
    as Strong's Bluff at one time. Fred I. Massengill, Texas Towns, p.
    137. Massengill also states that Orange was once known as Jefferson,
    but the Cow Bayou settlement seems well established as the town of
    Jefferson. The town is also said to have been called Pine Bluff.
    Russell, "History of Orange," Leader, Aug. 30, 1940.

Courthouses

A number of sessions of district court were held under shade trees in Madison. County business during the first year was transacted in the upper story of a sagging frame business house on Water Street.[45] The next year, the county shared this ramshackle structure with the newly organized Masonic Lodge.[46]

On October 31, 1853, the commissioners adopted a resolution to build a courthouse in Madison. They appointed William Smith and William Hewson agents to purchase lots and superintend construction, and pledged the county for $300. Aware that the amount appropriated was insufficient, the court "do hope said Agents will . . . get as much as possible subscription to aid the erection of said building." But the plan was apparently too ambitious; on November 21, 1853, the commissioners ordered the agents to finish only the lower part of the building.[47] This first county building was a frame house located at Market and Henderson Streets; a single room served the district, county, and commissioners courts; and a lean-to addition was used when juries met in secret session. The courthouse was frequently used for church services.[48]

Early in 1859 the county in some manner lost its courthouse. During 1858 the clerk usually recorded sessions of the commissioners court as "begun and holden at the Court house";[49] then, on February 21, 1859, court was held "at the House of M Wilson . . . the place set apart for the time being," and when court was called there again in the following month, Wilson's residence was designated as the place set apart "for holding Courts there being no Court house."[50]

The court authorized construction of a 2-story log jail, 16 feet square, in November 1860. In December $350 was appropriated to buy the

---

45. "Court Held in Masonic Hall Here in 1852," Orange (Tex.) Leader, Aug. 30, 1940.
46. "Local Masonic Lodge Organized in 1853 When Town was Known as Madison; Membership Totals 192," Orange (Tex.) Leader, May 29, 1936. First officers of the lodge were Hugh Ochiltree, acting deputy grand master; George A. Pattillo, senior warden; William Smith, junior warden; A. H. Reading, secretary; I. H. Hutchings, treasurer; S. Fairchilds, senior deacon; Charles H. Saxon, tiler.
47. Comr's. Ct. (1852-60), vol. A, pp. 39, 40, 44, in Commissioners Court Minutes, see entry 1.
48. "Court Held in Masonic Hall Here in 1852," Orange (Tex.) Leader, Aug. 30, 1940.
49. Comr's. Ct. (1852-60), vol. A, passim, in Commissioners Court Minutes, see entry 1.
50. Ibid., pp. 157, 158, 167.

lumber; and on March 22, 1861, the jail was complete, and commissioners were appointed to accept it.[51]

During the early eighties, the commissioners court gave considerable attention to regularizing finances and calling to account various officers who seemed to be neglecting their records. At a special term on January 6, 1885, investigation was made of the loss by theft in 1883 of important documents belonging to the county; and an investigation was ordered to ascertain the county's legal indebtedness, concerning which the court observed, "the system provided by law for the registration of claims against the County, has at times for many years been loosely and irregularly kept."[52]

By the time these matters had been straightened out, the county officers were established in a new courthouse. In 1883 a special ad valorem tax of $\frac{1}{4}$ of 1 percent had been levied for a courthouse and jail building fund.[53] The courthouse plans and specifications of James J. Sigon, of Orange, were adopted on August 21, 1883, and County Judge D. R. Wingate was authorized to advertise for bids. J. A. Robinson submitted the only bid, $6,200, for which price he offered, beyond specifications, to "sheath the out side of building walls with unfaced pine boards put on at right Angles at Corner to strengthen build," and to construct a records vault. His bid was accepted on September 11, on condition that he furnish $5,000 bond and complete the building by March 1, 1884. Judge Wingate was authorized to sell the old courthouse and the brick vault connected with it.[54] The new courthouse was accepted on July 21, 1884, and the balance of $2,200 then due Robinson was paid at this time.[55] The new building had been furnished and occupied a month before.[56] It was a 2-story structure containing a large substantial steel vault.[57]

In the latter part of the 1890's this courthouse burned, but the steel vault preserved the county records, a few only being slightly scorched.[58] Bonds were issued to build a 3-story brick, tile, and concrete structure, which was soon erected. It served the county until 1937, when it was replaced by a new stone building costing $250,000.[59]

---

51. Minutes of County Court of Orange Co. (1860-66), vol. B, pp. 19, 23, 33, in Commissioners Court Minutes, see entry 1.
52. Commissioners Court Minutes, vol. B (2d), pp. 68, 69, see entry 1.
53. Ibid., p. 4.
54. Ibid., pp. 19-22.
55. Ibid., pp. 47, 48.
56. "Memories of Old Timers Drawn Upon for Old Records," Longview (Tex.) Daily News, May 31, 1936.
57. Commissioners Court Minutes, vol. B (2d), pp. 20, 21, see entry 1.
58. "Court Held in Masonic Hall Here in 1852," Orange (Tex.) Leader, Aug. 30, 1940.
59. "Orange County Dedicates New Courthouse," County Progress, XV (February 1938), 7, 8; see pp. 26-28, for description of present courthouse.

Civil War and Reconstruction

Orange County's vote on the question of Secession was 142 to 3 in favor of withdrawing from the Union.[60] The commissioners court, however, took no official notice of the new status of the county until September 6, 1861, when the court organized a home guard by reviving the beat patrol system. A. C. Swearinger, Richard Adcock, and Leroy Pattillo were captains, each with a command of five men.[61] No other indication is given of official recognition of the war until March 12, 1862, when the court appointed census-takers to determine the number of small arms fit for service, the number out of order, and the "number of persons still left capable of bearing arms."[62] Jury lists shrank, and the county officers changed frequently, presumably because of the resignation of able-bodied men.[63]

Orange County - as did the rest of East Texas during the war years - toiled to load the blockade runners on the Sabine and Neches with lumber, cotton, beeves, and grain, while the same vessels brought in goods from Europe and Northern States at greatly increased prices. For a time the county rested in comparative security behind natural defenses - the Louisiana marshes to the east and the easily guarded Sabine Pass some 30 miles southeast. In addition, the Confederate forces had an unwelcome ally in the summer of 1862 - yellow fever, which reached epidemic proportions at Sabine Pass and Galveston and caused the Federals to withhold attack until the "sickly season" had passed.[64]

Then late in September 1862, the roar of cannon was heard in the county as Federal gunboats attacked Sabine Pass. On October 4, a Union landing party captured Galveston; and the Confederates began intensive preparation in the Sabine-Neches area in anticipation of a general invasion of East Texas.[65] Recapture of Galveston on New Year's Eve lessened the danger; but "except at the lumber mills, industry by this time was virtually at a standstill; most of the men were in uniform."[66]

Five miles from the county seat, the main road from Louisiana reached the Sabine at Niblett's Bluff, the only high ground along Orange County's eastern border.[67] Here, since the outbreak of the Civil War, a company of Texas troops had been stationed. In the fall of 1863, Niblett's Bluff

60. E. W. Winkler, ed., Journal of the Secession Convention of Texas, 1861, pp. 7, 8, 89.
61. Minutes of County Court of Orange Co. (1860-66), vol. B, pp. 56, 57, in Commissioners Court Minutes, see entry 1.
62. Ibid., p. 86.
63. Ibid., pp. 60-100, passim.
64. WPA Writers' Program, comp., Beaumont, pp. 64-69.
65. Ibid.
66. Ibid., p. 68.
67. U. S. Geological Survey Map, Orange Quadrangle, 1926.

was headquarters for the Confederate Army's line on the Sabine, with Col. Augustus Buchel, Mexican War veteran, in command. Among the companies stationed here in 1863 was one of Orange militiamen commanded by Capt. John Bland,[68] pioneer citizen, and veteran of the Texas Revolution.[69] Captain Bland steadfastly refused to allow his company to be sent farther from Orange than Niblett's Bluff or Sabine Pass.[70]

When the war ended all industry was paralyzed; and for a time returning soldiers and the few Freedmen went back to the pioneer trade of shingle- and stave-making.[71] A member of the John Harmon family, who a few years before had sold 12,000 acres of land for $600 in Confederate money, sadly deposited the worthless currency in the Neches River.[72] Then in September 1865 further misfortune struck.

> By the ravages of a tornado . . . the dwelling houses, corn cribs, barns, stables and fences, together with the crops in the fields, and the timber on almost every farm or plantation in the County of Orange, were either destroyed or greatly damaged, and in the town of Orange only four houses were left standing . . .[73]

The storm left scarcely a leaf on the trees, and even the grass was uprooted.[74] Because of this catastrophe the Constitutional Convention on March 31, 1866, relieved the county of State taxes then due and any others that might be assessed for the year 1866.[75] To add to the bleakness of the picture, rails of the Texas and New Orleans Railroad, which had been laid in 1860, lay rusted and unused along the main street of Orange.[76]

Economic and Social Development

The county slowly recovered from the war and the storm. During 1866 a small shipping trade augmented traffic on the Neches and the Sabine,

---

68. War of the Rebellion, Official Records of the Union and Confederate Armies, ser. I, vol. XXVI, pt. II, pp. 133, 347.
69. Burns, "Mr. and Mrs. J. C. Turner Believed To Be Oldest Native Born Couple Now Residing in Orange County," Orange (Tex.) Leader, May 29, 1936.
70. War of the Rebellion, Official Records of the Union and Confederate Armies, ser. I, vol. XXVI, pt. II, pp. 346-348, 366, 370.
71. Johnson and Barker, Texas and Texans, II, 697.
72. Russell, "History of Orange," Leader, Aug. 30, 1940.
73. Gam. Laws, V, 905.
74. Russell, "History of Orange," Leader, Aug. 30, 1940.
75. Gam. Laws, V, 905.
76. Charles S. Potts, Railroad Transportation in Texas, pp. 31, 38.

which since the war had been largely limited to the rafting of shingles
down to Bunn's Bluff and Orange.[77] Finally, in 1876, the Texas and New
Orleans brought in the first train over their line, and thereafter on
alternate days the train whistled its arrival from Houston, 12 hours
distant, at 7 p. m.[78]

The lumber industry developed rapidly after the railroad entered
the county. Alexander Gilmer, a former ship's carpenter who had already
made a fortune in merchandise and shipping, and James Woods, who had operated lumber mills in Mississippi in the first half of the century, were
the owners of Orange's chief mill - a small plant by present standards,
cutting an average of 7,000 feet of boards and scantling, or about 10,000
railroad ties in a 14- or 15-hour day.[79] In 1871 William H. Stark, a
20-year-old mail rider from Burkeville, made a trip to Orange and decided
to cast his lot with the development of the lumber industry.[80] At about
the same time, T. Bancroft, an English piano-tuner, made a similar deci-
sion after a visit to Duncan's Woods.[81] These men remained to become two
of the leaders in the lumber industry. Stark became associated with Henry
J. Lutcher and G. Bedell Moore, Pennsylvania lumbermen, whose arrival in
1877 marked the beginning of large-scale commercial production. At the
beginning of the Lutcher and Moore mill building operations, young Stark
was a sawyer in the R. B. Russell mill, and turned out the lumber for the
framework of Lutcher's first mill.[82]

As business conditions improved, schools and churches began to dot
the county. A public school was opened at Orange in 1872.[83] Previously,
during Reconstruction, a school for Negroes had been organized in Orange
in the Mount Zion Baptist Church, with a Professor Washington as principal.[84] The earliest church in the county was organized in the Big Woods
community of Louisiana in the 1860's and later moved to "Aunt Jennie Jett's
Island." Rev. F. A. Burton was the pastor while the church was on Jett's

---

77. Johnson and Barker, Texas and Texans, II, 697.
78. Potts, Railroad Transportation in Texas, p. 38; A. F. Burns, "First
     Train Is Brought Here in Early '70's," Orange (Tex.) Leader, May 29,
     1936.
79. Jerome Swinford, "A. Gilmer Pioneer in Early Saw Mill History,"
     Orange (Tex.) Leader, May 29, 1936.
80. "Life Story of W. H. Stark Is History of East Texas," Orange (Tex.)
     Leader, May 29, 1936.
81. A. F. Burns, "Tuning of Piano in Orange in Early 70's Resulted in
     Establishment of Lumber Manufacturing Industry," Orange (Tex.)
     Leader, May 29, 1936.
82. "Saw Mill Industry Plays Major Part in Texas History," Orange (Tex.)
     Leader, May 29, 1936.
83. "First Public School Established in Orange in 1872," Orange (Tex.)
     Leader, May 29, 1936.
84. "School for Negroes Formed Here in 1870," Orange (Tex.) Leader, May
     29, 1936.

Island. In the 1870's the church moved east to a point near the home of John Lyons.[85]

The First Presbyterian Church of Orange was organized on April 3, 1878, by Rev. D. McGregor, an evangelist sent by the Brazos Presbytery. The church building, erected the following year, was the first in Orange proper.[86] Rev. Daniel Morse, who had been doing missionary work in Orange and other towns of the area, was named presiding elder of the "Alligator Circuit" of the Methodist Church in 1879, and Rev. Lensy Nurke was appointed to take charge of the work in Orange.[87]

On June 1, 1880, A. P. Harris, owner and editor, presented the first issue of the Orange Daily Tribune, declaring in a salutatory column that Orange was destined to become a great city. The town's population was given as 3,000, although the 1880 census listed only 2,000 residents; but the editor explained that he was claiming a metropolitan area which included many families living near the two sawmills across the river. One article stated that 10 of the 12 saw and shingle mills were in operation, and that Gilmer and Woods were rebuilding a mill on Conway's Bayou to replace one that had burned. Twenty-five new houses were in the course of construction. Capt. Tom Davis reported the sinking of his steamboat, the Laura, above Dead Eddy in the Sabine Narrows. Orange excursionists journeying to Lake Charles were requested not to shoot from car windows. Other articles told of meetings of the Orange Rifles and the Orange Fire Company.[88]

The lumber industry, dominant in the county since the days of the fur trappers, received a challenge about 1882 when a large rice mill was put in operation at Orange.[89] Larger vessels were docking on the Sabine and Neches as a result of a new 12-foot channel which Federal grants had made possible, and Orange had secured a rail outlet to the east with the completion of the Mobile, New Orleans, and Texas Railroad.[90]

A terrible storm, reminiscent of the tornado which all but wiped out the county seat in 1865, skimmed past Orange in 1886, breaking a drought

85. A. F. Burns, "Oldest Church in County Is Near McLewis," Orange (Tex.) Leader, May 29, 1936.
86. "Presbyterians Organize Church Here in 1878," Orange (Tex.) Leader, May 29, 1936.
87. "Local Methodist Program Dates Back to 1877," Orange (Tex.) Leader, May 29, 1936.
88. A. F. Burns, "News Items in First Copy of Orange Daily Tribune Give Interesting Facts about Early History of Town," Orange (Tex.) Leader, May 29, 1936.
89. Orange (Tex.) Chamber of Commerce, Orange County, Where the Best Comes From, p. 16, hereinafter cited as Orange Chamber of Commerce, Orange County.
90. Johnson and Barker, Texas and Texans, II, 697, 698.

which had destroyed about a third of the county's crops. Worms destroyed
more than half of what was left of the cotton crop. Nevertheless, the
county made a creditable showing in the 1888 agricultural report, with
corn, garden crops, and sweet potatoes topping cotton, and a heavy production of sugar cane and dairy products. Neither rice nor orange production
was noteworthy. The manufacture of lumber and shingles was the "engross-
ing pursuit of the people."[91]

By 1890 Orange had a National bank capitalized at $25,000, 4 schools
taught by 15 teachers, 5 sawmills, 4 shingle mills, 5 planing mills, 6
lawyers, 2 dentists, 30 mercantile establishments, 6 retail liquor dealers,
and 1 beer dealer. The assessed value of property was $1,285,287, an in-
crease of $530,799 in 10 years. The population of the county was 4,768;
that of Orange, 2,000.[92]

The first 3 years of the new century saw an unprecedented industrial
development. In 1901 the Spindletop oil field - greatest in the world -
came in, just across the county line in Jefferson County.[93] While this
did not lead to immediate discovery of oil in Orange County, it did lead
to construction of a million-dollar refinery at Orange. Orange, the
largest lumber market in Texas, paid more than $3,600,000 on outgoing
freight in 1902, and by 1903 boasted the investment of almost a million
dollars in brick buildings in 18 months. Early that year the Orange
Cotton Mill Company was organized with a capital of $400,000 and began
to erect a mill. A Government appropriation of $125,000 was made to
initiate the dredging of a channel across Lake Sabine. In addition to
the Southern Pacific and the Texas and New Orleans Railroads, the Orange
and Northwestern, a locally financed line, was pushed eastward 61 miles
to Burkeville. Two other roads, the International and Great Northern out
of Houston and the Cotton Belt from Lufkin, were built through Orange.[94]

The county's "providence" rice farms gave way to irrigated tracts
soon after the turn of the century. Between 1907 and 1909 rice production became the chief agricultural pursuit. In 1907 K. Kishi, a Japanese
nobleman of wealth, established a Japanese colony at Terry, in central
Orange County, and began intensive cultivation of rice.[95] Throughout

---

91. Texas Department of Agriculture, Insurance, Statistics, and History,
        Agricultural Bureau, Texas Agricultural and Statistical Report, 1888,
        pp. 173, 174.
92. Texas Department of Agriculture, Insurance, Statistics, and History,
        Agricultural Bureau, Texas Agricultural and Statistical Report, 1890,
        pp. 193, 194.
93. WPA Writers' Program, comp., Beaumont, pp. 99-104.
94. W. W. Dexter, ed., The Coast Country of Texas, p. 127.
95. Lillie Mae Tomlinson, "The Japanese Colony in Orange County," Texas
        History Teachers' Bulletin, XIV (1927), 141-145, hereinafter cited
        as Tomlinson, "Japanese Colony," Teachers' Bulletin.

southeast Texas, other growers planted increased acreage, with the result
that the bumper crop of 1909 paralyzed the market. This led to the organization of the Southern Rice Growers Association. Soon after, over-produc-
tion was lessened somewhat by salt water inundation from the large new
irrigation and navigation canals.[96]

In 1918 the Southern Rice Growers Association launched a widespread
educational campaign to advance its product, and the following year rice
reached a new peak of production, leading again to falling prices.[97]
Thereupon Kishi renounced rice farming and turned to truck gardening.
Diversification of Orange County farming has proved lucrative, and bumper
crops of strawberries, cabbages, and figs are produced.[98] In 1939, 67
farms produced 149,492 barrels of rice. The county also raised 24,369
bushels of potatoes, 36,679 bushels of corn, and 190 square bales of
cotton.[99]

In the meanwhile, Port Orange was coming into its own. A project
for deep water in the entire Sabine-Neches channel began with the Federal
River and Harbor Act of February 27, 1911.[1] In anticipation of this, the
county commissioners had organized a county navigation board in 1909.
W. H. Stark, who had become the president of the Lutcher and Moore Lumber
Company upon the death of Henry J. Lutcher in 1912, carried on Lutcher's
fight for deep water in the Sabine-Neches district, and on January 3,
1916, the lumber company brought into Orange five schooners to be loaded
at the mill wharves, with the promise of the Government engineers that
the 26-foot channel would be completed before they could load. The ships
went out loaded, the first to navigate the Sabine-Neches channel; and
Orange notified the shipping world that it was the first port on the
channel open to serve.[2]

On March 13, 1917, a city ordinance created the Orange Wharf and
Dock Commission to control the port and work jointly with the county
navigation board, which exercised jurisdiction over navigation on the
Sabine River.[3] With the advent of World War I, Eastern capitalists

_____

96. WPA Writers' Program, comp., Beaumont, p. 116.
97. Ibid., p. 117.
98. Tomlinson, "Japanese Colony," Teachers' Bulletin, XIV (1927), 142,
        143.
99. U. S. Department of Commerce, Sixteenth Census of the United States,
        1940, Reports on Agriculture, Texas, pp. 148, 168.
 1. Corps of Engineers, U. S. Army, The Ports of Port Arthur, Sabine,
        Beaumont, and Orange, Texas, p. 5, hereinafter cited as Corps of
        Engineers, Ports.
 2. "Saw Mill Industry Plays Major Part in Texas History," Orange (Tex.)
        Leader, May 29, 1936; see also entry 71.
 3. Corps of Engineers, Ports, pp. 136, 137.

(First entry, p. 37)   Historical Sketch - Economic and
                                                                      Social Development

constructed a shipyard at Port Orange. This yard was building ships before the Government shipbuilding program started, and launched many
wooden vessels.[4]

An extensive oil field was discovered 6 miles west of Orange in 1913,
and in 1921 this field began heavy production of high-grade petroleum.[5]
Since the oil field was in an orange-producing area, the town which grew
up near it came to be called Orangefield.[6] In 1940 the county produced
1,195,590 barrels of oil.[7]

A large school grew up at Orangefield. In March 1926 the schoolhouse
was damaged by a tornado, and the following year it was destroyed by fire.
Even before the new building was erected with the aid of a $50,000 bond
issue, Orangefield became an independent school district.[8] Consolidation
of the Oilla and Duncan's Woods schools with the Orangefield school soon
made it one of the outstanding educational institutions in East Texas.
Orange, Mauriceville, and Vidor are also high school districts.[9] Orange
High School is best known for its bands, the Bengal Lancers, an all-male
aggregation, and the Bengal Guards, composed of more than 100 girls. The
bands are sponsored and financed by H. J. Lutcher Stark, son of William
H. Stark and Miriam M. Lutcher.[10]

Beginning about 1927 and extending through the depression of the
early 1930's the lumber industry declined seriously, and Port Orange
shipments fell off.[11] Within a few years, however, public improvements
showed Orange was shaking off the slump. In 1936 the first section of
municipal levee extension was completed, making possible the reclamation
of some 80,000 acres of rice lands and better flood and malaria protec-
tion.[12] Recently a $2,750,000 bridge, the highest in the South, was
completed to link Port Arthur to Orange County.[13]

---

4. "Saw Mill Industry Plays Major Part in Texas History," Orange (Tex.)
    Leader, May 29, 1936.
5. Louis J. Wortham, A History of Texas from Wilderness to Commonwealth,
    V, 192, 282.
6. Massengill, Texas Towns, p. 137.
7. The Texas Almanac for 1941-42, p. 492.
8. "Orangefield Has Fully Accredited High School," Orange (Tex.) Leader,
    May 29, 1936.
9. "Orange County Schools Make Splendid Progress," Orange (Tex.) Leader,
    May 29, 1936.
10. Ben S. Woodhead, "Orange Bengal Guards To Appear at Fat Stock Show,"
    Houston (Tex.) Post, Feb. 2, 1941; "The Pride and Joy of Orange, Texas,
    Is the Wonderful Girls' School Band," Life, IX (Oct. 14, 1940), pp.
    48-50.
11. Corps of Engineers, Ports, pp. 137, 156.
12. "Municipal Levee Protects City from Sabine Overflow," Orange (Tex.)
    Leader, May 29, 1936.
13. Orange Chamber of Commerce, Orange County. The bridge is 183 feet
    above normal tide.

Although the 1940 census gave Orange a population of 7,472, a rush of laborers to the city following the opening of a large shipbuilding plant late in 1940 has increased the number of its residents 100 percent.[14] Orange is an important shipping center. The old line of the Texas and New Orleans has been taken over by the Southern Pacific, which, with the Missouri Pacific, connects the city with Northern markets. The port, municipally controlled, centers on the city wharf, 2 miles south of Orange. The wharf is 1,502 feet long, with 30 feet of water alongside, and has 2 transit sheds with a total floor space of 72,000 square feet. The city also owns a small wharf at the foot of Fourth Street, used as a terminal for river and canal boats engaged in local traffic; several street ends in the city proper; and about 3,000 feet of frontage on the south side of a slip dredged off the right bank of the Sabine River, approximately 2 miles below the turning basin. The remainder of the waterfront is owned by private interests.[15]

The city of Orange also owns Stark Field, a municipal airport, $2\frac{1}{2}$ miles west of the city.[16]

Present-day industries include lumber mills, paper mills, rice mills, shipyards, woodworking plants, canneries, and crate factories.[17] A description of the county seat written in 1930 still applies:

> There is probably no other city in the state or in the South, according to population, with so many aristocratic old Southern families and such a number of beautiful and palatial homes. Though Orange has ample city parks, it is said that there is less need for them there than in any other Texas city, because of the spacious and tree-shaded lawns with which practically every home is surrounded. Mammoth, age-old live-oaks and stately magnolias line the streets and country drives; while the winding, shaded roads leading to the city are bordered for miles with exquisite, fragile, purple water-hyacinths, blooming in the ditches as luxuriantly and with as beautiful effects as those carefully planted and tended in private yards or parks.[18]

---

14. The Texas Almanac for 1941-42, p. 492.
15. Corps of Engineers, Ports, pp. 132, 153, 154.
16. Ibid., p. 154.
17. The Texas Almanac for 1939-40, p. 445.
18. Ethel Osborn Hill, "The Wonderland of the Sabine District," East Texas, IV (May 1930), p. 11.

(First entry, p. 37)

2. GOVERNMENTAL ORGANIZATION

Orange County was created in February 1852,[1] and organized in May.[2] The keystone of its governmental structure is the county commissioners court, which consists of a county judge and four commissioners. Each of the latter represents one of the four commissioners' precincts into which the county is divided.[3] The court has many diverse functions, the most important dealing with finance, taxation, welfare, public improvements, contracts, and elections. A brief examination of each of these will reveal the interrelationship of the various county offices as they revolve around the court.

The commissioners court has been designated as the custodian of the county's funds,[4] which may be classified according to source or origin. The first class is set up by the Constitution,[5] the second by statutes,[6] and the third by order of the court.[7] It may transfer money from statutory funds of the various classifications;[8] it directs the treasurer to make disbursements;[9] it may, for certain purposes, issue non-negotiable interest-bearing county warrants,[10] independently of the voters' approval;[11] it must approve claims against the county;[12] it supervises the keeping of the finance ledger;[13] it receives reports of collections and of the financial condition of the county;[14] and it may employ public accountants "to audit all or any part of the books, records, or accounts of the county."[15]

In order to finance the county, the commissioners court has been empowered to levy certain taxes, which may be divided, according to the purpose for which the disbursement is to be made, into four classes: 1) General, 2) road and bridge, 3) jury, and 4) permanent improvements. The total maximum of these four is 95 cents on the $100 valuation, distributed as follows: 1) General, 25 cents; 2) road and bridge, 30 cents; 3) jury, 15 cents; and 4) permanent improvements, 25 cents. With the exception of the special road and bridge tax, the commissioners court

---

1. Acts 1852; Gam. Laws, III, 926.
2. Comr's. Ct. (1852-60), vol. A, p. 1, in Commissioners Court Minutes, see entry 1.
3. Const. 1876, art. V, sec. 18.
4. Hurley et al. v. Buchanan et al., 233 SW 590 (1921).
5. Const. 1876, art. VIII, sec. 9.
6. Vernon's Texas St. 1936, RCS, art. 1628.
7. Ibid., art. 1629.
8. Ibid., art. 1630.
9. Ibid., art. 1709.
10. Lasater v. Lopez, 110 Tex. 179, 217 SW 373 (1919).
11. Commissioners Court of Floyd County et al. v. Nichols et al., 142 SW 37 (1911).
12. Vernon's Texas St. 1936, RCS, art. 2351, sub. 10.
13. Ibid., art. 1607.
14. Ibid., art. 1665.
15. Ibid., art. 1641.

GOVERNMENTAL ORGANIZATION
OF
ORANGE COUNTY, TEXAS
1941

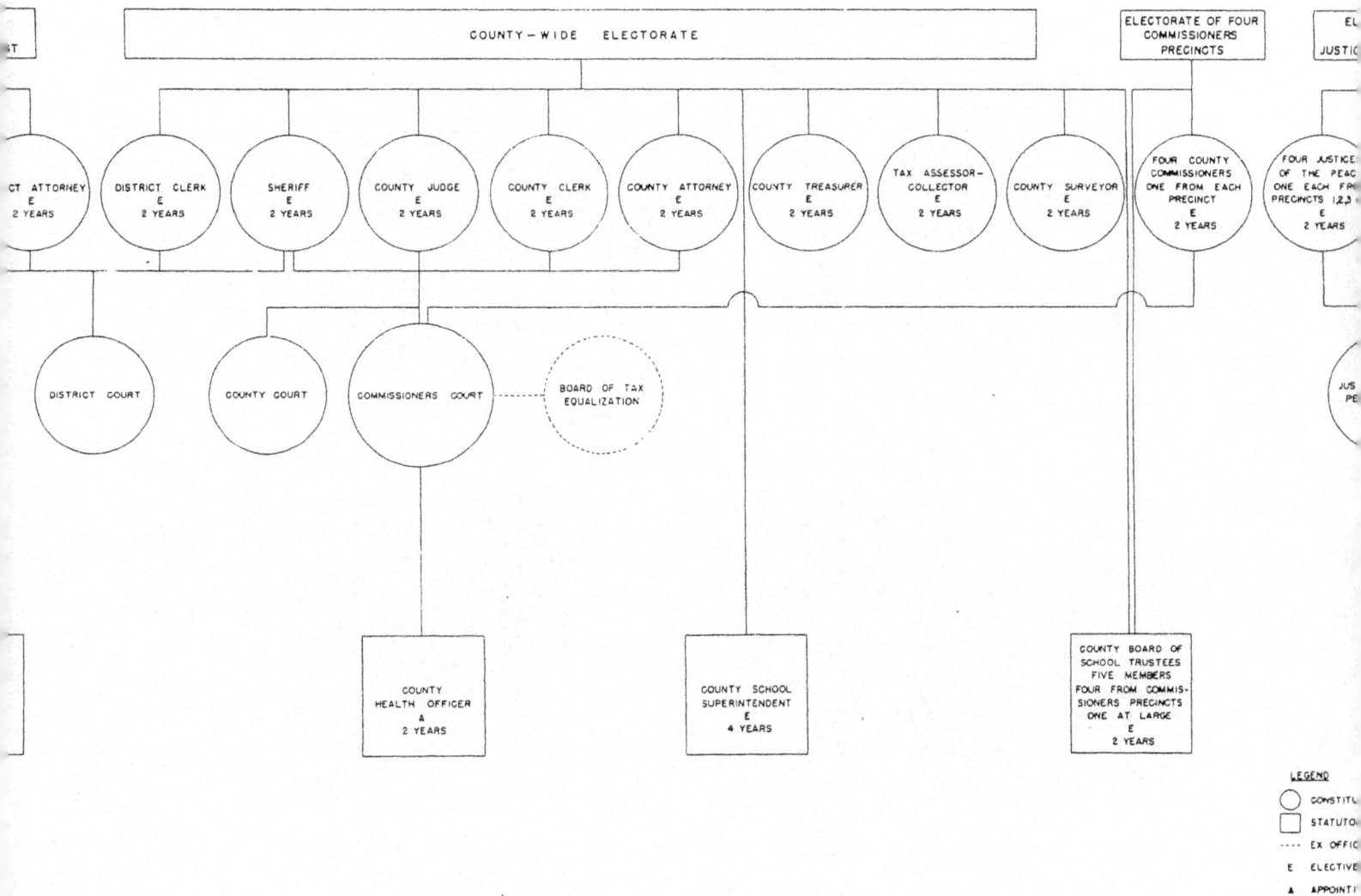

COUNTY—WIDE ELECTORATE	ELECTORATE OF FOUR COMMISSIONERS PRECINCTS	EL...JUSTIC...

CT ATTORNEY
E
2 YEARS

DISTRICT CLERK
E
2 YEARS

SHERIFF
E
2 YEARS

COUNTY JUDGE
E
2 YEARS

COUNTY CLERK
E
2 YEARS

COUNTY ATTORNEY
E
2 YEARS

COUNTY TREASURER
E
2 YEARS

TAX ASSESSOR-COLLECTOR
E
2 YEARS

COUNTY SURVEYOR
E
2 YEARS

FOUR COUNTY COMMISSIONERS
ONE FROM EACH PRECINCT
E
2 YEARS

FOUR JUSTICE...
OF THE PEAC...
ONE EACH FR...
PRECINCTS 1,2,3...
E
2 YEARS

DISTRICT COURT

COUNTY COURT

COMMISSIONERS COURT

BOARD OF TAX EQUALIZATION

JUS...
PE...

COUNTY
HEALTH OFFICER
A
2 YEARS

COUNTY SCHOOL SUPERINTENDENT
E
4 YEARS

COUNTY BOARD OF SCHOOL TRUSTEES
FIVE MEMBERS
FOUR FROM COMMIS-SIONERS PRECINCTS
ONE AT LARGE
E
2 YEARS

LEGEND

○ CONSTITU...
□ STATUTO...
---- EX OFFIC...
E ELECTIVE...
A APPOINTI...

O.P. 265-1-66-60   10/15/1941

may impose up to the maximum by its own order. The court may levy the
additional 15-cent tax for the special road and bridge fund only after
authorization by a majority of the taxpaying property owners.[16] The
court may also, after a majority vote by the voters in the district, levy
a tax not to exceed $1 on the $100 valuation for the common school districts.[17]

In addition, if a majority of the property tax payers participating
in an election consent, road and bridge bonds may be issued for which an
additional 15-cent maximum tax shall be levied to pay the interest and
create a sinking fund for their redemption.[18]

In order to equalize "the valuation of all property subject to or
rendered for taxation," the court each May meets as a board of equalization.[19]

The court is responsible for furnishing the necessary support for,[20]
and the burial of resident paupers.[21] It may make contracts for the medical care of indigents.[22] While the court is not required to provide hos-
pitalization for the indigent sick, it must extend to them the benefits
of such public hospital facilities as the county may possess.[23] The
court may, upon the approval of the taxpayers, issue bonds to establish
poor houses and farms.[24] In 1917 a law was passed permitting counties to
pay small pensions to widowed mothers. The commissioners court authorizes
their payment from county funds.[25]

The county health officer is appointed by the court.[26] He is required by law to attend sick county prisoners and indigents, to discharge
duties relating to quarantine, and to perform such other functions as
the State Board of Health may prescribe for the general welfare of the
county.[27]

The power of a county to establish and maintain roads and bridges
is vested in its commissioners court. The court is empowered and directed
to "order the laying out and opening of public roads," and, subject to

---

16.   Const. 1876, art. VIII, sec. 9.
17.   Ibid., art. VII, sec. 3; Vernon's Texas St. 1936, RCS, art. 2784.
18.   Ibid., arts. 718, 719, 722, 723.
19.   Const. 1876, art. VIII, sec. 18.
20.   Vernon's Texas St. 1936, RCS, art. 2351, sub. 11; Galveston County
        v. Ducie, 91 Tex. 665, 45 SW 798 (1898); Willacy County v. Valley
        Baptist Hospital et al., 29 SW (2d) 456 (1930).
21.   Vernon's Texas St. 1936, RCS, art. 2351, sub. 12.
22.   See footnote 20.
23.   Vernon's Texas St. 1936, RCS, art. 4438.
24.   Ibid., art. 718, sub. 3.
25.   Ibid., art. 6228.
26.   Ibid., art. 4423.
27.   Ibid., art. 4427.

certain limitations, to discontinue or alter them, when necessary. In
Orange County, each commissioner's precinct is a road district, and each
county commissioner is ex-officio road superintendent in his district.
It is his duty to superintend the construction of such county roads and
bridges in his district as the commissioners court may provide for. The
court may acquire property for rights-of-way or road material by purchase
or expropriation. It is expressly authorized to adopt the system of working county roads through the compulsory service of citizens and convict
labor, but in actual practice road work is done by labor employed by the
court, and is paid for from moneys belonging to the road and bridge fund.[28]

Only the commissioners court may make contracts binding the county;
these must be authorized by formal resolution of the court and recorded
in its minutes.[29] Other county officials are powerless to make enforce-
able contracts, unless these be ratified by the court.[30]

The commissioners court also has important electoral functions. It
must divide the county into election precincts,[31] appoint election officers in each of these precincts,[32] and in all elections, except primary
elections, must tabulate the returns from all the precincts.[33] The county
judge must, within 48 hours after such returns have been canvassed by the
court, report the results to the Secretary of State.[34] The judge issues
certificates of election to the successful candidates for county and precinct offices.[35]

In general the county clerk serves as clerk of both the county[36] and
the commissioners courts[37] and as custodian of the records of both courts;[38]
he issues deposit warrants to the treasurer;[39] the clerk, together with
the county judge and sheriff, serves on the county board which furnishes
supplies to election officials,[40] at county expense;[41] and as recorder
for the county he keeps many permanent records.[42]

---

28. Vernon's Texas St. 1936, RCS, art. 2351, subs. 3-6, and arts. 6702-
    6789, 6794-6797c.
29. Ibid., art. 2365; Fayette County v. Krause et al., 73 SW 51 (1903).
30. Germo Mfg. Co. v. Coleman County, 184 SW 1063 (1916).
31. Vernon's Texas St. 1936, RCS, art. 2351, sub. 1, and arts. 2933, 2934.
32. Ibid., arts. 2937, 2938.
33. Ibid., art. 3030.
34. Ibid., art. 3026a.
35. Ibid., art. 3032.
36. Const. 1876, art. V, sec. 20; Vernon's Texas St. 1936, RCS, art. 1935.
37. Const. 1876, art. V, sec. 20; Vernon's Texas St. 1936, RCS, art. 2345.
38. Ibid., art. 1942.
39. Ibid., art. 1657.
40. Ibid., art. 2992.
41. Ibid., art. 2996.
42. Const. 1876, art. V, sec. 20; Vernon's Texas St. 1936, RCS, art. 1941.

The trial courts in Orange County are the district court,[43] the county court,[44] and the justice courts.[45] Orange County is in the 1st judicial district,[46] the 9th supreme judicial district,[47] and the 2d administrative judicial district.[48]

Generally, the jurisdictional powers of the trial courts in civil actions are made to depend either upon the nature of the subject matter of the action or upon the amount in controversy between the parties, but in one instance, namely, the trial of the right of property seized under levy, they depend upon both. Insofar as they depend solely upon the nature of the action, jurisdictional powers in civil cases are distributed among the trial courts of Orange County as follows: The district court has exclusive jurisdiction in cases involving the title to, and for the enforcement of liens upon lands,[49] for the partition of lands,[50] for the recovery on behalf of the State of penalties, forfeitures, and escheats, for the recovery of damages for slander or defamation of character, of divorce, contested elections,[51] adoptions,[52] juvenile dependency,[53] and of all other cases over which jurisdiction has not been conferred upon some other court.[54] The county court has exclusive jurisdiction in probate cases, in apprenticing minors,[55] and in suits brought under the general law regulating the exercise of the right of eminent domain;[56] and the justice courts have exclusive jurisdiction in cases of forcible entry and detainer.[57] As they have been made to depend solely upon the amount in controversy, jurisdictional powers are distributed as follows: Those of the district court extend to all cases involving $500 or more.[58] In cases involving amounts ranging from $500 to $1,000, the district and county courts have concurrent jurisdiction;[59] above $1,000 the jurisdiction of the district court is exclusive.[60] The jurisdiction of the county court extends to cases involving not less than $200 nor more than $1,000; in cases involving amounts ranging from $200 to $500, it is exclusive,[61]

---

43. Const. 1876, art. V, sec. 7.
44. Ibid., sec. 15.
45. Ibid., sec. 18.
46. Vernon's Texas St. 1936, RCS, art. 199, sub. 1.
47. Ibid., art. 198.
48. Ibid., art. 200a.
49. Const. 1876, art. V, sec. 8.
50. Vernon's Texas St. 1936, RCS, art. 6083.
51. Const. 1876, art. V, sec. 8.
52. Vernon's Texas St. 1936, RCS, art. 46a; and 1939 Supp., RCS, art. 46a.
53. Vernon's Texas St. 1936, RCS, art. 2329.
54. Const. 1876, art. V, sec. 8.
55. Ibid., sec. 16.
56. Vernon's Texas St. 1936, RCS, arts. 1960, 3264-3271.
57. Ibid., art. 2385.
58. Const. 1876, art. V, sec. 8.
59. Ibid., sec. 16.
60. Ibid., sec. 8.
61. Ibid., sec. 16; Acts 1903, 28th Leg., p. 41.

but in cases involving $200 or less, the justice courts are the courts of exclusive jurisdiction.[62]

In suits for the trial of the right of property seized under levy, the jurisdiction of the district court is exclusive when the value of the property is $500 or more; when it is less, jurisdictional powers are divided between the county court and the justice courts, as in other cases in which jurisdiction depends upon the amount in controversy alone.[63]

In Orange County the criminal jurisdiction of the district court is confined to felonies, and misdemeanors involving official misconduct, and over these two kinds of offenses its jurisdiction is exclusive;[64] other misdemeanors fall within the jurisdiction of the county and justice courts. The justice courts are invested with jurisdiction, concurrent with the county courts, over misdemeanors punishable by fine only and in which the fine imposed does not exceed $200;[65] in misdemeanors of higher grade, the jurisdiction of the county court is exclusive.[66] In juvenile delinquency cases, jurisdiction is exercised concurrently by the district and county courts.[67]

The district court has appellate jurisdiction and supervisory control over the county commissioners court, but its appellate jurisdiction over the trial courts extends to probate matters only.[68] The county court has appellate jurisdiction in civil and criminal cases over which the justices of the peace have original jurisdiction, but in civil cases, only when the judgment appealed from or the amount in controversy exceeds $20, exclusive of costs.[69]

Generally, appeals in civil cases lie from the county and district courts of Orange County, when the amount in controversy or the judgment rendered exceeds $100 exclusive of interest and costs, to the Court of Civil Appeals of the 9th supreme judicial district.[70] Under the conditions and in the instances specified by constitutional and statutory provisions, cases may be taken by writ of error from the Court of Civil Appeals to the Supreme Court. The jurisdiction of the Supreme Court extends to questions of law only.[71]

---

62. Const. 1876, art. V, sec. 19.
63. Ibid., sec. 8.
64. Ibid., sec. 8.
65. Ibid., sec. 19; Ballew v. State, 9 SW 294 (1888).
66. Const. 1876, art. V, sec. 16; Acts 1897, Gam. Laws, X, 1146.
67. Vernon's Texas St. 1936, RCS, art. 2329.
68. Const. 1876, art. V, sec. 8.
69. Ibid., sec. 16; Acts 1897, Gam. Laws, X, 1146; Acts 1903, 28th Leg., p. 41.
70. Ibid., sec. 6; Vernon's Texas St. 1936, RCS, art. 1821.
71. Const. 1876, art, V, sec. 3; Vernon's Texas St. 1936, RCS, art. 1728.

Appeals in criminal cases originating in the district and county courts lie to the Court of Criminal Appeals. Cases brought to the county court on appeal may be further appealed to the Court of Criminal Appeals only if the fine imposed by the county court amounts to $100 or more; otherwise the decision of the county court is final.[72]

The district attorney represents the State in all civil and criminal cases in the district court in which the State is interested, and in examining trials and habeas corpus actions;[73] he also makes various reports on collections and disbursements,[74] and keeps records of his official acts,[75] fees, costs, and commissions;[76] the district clerk serves as the recorder of the court.[77]

The county attorney represents the State in all courts within the county below the grade of district court;[78] he gives legal advice to county officials;[79] he may institute proceedings against them for official misconduct;[80] and he may issue subpoenas in certain cases.[81] He also files and prosecutes delinquent tax suits for the State and the county.[82]

The sheriff acts as process and attendance officer for the courts;[83] he is the custodian of the jail[84] and the courthouse, subject to the rules and regulations of the commissioners court;[85] and he serves on the board of election supplies.[86]

The judge of the 1st judicial district presides over the district court.[87] The district clerk serves as its recorder.[88]

The tax assessor-collector is the assessing officer for State and county ad valorem taxes levied upon physical properties within the county;[89] in the case of ad valorem taxes upon intangible property, he

---

72. Const. 1876, art. V, sec. 5; Vernon's Texas St. 1936, CCP, art. 53.
73. Ibid., art. 25.
74. Ibid., RCS, art. 337.
75. Ibid., art. 338.
76. Ibid., art. 335.
77. Const. 1876, art. V, sec. 9.
78. Vernon's Texas St., CCP, art. 26.
79. Ibid., RCS, art. 334.
80. Ibid., CCP, art. 27.
81. Ibid., PC, art. 978.
82. Ibid., RCS, art. 7326.
83. 38 Texas Jurisprudence 431.
84. Vernon's Texas St. 1936, RCS, art. 6871.
85. Ibid., art. 6872.
86. Ibid., art. 2992.
87. Const. 1876, art. V, sec. 7.
88. Ibid., sec. 9.
89. Vernon's Texas St. 1936, RCS, title 122, ch. 7.

prorates the State and the county taxes fixed by the State board;[90] he must list all property within the county[91] and, subject to the approval of the board of equalization, he determines the value of it and the amount of the tax due;[92] after the approval of the lists of taxable property, he prepares in triplicate the tax roll, one remaining with him, another going to the State Comptroller, and the third to the county clerk;[93] he may seize and sell the personal property of delinquent tax payers;[94] and he is required to dispose of money received by him from taxes to accountable officers and depositories.[95]

The treasurer receives all money belonging to the county and pays it out upon orders from the commissioners court, which is responsible for the finances.[96] The treasurer may receive deposits only upon the authority of warrants issued by the county clerk.[97] All claims must be registered by the county treasurer in his claim register, in the order of presentation.[98] He may not pay out money except in pursuance of a warrant. Should he doubt the legality of any warrant he must withhold payment and report the matter to the commissioners.[99] The county depository serves as the treasury of the county funds.[1]

The auditor[2] of Orange County is responsible for its accounting system. He receives and records deposit warrants;[3] he examines and approves all claims, bills, and accounts before the commissioners court meets to act upon them;[4] he keeps, under the general supervision of the court, the finance ledger;[5] he oversees the enforcement of the law governing county finances;[6] he examines all reports of collections as made to the court;[7] he counts the cash in the possession of the treasurer and checks up on the money in the depository;[8] and he keeps many records, including a register of warrants issued.[9] Furthermore, he must make quarterly and annual reports to the court concerning the financial condition

---

90. Vernon's Texas St. 1936, RCS, arts. 7098, 7110-7113.
91. Ibid., art. 7189.
92. Ibid., arts. 7193, 7218.
93. Ibid., art. 7219.
94. Ibid., art. 7266.
95. Ibid., art. 7249a.
96. Ibid., art. 1709.
97. Ibid., art. 1657.
98. Ibid., arts. 1625-1627.
99. Ibid., art. 1713.
 1. Ibid., arts. 2828, 2829.
 2. Ibid., art. 1646.
 3. Ibid., art. 1657.
 4. Ibid., art. 1660.
 5. Ibid., art. 1663.
 6. Ibid., arts. 1651, 1653.
 7. Ibid., art. 1654.
 8. Ibid., art. 1655.
 9. Ibid., arts. 1662, 1666.

of the county;[10] each year he must submit to the commissioners court an estimate of all county revenues and expenditures; and he must see that no department exceeds its budgetary appropriation.[11]

Heading the local public school organization is the county school superintendent, who is charged with the immediate supervision of the schools in the county.[12] He appoints the members of the county board of examiners,[13] apportions the county's share of the State available school fund to the common school districts and the county funds to the common and independent districts,[14] and distributes free textbooks.[15] In addition, he serves as secretary to the county board of school trustees,[16] which consists of five elective members.[17]

The board is incorporated and in its corporate capacity may, for school purposes, acquire and own property, make contracts, sue and be sued, and do all other things necessary in the management of the common schools in the county.[18]

Each of the common school districts has its own board of trustees elected from the district.[19] Its powers within the district are similar to those of the county board.[20] It manages and disburses district school funds, directs and controls the public school buildings and grounds in the district, determines the number of schools needed and their locations, employs teachers, passes upon claims for district money,[21] and may make such rules and regulations as are necessary for the government of the district schools.[22]

The county board of school examiners, which serves "during the pleasure of the county superintendent," represents the State Board of Examiners in the county in giving examinations to applicants for teaching positions.[23]

---

10. Vernon's Texas St. 1936, RCS, art. 1665.
11. Ibid., art. 1666.
12. Ibid., art. 2690.
13. Ibid., art. 2878.
14. Ibid., art. 2692.
15. Ibid., arts. 2693, 2875.
16. Ibid., art. 2681.
17. Ibid., art. 2676.
18. Ibid., art. 2683.
19. Ibid., art. 2745.
20. Ibid., art. 2748.
21. Ibid., arts. 2749, 2754.
22. Bishop v. Houston Independent School District, 119 Tex. 403, 29 SW (2d) 312 (1930).
23. Vernon's Texas St. RCS, arts. 2878-2881.

Orange County uses the county school superintendent, and the peace
officers of the county and of the justice precincts to enforce the compulsory education laws of the State.[24]

The county surveyor performs important functions relating to boundaries, roads, and highways. His records frequently are invaluable in
settling title claims.[25]

In 1909 Orange County became a navigation district. The district
was established to finance improvements of the Sabine River designed to
make its waters navigable. Bonds were issued against the credit of the
district, and a tax was levied by the commissioners court to pay the interest upon the bonds and to create a sinking fund for their retirement.
Taxes so levied are assessed and collected for the district by the county
tax assessor-collector.[26]

The Orange County Conservation and Reclamation District, like the
navigation district, comprises Orange County alone. The greater part of
the bonded indebtedness of the navigation district has either been assumed by the conservation and reclamation district, or has been paid.
Indeed, the navigation district continues its existence for the sole purpose of liquidating the small balance of indebtedness remaining unpaid
or unassumed; it will be completely supplanted by the conservation and
reclamation district when this balance has been paid off.[27]

3. HOUSING, CARE, AND ACCESSIBILITY OF RECORDS

The records of Orange County are unusually well housed in the modern
courthouse at the city of Orange. This brick and concrete building is
145 feet long, 65 feet wide, and 3 stories high; was completed in 1937 at
a total cost of $250,000. It is considered 90 percent fireproof, and
most of the permanent archives of the county are kept in fireproof vaults.
Inside walls and ceilings of plaster and floors of terrazzo eliminate
much of the dampness prevalent along the Texas coast which is so des-
tructive to records. Modern steel roller-shelving, cabinets, and file
drawers are used throughout the building for housing records. Lighting
and ventilation are excellent. Tables and chairs are provided in most
of the depositories for persons desiring to consult the records.

---

24. Vernon's Texas St. 1936, RCS, arts. 2895-2897.
25. Ibid., arts. 5277-5280, 6706.
26. Const. 1876, art. XVI, sec. 59; Vernon's Texas St. 1936, RCS, arts.
    8198, 8213, 8222, 8224; Commissioners Court Minutes, vol. E, pp. 299,
    300, see entry 1.
27. Information obtained from County Judge, Orange County, February
    1941. And see Const. 1876, art. XVI, sec. 59; Vernon's Texas St.
    1936, RCS, art. 8194 et seq.; Commissioners Court Minutes, vol. H,
    p. 314, see entry 1.

County Commissioners Court. The commissioners' department consists
of a courtroom and four small offices, on the southwest side of the second floor. Records of the court are in the custody of the county clerk
and are kept in the clerk's office, in his vault, and in his annex vault,
on the first floor, for the most part; but a few papers and books identified with the court were found elsewhere - in the witness room on the second floor, in the basement storage space, and in the district clerk's office on the second floor.

County Clerk. The county clerk has a large vault, a small annex
vault, and a small office, on the east side of the first floor. These
depositories are well equipped to handle the large volume of records
which the clerk makes and keeps as recorder for the county and clerk of
the county and commissioners courts. In the large vault volumes are kept
on steel roller-shelving along the walls and on counter-shelves; unbound
material is in steel file drawers, cabinets, and pigeonholes. Records
are well arranged and are not crowded. In addition to the clerk's records,
all of the records of the county surveyor are located here, and scattering
records identified with the sheriff, county school superintendent, county
treasurer, justices of the peace, and district court.

The annex vault has three sections of steel roller-shelving for bound
volumes along the west wall, and steel cabinets containing file drawers
for unbound material. Records other than the clerk's found here include a
few of those of the sheriff, constable, justices of the peace, district
court, tax assessor-collector, and county treasurer. Records here are
poorly arranged, some 83 volumes now being stacked on top a steel filing
cabinet. If the volumes were rearranged, however, shelving would afford
adequate space for present needs.

A steel cabinet holds the three volumes and five file drawers of records kept in the county clerk's office.

District Court. The district courtroom occupies the east end of the
second floor. Its records are kept by the district clerk in his office
on the south side of the same floor. The office is well equipped, with
steel roller-shelving in sections along the walls and in a counter-shelf,
cabinets, and file drawers; but it is crowded, and record books are now
stacked on the floor in the northwest corner. Retired records of the court
are located in the sheriff's office, the county clerk's vault and annex
vault, and in the basement. Three volumes of county clerk's records were
found in the district clerk's office.

County Court. The county courtroom is in the northwest wing, on
the second floor. The records of the court are in the custody of the
county clerk. Most of its books and papers are in the clerk's large
vault; a few are in the annex vault; about 15 file drawers are in the
basement; and 1 volume is in the district clerk's office.

Justices of the Peace. The justice of the peace of precinct 1 has
an office in the southwest corner of the first floor. Records here are

kept in 2 wooden cabinets and 3 steel cabinets; they consist of 45 volumes
and 20 file drawers of justice court records and 8 volumes of sheriff's.
Retired records of the justices of the peace are located in the second-
floor witness room, the county clerk's vaults, and the basement.

Sheriff. The sheriff's office is in the south center of the first
floor. Two steel cabinets accommodate his records and two volumes of
district court records. A few of the sheriff's records are in the county
clerk's vaults; a few in the office of the justice of the peace.

Constables. The constable of precinct 1 has no office in the courthouse. One record book identified with this office is in the county clerk's
vault.

Tax Assessor-Collector. This official's department occupies the entire northwest wing of the first floor and consists of two offices and a
vault. Records are kept in the vault and in the larger office. The vault
is very crowded; books and papers are piled and stacked on all available
shelving, a file cabinet, on top an iron safe, and on the floor. The office has steel cabinets, steel roller-shelving, and two counter-shelves.
A few tax records are in the county clerk's annex vault.

Board of Equalization. Records of this agency are kept by the county
clerk in his vaults.

County Treasurer. In the treasurer's office, on the north side of
the second floor, 35 bound volumes and 8 file drawers of papers are kept
in a steel cabinet. Other records identified with the treasurer are in
the second-floor witness room, in the county clerk's vault, and in the
basement.

County Auditor. At the time this inventory was taken, the office of
county auditor was vacant; records made by a former county auditor are
located in the county clerk's vault and in the second-floor witness room.

County Board of School Trustees. The minutes of this board are in
the office of the county school superintendent.

County School Superintendent. This official's department is in
the southwest wing of the first floor. Five steel cabinets hold papers,
and a glass-front bookcase accommodates bound volumes. Obsolete papers
of the superintendent are in the county clerk's vault; and one old book
is in the basement.

County Surveyor. The surveyor has no office in the courthouse.
His records are kept in the county clerk's vault.

up

24x44

up

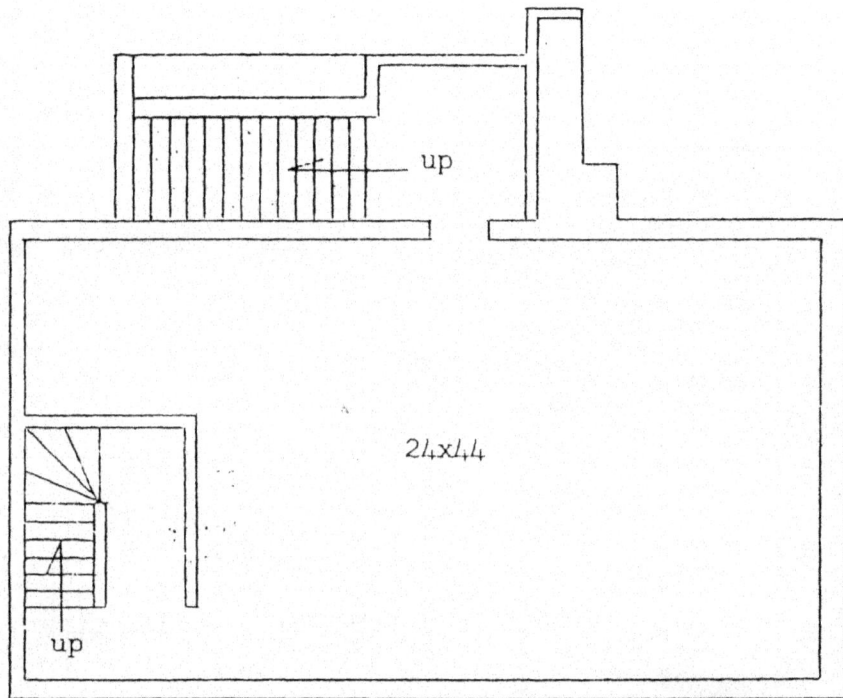

ORANGE COUNTY COURTHOUSE
Basement Floor Plan
Scale: 3/32" = 1'

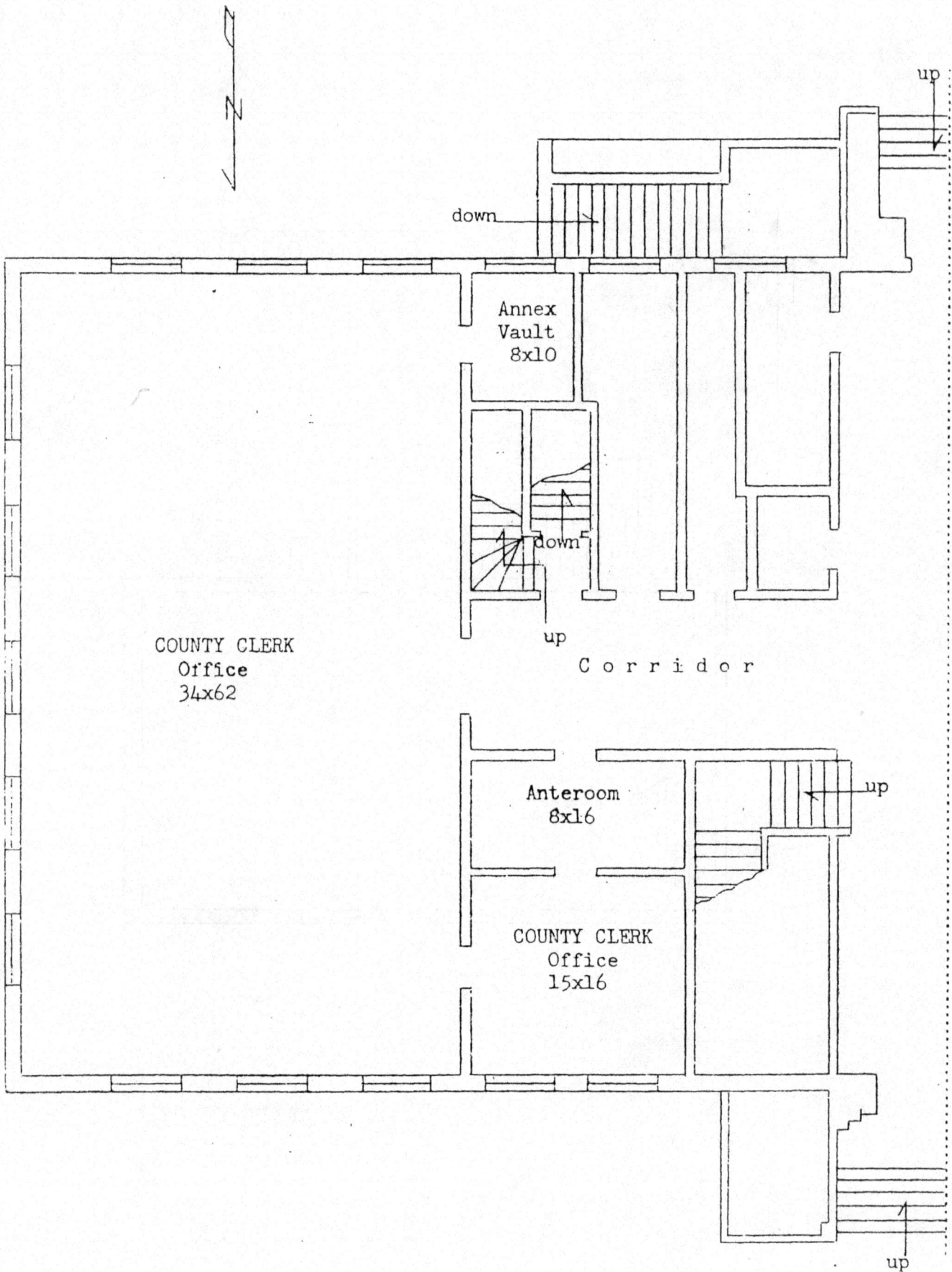

N

up

down

Annex
Vault
8x10

down

up

COUNTY CLERK
Office
34x62

C o r r i d o r

Anteroom
8x16

up

COUNTY CLERK
Office
15x16

up

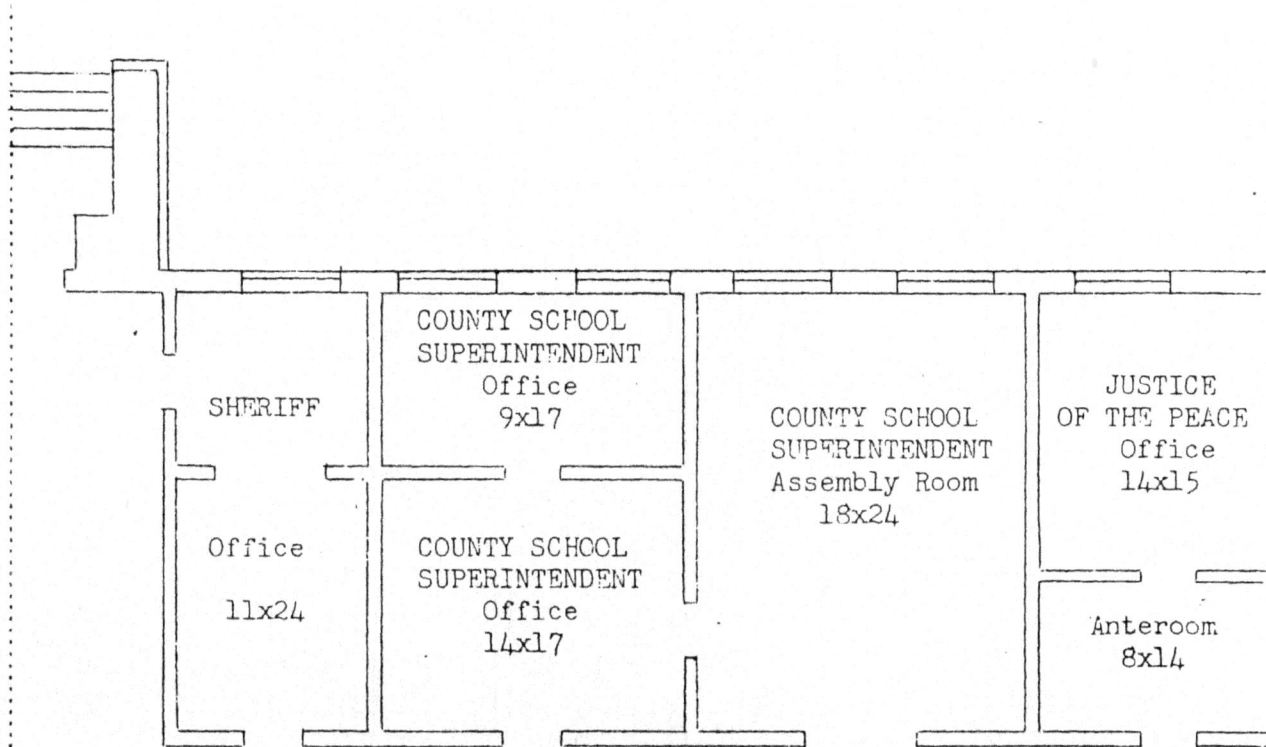

SHERIFF

Office

11x24

COUNTY SCHOOL
SUPERINTENDENT
Office
9x17

COUNTY SCHOOL
SUPERINTENDENT
Office
14x17

COUNTY SCHOOL
SUPERINTENDENT
Assembly Room
18x24

JUSTICE
OF THE PEACE
Office
14x15

Anteroom
8x14

Corridor

Elevator

Anteroom
8x8

Vault
5x15

T.A.C.
Office
12x15

TAX ASSESSOR-COLLECTOR

Office
24x42

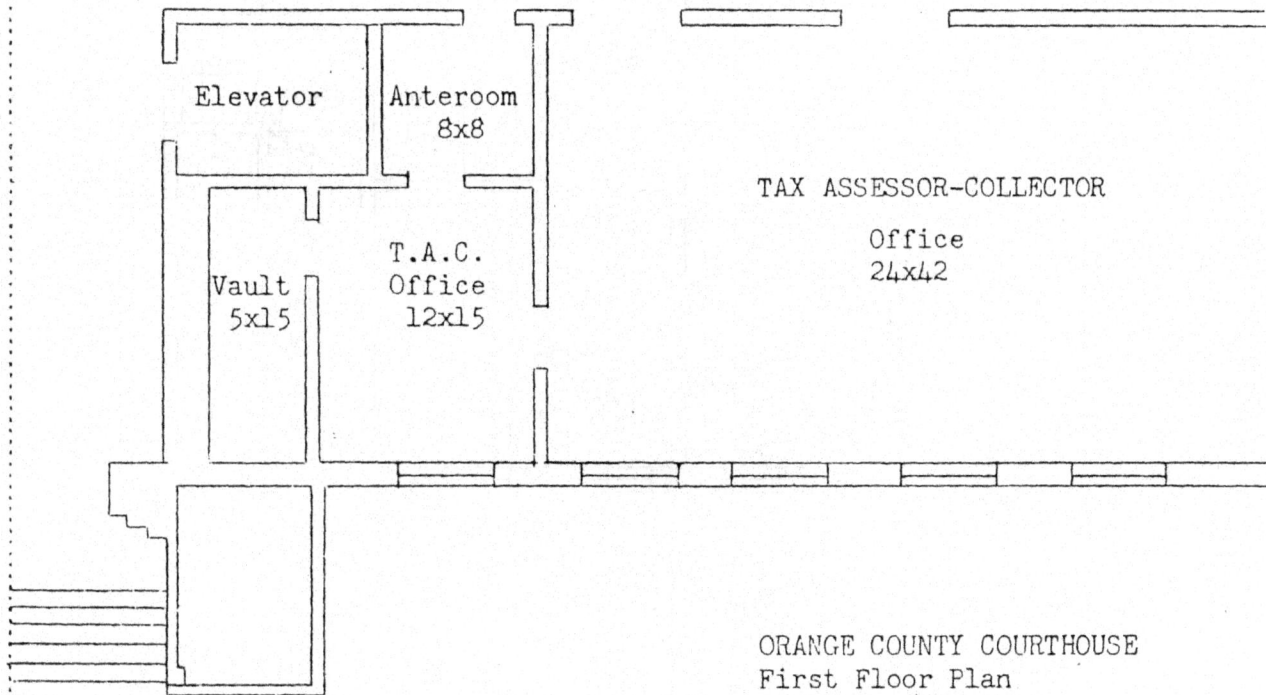

ORANGE COUNTY COURTHOUSE
First Floor Plan
Scale: 3/32" = 1'

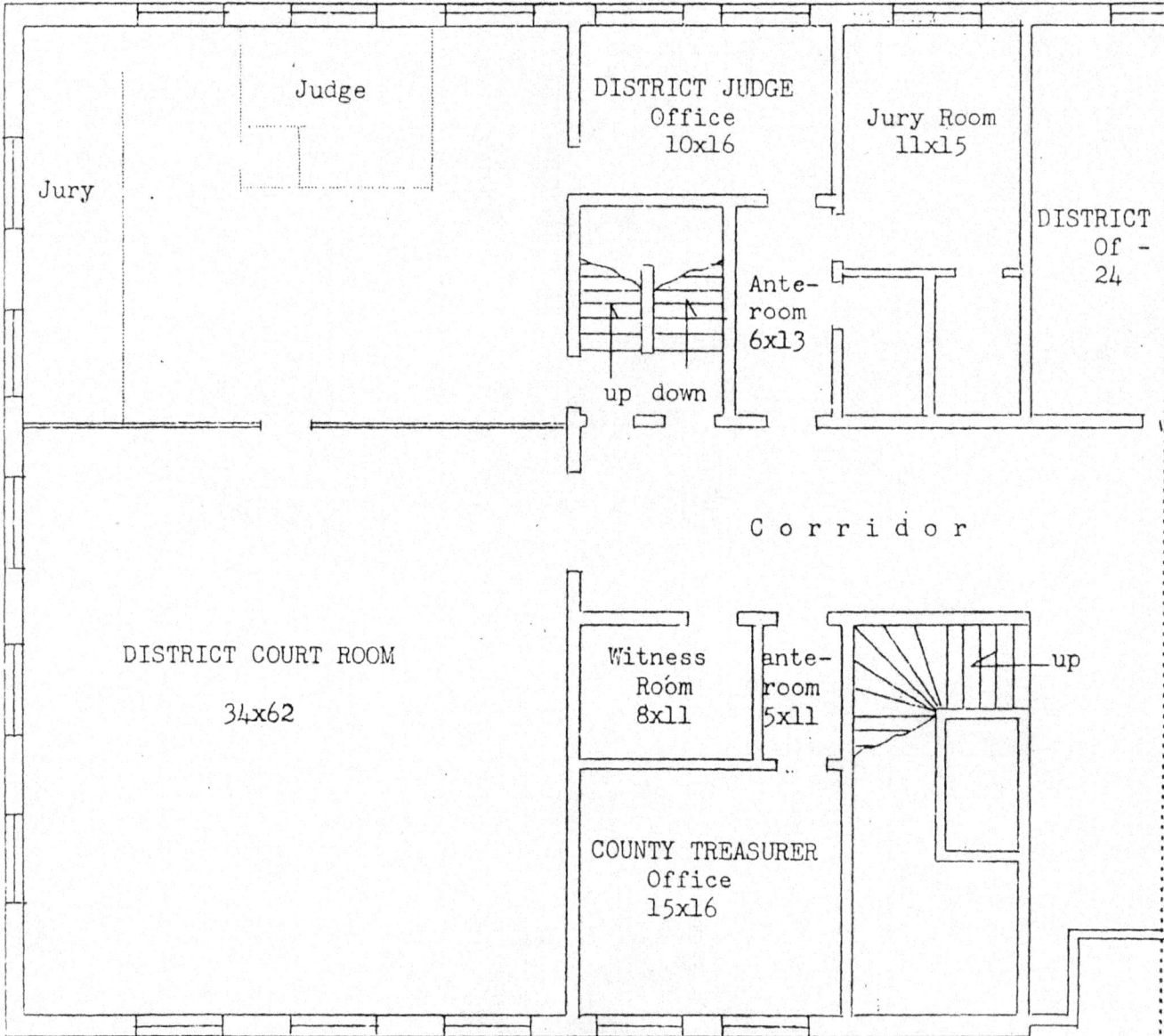

Judge

Jury

DISTRICT JUDGE
Office
10x16

Jury Room
11x15

DISTRICT
Of -
24

Ante-
room
6x13

up down

Corridor

DISTRICT COURT ROOM

34x62

Witness
Room
8x11

ante-
room
5x11

up

COUNTY TREASURER
Office
15x16

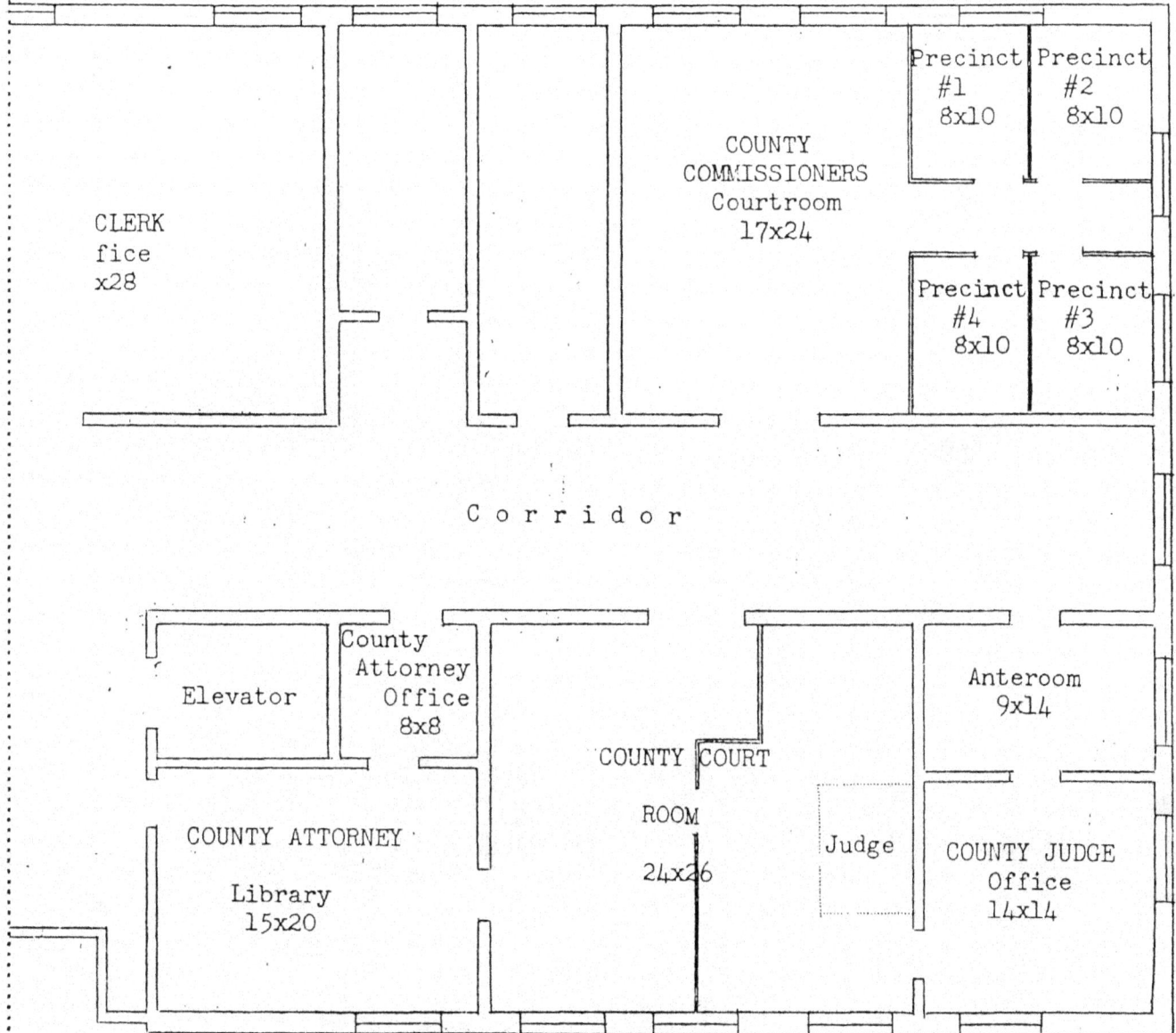

Precinct
#1
8x10

Precinct
#2
8x10

COUNTY
COMMISSIONERS
Courtroom
17x24

CLERK
fice
x28

Precinct
#4
8x10

Precinct
#3
8x10

C o r r i d o r

Elevator

County
Attorney
Office
8x8

Anteroom
9x14

COUNTY ATTORNEY

COUNTY COURT

ROOM

24x26

Judge

COUNTY JUDGE
Office
14x14

Library
15x20

ORANGE COUNTY COURTHOUSE
Second Floor Plan
Scale: 3/32" = 1'

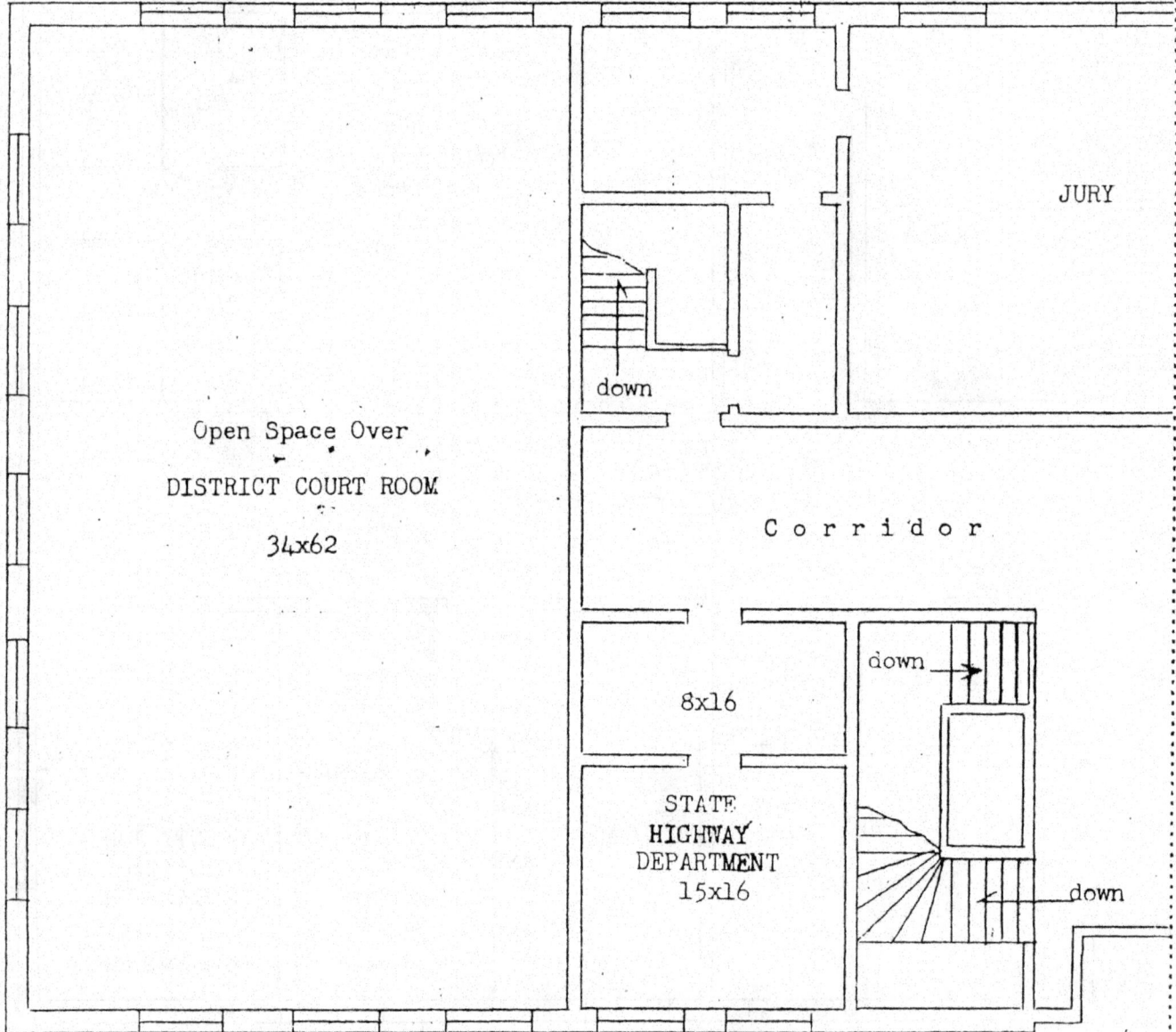

DORMITORY
24x40

BATH
17x24

WITNESS
ROOM
10x24

GRAND JURY
ROOM
23x24

Corridor

Elevator
8x11

TICK
ERADICATION
Office
20x24

CONSTRUCTION
UNIT
Office
16x24

HOME
DEMONSTRATION
AGENT
Office
12x24

COUNTY
FARM
AGENT
Office
12x24

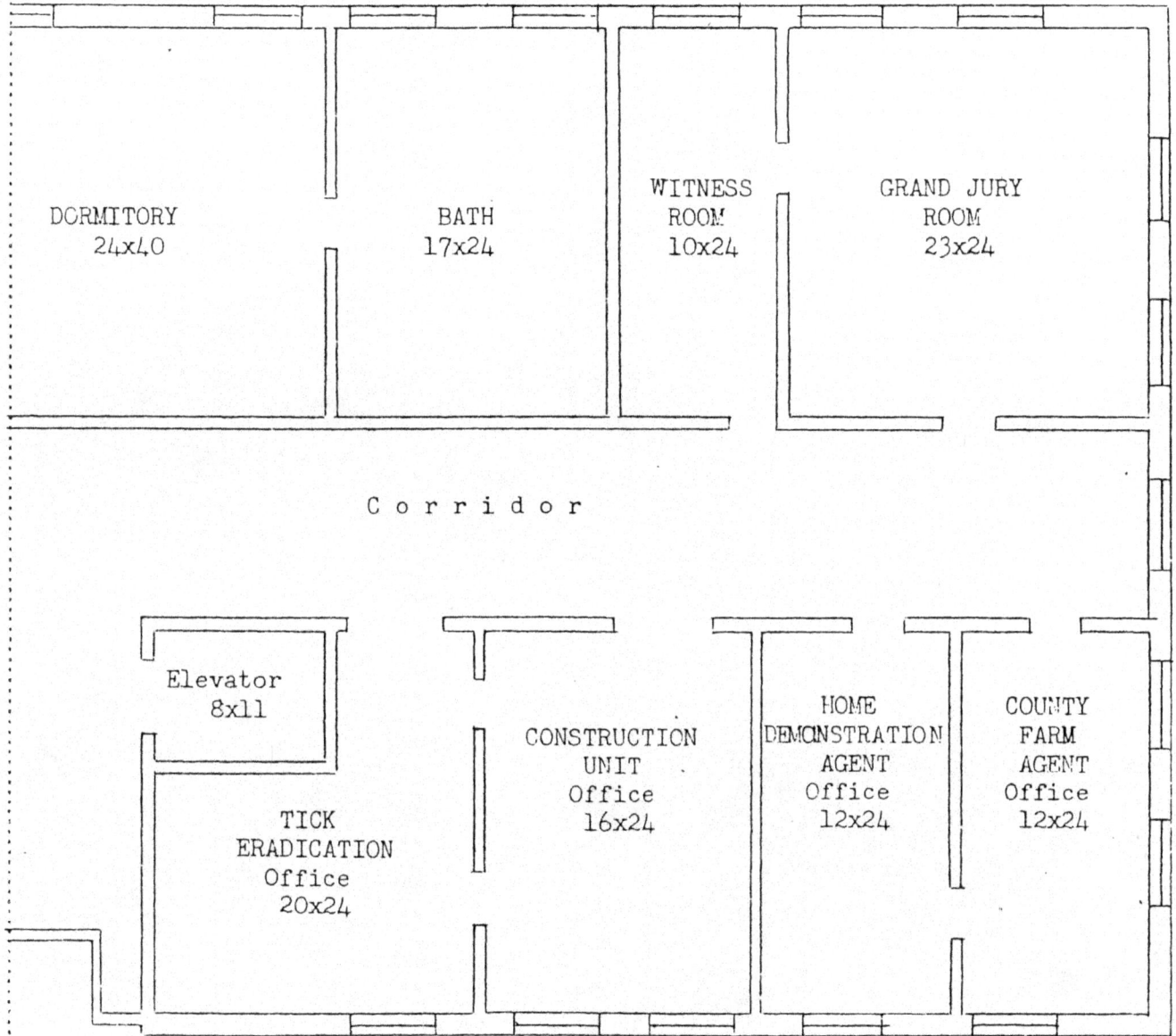

ORANGE COUNTY COURTHOUSE
Third Floor Plan
Scale: 3/32" = 1'

I. COUNTY COMMISSIONERS COURT

Since 1852, when Orange County was created and organized, the governmental functions of Texas counties have been performed, and their corporate affairs managed under the general direction of a governing court or board.[1] Orange County's first governing court was organized at a meeting held at Madison, May 7, 1852.[2]

The present governing court, the county commissioners court, was established in 1876. It is composed of the county judge and four county commissioners, all elected at each biennial general election. Each county is divided into four commissioners' precincts, and a commissioner is elected from each.[3] The county judge is chosen from the county at large and is the presiding officer of the court.[4] The county clerk is ex-officio clerk of the court.[5] The sheriff and the constables are its process officers.[6]

All of the records of the court are in the county clerk's vault except as otherwise indicated in the entries.

General Proceedings

1. COMMISSIONERS COURT MINUTES, May 7, 1852-May 28, 1866, Feb. 12, 1883--. 10 vols. (A, B, B-I). Title varies: Comr's. Ct., May 7, 1852-Feb. 22, 1860, 1 vol.; Minutes of County Court of Orange Co., Mar. 5, 1860-May 28, 1866, 1 vol.

Minutes of commissioners court in regular and special meetings, showing date and place of meeting, names of members present, disposition of business, judge's approval of minutes, and clerk's attest; business transacted includes classification and expenditure of county funds, approval of claims, levy of taxes, care of paupers, construction and maintenance of public buildings and roads and management of other county works, calling of bids and letting of contracts, designation of election precincts, appointment of election judges, calling of elections, and approval of bonds of county officials. Also contains: Tax equalization minutes, 1883-1908, entry 404. Arr. chron. by court term. No index, 1852-66, 1883-95, 1935--; for index 1896-1935, see entry 2. Hdw. 1852-66, 1883-

---

1. Acts 1846, Gam. Laws, II, 1639; Const. 1866, art. IV, sec. 17, Gam. Laws, V, 868; Const. 1869, art. V, sec. 20, Gam. Laws, VII, 414; Const. 1876, art. V, sec. 18; Vernon's Texas St. 1936, RCS, art. 2339, et seq.
2. Comr's. Ct., vol. A, p. 1, in Commissioners Court Minutes, see entry 1.
3. Const. 1876, art. V, secs. 1, 18; Vernon's Texas St. 1936, RCS, arts. 1927, 2339, 2342.
4. Const. 1876, art. V, sec. 15; Vernon's Texas St. 1936, RCS, art. 2342.
5. Const. 1876, art. V, sec. 20; Vernon's Texas St. 1936, RCS, art. 2345.
6. Ibid., art. 2346.

(2, 3)

1912; typed 1912--. Pages torn and writing faded, 1852-66, 2 vols.
634 pp. 18 x 14 x 4.

2. INDEX TO MINUTES COMMISSIONERS COURT, Sept. 4, 1896-Nov. 29,
1935. 1 vol. (1). Discontinued.
Index by subject of business to Commissioners Court Minutes, vols. D-H,
entry 1; page headings show printed alphabetical list of subject headings, with beginning page reference for each; each entry shows date of
proceedings, names of interested parties, nature of proceedings, and volume and page reference. Arr. alph. by first letter of subject and thereunder chron. by date of proceedings. Hdw. pr. hd. 640 pp. 18 x 14 x 4.

3. (MISCELLANEOUS PAPERS), 1852--. 23 f.d. (1-10; 13 f.d. unlabeled) and 64 pigeonholes (unlabeled).
Commissioners court papers, including:
   i. Confederate States, oath of allegiance to support, by aliens
      Frederick Sack and William de Carcamo, June 5, 1861.
   ii. Convict bonds executed in favor of the county judge by persons
       hiring county convicts through the commissioners court, 1925-26,
       showing amount of bond, names of principal and sureties, name
       of convict, rate of pay per month, total amount of fine and
       costs and court of assessment, term of court, date due, con-
       ditions of bond, signatures of principal, sureties, and county
       judge, and filing date. For minutes of convict hire, see
       entry 82.
   iii. Convict hire, reports of fines and bonds collected on, made
        monthly or quarterly by county judge to commissioners court.
        For register of reports, see entry 85.
   iv. County auditor, copy of district judge's order discontinuing
       office of, May 30, 1925, as recorded in Minutes District
       Court, vol. O, p. 84, in Civil Minutes Dist. Court, entry 187.
   v. County officials, appointments of, 1884, 1894; resignations of,
      1853-88; bonds, notices to make, 1857, 1881, and petitions
      for release as sureties on, 1852-81.
   vi. Cow Bayou, plan of bridge over, Sept. 1, 1893.
   vii. District court jury lists, 1900-1909, 1928--, copies of, filed
        with county clerk for use of county court jury commissioners,
        showing information as in entry 250.
   viii. Franchise for railroad right-of-way, copy of ordinance of city
         of Orange for.
   ix. Justice of peace, applications for appointment as, 1908-27.
   x. Justice of peace precincts, petitions to create, 1907-26.
   xi. Justices' of peace jury service reports, 1892-1925, showing
       name of reporting officer, court, month date of report, name
       of each juror, number of days served, and case number.
   xii. Road papers, including petitions for roads, road repairs, and to
        change boundaries of roads, plat to accompany field notes of
        road, orders for road work, and specifications for bridge work.
   xiii. School district no. 19, common, petition to levy maintenance
         tax for.

xiv. Tick eradication, petition to inaugurate.
xv. Tiger Creek, petition for new voting box at.
Also contains: County treasurer's county fund reports, 1913-16, entry
13; county clerk's county fund report, 1917, entry 16; county depository's
school fund reports, 1921, 1926, entry 19; assessor-collector's county
tax collection statements, 1853-58, 1861-94, entry 26; district clerk's
collection reports, 1861-94, entry 37; justices' of peace collection
reports, 1870-80, entry 39; county attorney's collection reports, 1861-
94, entry 41; sheriff's collection reports, 1861-94, entry 43; paid
county bills, 1852-1924, entry 45; canceled county warrants, 1861-74,
1914-29, 1937, entry 49; desposit slips, 1933-37, entry 55; check stubs,
1927-37, entry 56; insurance policies, 1886-1922, entry 58; road overseers' commissions, 1876-90, entry 63; road overseers' reports, 1852-
1924, entry 64; road bids and contracts, 1927--, entry 68; election
papers, 1852-1939, entry 73; instruments unclaimed, 1852-1934, entry 98;
public school land applications, 1916-27, entry 109; county officials'
bonds, 1936-37, entry 159; district court civil case papers, 1852-1911,
entry 172; district court criminal case papers, 1854-96, entry 214; probate case papers, 1915-21, entry 259; wills filed for probate, 1873,
1898, 1907, 1924--, entry 262; lunacy papers, 1867-93, entry 273; county
court civil case papers, 1886-1928, entry 278; county court criminal
case papers, 1852-89, entry 295; county court jury lists, 1922-35, entry
311; petitions for beer and wine licenses, 1933-35, entry 315; justice
court civil case papers, 1857-1929, entry 319; justice court criminal
case papers, 1860-1912, entry 323. Arr. chron. by filing date, 1852-
1934, 10 f.d.; no obvious arr., 1852--, 13 f.d. and 64 pigeonholes. No
index. F.d. 11 x 5 x 14; pigeonholes 5 x 5 x 5. 10 f.d., 1852-1934,
annex va.; 13 f.d. and 64 pigeonholes, 1852--, c.c. va.

4. APPLICATIONS FOR JOBS, Oct. 27, 1937-Sept. 2, 1938. 1 f.d.
Applications submitted to commissioners court for positions as stenographer to county attorney, caretaker of courthouse yard, house engineer,
and janitor; show name of applicant, position applied for, date, applicant's signature, and clerk's filing certificate. Arr. chron. by date
of application. No index. Typed. 11 x 5 x 14.

5. GRAND JURY REPORT, Oct. 13, 1937--. 10 reports in 1 f.d.
Copies of reports of grand jury investigations, made to district judge
by grand jury foreman, on felonies investigated, on condition of county
buildings, on examination of county finances, and recommendations relative
to enforcement of criminal laws, showing information as in entry 182-i.
Arr. chron. by date of report. No index. Typed. 11 x 5 x 14.

6. RECEIPTS, June 15, 1855-June 15, 1858. 1 vol.
Receipts taken by chief justice upon distribution of copies of session
acts of the legislature to county officers, showing date of receipt, number of copies, and officer's signature. Arr. chron. by date of receipt.
No index. Hdw. Pages torn and writing faded. 150 pp. 6 x 8 x 2.

(7)

Financial Supervision

Budgets

7. YEARLY REPORTS TO STATE AUDITOR, 1933-39. 150 reports in 1 f.d.
Copies of annual reports of taxing agencies to the State Auditor, forward-
ed with summaries made by county clerk when there is no county auditor:
  i. Form 396, statement of tax collections and delinquent taxes for
     conservation and reclamation districts, navigation districts,
     and road bond districts, showing total collections on real
     and personal property for all purposes, total interest and
     earned interest on investments, grand total of collections
     and interest, total delinquent and unpaid taxes for fiscal
     year ending June 30 of report, total delinquent taxes from
     1919 to beginning date of report as shown by compiled delin-
     quent tax rolls, entries 23, 389, grand total of delinquent
     and unpaid taxes at end of fiscal year covered by report, and
     assessor-collector's affidavit.
  ii. Form 396a, statement of indebtedness and sinking funds of con-
     servation and reclamation districts, navigation districts,
     and road bond districts for fiscal year ending June 30 of re-
     port, showing total amounts of checks and warrants outstand-
     ing, amount of cash on deposit, total amount of time warrants,
     bank notes, and other obligations classed as time indebted-
     ness, total outstanding bonded indebtedness, total amount of
     cash and securities to credit of sinking funds, and county
     treasurer's affidavit.
  iii. Form 397, statement of tax collections and delinquent taxes for
     common and independent school districts for fiscal year ending
     August 31, showing items of information as in subentry i, and
     school superintendent's affidavit.
  iv. Form 397a, statement of indebtedness and sinking funds of com-
     mon and independent school districts for fiscal year ending
     August 31, showing items of information as in subentry ii,
     and school superintendent's affidavit.
  v. Form 399, summary statement of tax collections and delinquent
     taxes for conservation and reclamation districts, navigation
     districts, and road bond districts, made from form 396, sub-
     entry i, showing total collections of all classes and for all
     purposes, total delinquent taxes for fiscal year, total amount
     delinquent from 1919 to year of report, grand total of delin-
     quents, and clerk's affidavit.
  vi. Form 399a, summary statement of indebtedness and sinking funds
     of conservation and reclamation districts, navigation districts,
     and road bond districts made from form 396a, subentry ii,
     showing totals of all classes of indebtedness, amount of sink-
     ing funds, and clerk's affidavit.
  vii. Form 400, summary statement of tax collections and delinquent
     taxes for common and independent school districts, made from
     form 397, subentry iii, showing items of information as in
     subentry v.

   viii. Form 400a, summary statement of indebtedness and sinking funds
of common and independent school districts made from form
397a, subentry iv, showing items of information as in subentry vi.

     ix. Form 401, summary statement of tax collections and delinquent
taxes of cities and towns, made from form 398, showing items
of information as in subentry v.

      x. Form 401a, summary statement of indebtedness and sinking funds
of cities and towns, made from form 398a, showing items of
information as in subentry vi.

    xi. Form 402, statement of county ad valorem taxes, occupation taxes,
and poll taxes, and amounts of depository interest and delinquent taxes, showing items of information as in subentry i,
and tax assessor-collector's affidavit.

   xii. Form 402a, statement of county funds, such as road and bridge,
general, and courthouse (but not including road bond districts,
school districts, or improvement districts), showing items of
information as in subentry ii, and tax assessor-collector's
affidavit.

  xiii. Form 403, statement of tax collections and delinquent taxes
administered for the State by county tax assessor-collector,
showing total amount of State ad valorem taxes on real and
personal property, occupation taxes, poll taxes, inheritance,
and liquor, amount of depository interest on all funds, amounts
of delinquent taxes as shown on form 396, subentry i, and
assessor-collector's affidavit.

   xiv. Form 404, recapitulation of tax collections and delinquent
taxes of local taxing agencies, showing name of agency, totals
as taken from reports, and clerk's affidavit.

    xv. Form 404a, recapitulation of indebtedness and sinking funds,
showing name of taxing agency, totals of indebtedness and
sinking funds as taken from reports (county, cities and towns,
road bond districts, school districts, navigation, and conservation and reclamation districts), grand totals of all taxing
agencies, and clerk's affidavit.

Arr. chron. by date of report. No index. Typed pr. fm. 11 x 5 x 14.

    8. BUDGETS FOR ORANGE COUNTY SCHOOLS, Aug. 20, 1932-Sept. 28, 1938.
        100 budgets in 1 f.d.
Copies of budgets for common and independent school districts, prepared
by the county school superintendent and superintendents of independent
school districts, as budget officers, showing year date of budget, date
of approval, amounts and classifications of expenditures for preceding
year, amounts and classifications of budget appropriations, recapitula-
tions of total expenditures and appropriations, amounts and sources of
revenue receipts for preceding year and estimates for current year,
totals of actual and estimated receipts, budget officer's signature, and
notarization. Arr. chron. by date of budget. No index. Hdw. pr. fm.
11 x 5 x 14.

    For other school budgets, see entry 441.

Fund Accounts & Reports

9. FINANCE LEDGER, July 24, 1879-Nov. 3, 1920. 7 vols. (6 vols.
    unlabeled; 3). Discontinued.
Clerk's ledger accounts with tax collector, occupation tax, sheriff, justice of peace, constable, county clerk, district clerk, county attorney,
county treasurer, and miscellaneous; each shows name of account, and for
debit entries, date, amount, and source of payment, and total debits; for
credit entries, date and amount of credit, total credits, and treasurer's
receipt number. Arr. in sections by accounts and thereunder chron. by
date of entry. Indexed alph. by first letter of name of account. Hdw.
pr. fm. 300 pp. 18 x 14 x 4. Annex va.

10. INSERT FOR COUNTY CLERK'S QUARTERLY REPORT, Nov. 1, 1905-Aug.
     13, 1917, Nov. 3, 1919-Jan. 12, 1920. 29 vols. and 1 unbound
     report. Untitled, Nov. 1, 1906, 1 vol.
Reports of accounts with county fee officials made quarterly by county
clerk to commissioners court, showing name and title of officer, name of
fund; debit sheet shows dates and sources of receipts and collections;
credit sheet shows dates, items (treasurer's receipt number, bank deposit,
or commission), and amounts of credits. Arr. in sections by accounts.
No index. Typed pr. hd. Torn and faded, Nov. 1, 1906, 1 vol. 50 pp.
15 x 7 x 1. Annex va.

11. AUDITOR'S REPORT RECEIPTS AND DISBURSEMENTS, Feb. 12, 1923-Mar.
     31, 1925. 17 reports in 17 paper-bound vols.
County fund reports made monthly by county auditor to commissioners court,
showing name of fund, month ending date of report, balance on hand at
date of report, total disbursements, total receipts, and itemized list
of disbursements from each fund, giving date of payment, warrant number,
name of payee, purpose of payment, and amount paid. Arr. in sections by
funds. No index. Typed. 20 pp. 12 x 10 x 1. Annex va.

12. AUDIT REPORT OF ORANGE, Oct. 31, 1910-Mar. 31, 1921, Jan. 1-Dec.
     31, 1939. 1 f.d. and 1 vol.
Special audits of county funds made by public accountants, with comments
calling attention to certain special items and summary of work accomplished,
summaries of cash receipts and disbursements of county funds, statement
of ex-officio compensations paid, reconciliations of receipts, disbursements, and remittances with bank statements and with treasurer's records,
summary statements of fees of office of all fee officials, and summary
statements of tax collections. Arr. in sections by summaries. No index.
Typed. F.d. 11 x 5 x 14; vol. 150 pp. 12 x 8 x 1. 1 f.d., 1910-21,
annex va.; 1 vol., 1939, c.c. va.

13. (COUNTY TREASURER'S QUARTERLY COUNTY FUND REPORTS), 1870-1916,
     Oct.-Dec. 1925. 1870-1916, Oct.-Dec. 1925 in (Treasurer's
     Reports &C), entry 15; 1913-16 also in (Miscellaneous Papers),
     entry 3.
County treasurer's county fund reports made quarterly to commissioners
court, showing name and county of treasurer, inclusive dates covered by

report, and for each fund, balance on hand from last report, amounts received and paid out during quarter, amounts of treasurer's commissions, credit and debit balances, and treasurer's affidavit.

   For recorded copies, 1905-19, see entry 14; for orders approving reports, from 1936, which serve as clerk's copies, see entry 15-iii.

   14. MINUTES COMRS. COURT FINANCES, Feb. term-Nov. term 1898, Aug.
       term 1905-Feb. term 1919. 4 vols. (1, 1-3).
Minutes of commissioners court examining and approving treasurer's quarterly reports of county funds; 1898 shows name of treasurer, court term, beginning and ending dates of quarter, name of fund (jury, road and bridge, general, buildings, bond sinking, ad valorem, indebtedness, road and bridge bond, stationery, jail, pauper and lunatic, salary, incidental, old 3d class, and quarantine), balance in each fund from previous quarter, amount of receipts, amount of disbursements, and balance on hand in each fund at end of quarter, and order to clerk to enter report and order upon minutes and properly credit the accounts of the county treasurer, with date of order, commissioners court affidavit, filing date, and clerk's attest; 1905-19 shows, at beginning of each term, date of court term, county, place and date of proceedings, and names and titles of officers present, and under each term, recorded copies of orders, showing county, court term, name of treasurer, month, day, and year of proceedings, beginning and ending dates covered by report, filing date, statement of court's examination of report, of its correctness, and statement of approval of amounts received and paid out and balance on hand for each fund since filing of preceding report, further statement of approval ordering clerk to enter report and order upon minutes and allowing credits taken in treasurer's accounts, and commissioners court affidavit; recorded copy of treasurer's report, showing information as in entry 13; and recorded copies of affidavits covering each report, showing information as in entry 15-ii. Arr. chron. by court term. No index. Hdw. pr. fm. 160 pp. 18 x 10 x 2.

   15. (TREASURER'S REPORTS &C), 1870--. 600 reports in 4 f.d.
Contains:
     i. County bonded indebtedness outstanding as of fiscal year ending June 30, copies of, made annually to State Comptroller by county treasurer, 1908-9.
    ii. County fund reports, affidavit of commissioners court to treasurer's quarterly, 1906-33, showing court term, county and name of treasurer, date report compared and examined, inclusive dates covered by report, statement that report is correct and that order of approval be entered on minutes, that court order recites separately the amounts received and paid out and balances on hand of each fund since last report, that cash and assets have been inspected and counted; with exhibit for each fund to prove inspection and counting of cash, showing amounts on hand from last report, totals received and paid out, debit and credit balances, and amount of cash on hand at date of examination; recapitulation of cash credits on hand, showing dates of balances, names of

funds, amounts on hand, and totals for all funds; commissioners court affidavit and clerk's attest.
iii. County fund reports, orders of commissioners court approving
treasurer's quarterly, 1936--, which serve as clerk's copies,
and show items of information as in entry 13. For treasurer's
copies, see entry 434.
iv. District clerk's reports of excess fees earned and deposited
with county treasurer, 1936--, showing report date, name of
clerk, case numbers, kind of fee (trial, fine, stenographer's),
amount for each case, grand total; and date and amount of
clerk's check to treasurer.
v. Expenses, actual and necessary, fee officials' monthly reports
of, showing court term, month date of report, date and kind
of disbursement (stamps, telephone, stationery, travel, and
other items), amount for each class, total expenditures, reporting officer's affidavit, notarization, judge's approval,
and clerk's filing certificate.
vi. Fee and expense report made annually by treasurer, 1938, showing items of information as in entry 32.
vii. Scholastic census, abstracts of, for years 1890-91, 1894-95,
made by tax assessor and approved by county judge, showing
scholastic year age groups 8 to 16, number male, female, and
total each group (white), number male, female, and total
each group (colored), grand totals; name, sex, color, post
office address and names of parents of deaf and dumb children.
Also contains: Treasurer's quarterly county fund report, 1870-1916, Oct.-
Dec. 1925, entry 13; quarterly school fund reports, 1887-94, 1898-1910, entry
17; annual school fund reports, 1905-7, 1918-19, 1925, entry 19; justices' of
peace collection reports, 1936--, entry 39. No obvious arr., 1870-1938, 2
f.d.; arr. by type of report and thereunder chron. by filing date, 1884,
1887-95, 1897-1902, 1918-19, 1 f.d.; arr. chron. by filing date, 1936--, 1
f.d. No index. Hdw., hdw. pr. fm., and typed. 11 x 5 x 14. 2 f.d., 1870-
1902, 1918-19, annex va.; 2 f.d., 1903--, c.c. va.

16. EXHIBIT (Clerk's Annual County Fund Report), 1909, 1914. 2 reports in 2 vols. 1917 in (Miscellaneous Papers), entry 3.
County fund reports made annually by county clerk to commissioners court
from totals in Finance Ledger, entry 9, showing name of fund, amounts
received or transferred from other funds, and total receipts; amounts
paid out or transferred to other funds, and total disbursements; and
debit or credit balances. Arr. in sections by funds. No index. Hdw.
pr. hd. 1909; typed pr. hd. 1914. 10 pp. 14 x 8 x 1. Annex va.

17. SCHOOL QUARTERLY REPORT, May 14, 1911--. 600 reports in 8 f.d.
1887-94, 1898-1910 in (Treasurer's Reports &C), entry 15.
School fund reports made quarterly to commissioners court by county depository (by treasurer prior to 1905), showing county, date, name of
depository, receipts, disbursements, and balances for each school fund
and each district, affidavit to report, and clerk's filing certificate.
Arr. chron. by date of report. No index. Typed pr. fm. 11 x 5 x 14.

18. MINUTES SCHOOL REPORTS, Nov. term 1905-Nov. term 1919. 2 vols.
    (1, 2).
Recorded copies of school fund reports made quarterly to commissioners
court by county depository, showing information as in entry 17, adding
date of court term, commissioners court approval, and clerk's attest
and recording certificate. Arr. chron. by court term. No index. Hdw.
pr. fm. 161 pp. 18 x 14 x 2.

19. ANNUAL STATEMENT OF SCHOOL FUNDS, Oct. 1, 1927--. 50 reports
    in 1 f.d. 1905-7, 1918-19, 1925 in (Treasurer's Reports &C),
    entry 15; 1921, 1926 in (Miscellaneous Papers), entry 3.
Copies of school fund reports made annually by county depository to State
Superintendent of Public Instruction, showing name of fund, date and
number of voucher, from whom received, to whom issued, total disbursements, date paid and amount, list of vouchers, district, and affidavits
of depository, county school superintendent, and clerk. Arr. chron. by
date of report. No index. Typed pr. fm. 11 x 5 x 14.

Tax Reports & Exhibits

20. CLERK'S COPY (of Annual Tax Reports), 1922-27, 1931-38. 10 vols.
    (subtitled by form numbers and titles of contained State Comp-
    troller's standard forms).
Copies of tax reports made annually to State Comptroller by assessor-
collector:
    i. Form F, supplemental assessment rolls of real and personal
        property, not assessed on regular rolls, 1924-27, 1931-38,
        showing items of information as in entry 357. For assessor-
        collector's copies, see entry 358.
    ii. Form 93, lands and town lots redeemed, 1924-27, 1931-38, show-
        ing information as in entry 393.
Also contains: Form 17, errors in assessments, entry 21; form 18, delinquent lands, 1924-27, 1931-38, entry 22; form 20, lands sold under judgment, 1931-38, entry 25. Arr. in sections by report forms and thereunder
alph. by taxpayer's name. No index. Hdw. and typed pr. fm. 100 pp.
18 x 14 x 1. 2 vols., 1922-27, annex va.; 8 vols., 1931-38, c.c. va.

21. ERRORS IN ASSESSMENTS (Form 17), 1901-21. 1 vol. 1922-27,
    1931-38 in Clerk's Copy (of Annual Tax Reports), entry 20.
Copies of annual reports (form 17) to State Comptroller by tax assessor-
collector, of errors found on tax rolls and of taxes uncollected thereon,
to be credited against totals charged on tax rolls, showing information
as in entry 386-ii. Arr. chron. by years and thereunder alph. by taxpayer's name. No index. Hdw. pr. fm. 100 pp. 18 x 14 x 1.

22. LAND SOLD TO STATE OR REPORTED DELINQUENT (Form 18), 1884-1923.
    12 vols. 1924-27, 1931-38 in Clerk's Copy (of Annual Tax Re-
    ports), entry 20.
Copies of annual reports (form 18) to State Comptroller by tax assessor-
collector, of lands and lots returned delinquent for year or reported

(23-26)

sold to State, showing information as in entry 387. Arr. alph. by taxpayer's name and chron. thereunder. No index. Hdw. and typed pr. fm. 18 x 12 x 1.

23. CLERK'S COPY DELINQUENT TAX RECORD (Form DTR), 1885-1932. 7 vols.
(3 vols. unlabeled; 4 vols. dated). Compiled 1929 and 1932.
Cumulative record (form DTR) of reports by tax assessor-collector to State Comptroller, of lands and lots returned delinquent or reported sold to State and not redeemed for years covered by compilation (made every 2 years), showing items of information as in entry 387. Arr. alph. by name of original grantee. No index. Typed pr. fm. 100 pp. 18 x 24 x 1.
For assessor-collector's copies, see entry 389.

24. ORANGE LEADER (called Orange Daily Tribune prior to September
1907), Mar. 1-31, 1904, Jan. 21, 1908, Apr. 3, 10, 17, 24, and
May 15, 1915, Aug. 14, 21, 28, 1924, June 15, 23, 29, 1926,
June 14, 21, 28, 1927, May 16, 23, 30, 1928, July 3, 1929. 8
vols. and 5 issues in 1 f.d.
Issues of the daily newspaper containing delinquent tax lists, as ordered published by the commissioners court, once a week for 3 weeks. Arr. chron. by publication date. No index. Pr. Vols. 100 pp. 18 x 24 x 1; f.d. 11 x 5 x 14. 8 vols., 1904, 1908, 1915, 1924, 1926-29, annex va.; 1 f.d., 1915, 1924, 1927, 1929, c.c. va.

25. LIST OF LOTS SOLD UNDER JUDGMENT (Form 20), 1903-19. 1 vol.
1931-38 in Clerk's Copy (of Annual Tax Reports), entry 20.
Copies of reports (form 20) to State Comptroller by tax assessor-collector of lands and lots sold by sheriff under delinquent tax judgment of the district court, on which State and county taxes, penalty, and interest have been paid to assessor-collector, showing reports of lands and town lots sold by sheriff under decree of district court and on which State and county taxes, penalty, and interest have been paid to assessor-collector, showing years sold for, in whose name assessed, to whom sold, abstract or lot number, certificate, tract, or block number, survey, division, or outlot; original grantee or city or town, subdivision or addition to city or town, acres sold; State ad valorem, poll, penalty; county tax, penalty, and interest; total State and county tax, penalty, and interest; total cost; date of sale; assessor-collector's receipt number; Comptroller's certificate number; commissioners court approval, and clerk's attest. Arr. chron. by date of report. No index. Hdw. pr. fm. 150 pp. 24 x 18 x 1. Annex va.

26. REPORTS FROM COUNTY OFFICERS, 1905-17, 1931-36. 250 reports in
1 f.d. 1853-58, 1861-94 in (Miscellaneous Papers), entry 3.
Annual statements of county taxes made to commissioners court by tax assessor-collector, 1905-17, showing total amounts received from all classes of tax collections, total charges, amounts of credits from insolvents and delinquents, amounts of commissions, amount paid county treasurer, and total credit. Also contains: Fee officials' annual reports, 1931-36, entry 32. Arr. chron. by filing date. No index. Hdw. pr. fm. and typed. 11 x 5 x 14.

County Commissioners Court -
Financial Supervision

27. CLERK'S COPY COLLECTOR'S MONTHLY REPORTS, 1902-17, 1919-22,
    1925--. 26 vols. and 23 unbound reports. Title varies slight-
    ly, 1902-17, 1919-22, 10 vols.; untitled, 1925-27, 23 unbound
    reports.
Copies of tax assessor-collector's sworn monthly reports to State Comptroller, examined and verified by county clerk, showing information as
in entry 394. Arr. chron. by date of report. No index. Typed pr. fm.
Aver. 150 pp. 18 x 14 x 1. 14 vols., 1902-6, 1909-10, 1930-35, 1938--,
c.c. va.; 12 vols. and 23 unbound reports, 1907-17, 1919-22, 1925-29,
annex va.

28. TEXAS LIQUOR CONTROL BOARD WEEKLY REPORT, Jan. 15-Aug. 7, 1937.
    11 reports in 1 f.d.
Copies of reports of fees collected for beer and liquor licenses, made
weekly by tax assessor-collector to Texas Liquor Control Board, showing date, county, amount of fee, license number, name of licensee, expiration date, State fees for permit, class, new or renewed, assessor-
collector's signature, and clerk's attest. Arr. chron. No index.
Typed pr. fm. 11 x 5 x 14.

29. TAX RECEIPTS, Jan. 24, 1903-Apr. 20, 1936. 3,700 receipts
    in 8 f.d. 1914-17 also in Tax Collector's Receipts, entry 31.
Copies and stubs of receipts issued upon payment of real and personal
property taxes, showing information as in entry 359. Arr. chron. by
date issued. No index. Hdw. pr. fm. 11 x 5 x 14.

30. POLL TAX RECEIPTS, May 6, 1916-Jan. 31, 1925, Dec. 10, 1935-
    Dec. 31, 1936. 3 f.d. 1915-18 also in Tax Collector's Re-
    ceipts, entry 31.
Copies of poll tax receipts issued, showing information as in entry 373.
Arr. numer. by receipt no. No index. Hdw. pr. fm. 11 x 5 x 14. 1 f.d.,
1916-25, c.c. va.; 2 f.d., 1935-36, annex va.

31. TAX COLLECTOR'S RECEIPTS, Jan. 8, 1903-Oct. 31, 1917, Dec. 2,
    1920-Mar. 15, 1935. 1,000 receipts in 6 f.d.
State Comptroller's invoices, 1903-8, of occupation tax receipt blanks
sent to tax assessor-collector by registered mail. Also contains: Property tax receipts, 1914-17, entry 29; poll tax receipts, 1915-18, entry
30. Arr. numer. by receipt no. No index. Hdw. pr. fm. 11 x 5 x 14.

Fee Officials' Reports (See also entry 15-iv, v, vi)

32. COUNTY OFFICERS FEE REPORTS (Annual), Jan. 20, 1939--. 50 re-
    ports in 1 f.d. 1931-36 in Reports from County Officers, entry
    26; 1931-37 also in District & County Clerk's Reports from May
    1899 to, entry 36.
Copies of reports of fees received and office expenses incurred, made
annually by county officers to commissioners court (and to State Auditor

and district court), showing year date of report, name and title of reporting officer, population of county, classes or kinds of fees, and for
each class amount earned, amount collected, and net collections, grand
totals of amounts earned and collected, and net collections; amounts of
deductions for office expense, maximum amount of fees allowed by law,
total authorized deductions, balance of excess fees due county, reporting officer's affidavit, notarization, and clerk's filing certificate.
Arr. chron. by filing date. No index. Typed pr. fm. 11 x 5 x 14.

33. (JUSTICES' OF PEACE ANNUAL REPORTS), 1932-35. In Justice of
         the Peace Reports, entry 39.
Copies of reports of fees received and office expenses incurred, made
annually by justices of the peace to commissioners court (and to State
Auditor and district court), showing items of information as in entry 32.

34. (COUNTY ATTORNEY'S ANNUAL REPORTS), 1932-38. In County Attor-
         ney's Reports, entry 41.
Copies of reports of fees received and office expenses incurred, made
annually by county attorney to commissioners court (and to State Auditor
and district court), showing items of information as in entry 32.

35. MINUTES OF QUARTERLY REPORTS, Aug. 3, 1907-Feb. 1, 1919.
         1 vol. (2).
Recorded copies of reports of fines, fees, and other collections, made
quarterly by county fee officials to commissioners court, showing name
and title of official, dates covered by report, number and style of case,
amount of judgment, fine, jury or trial fee, amount of officer's commission, by whom paid, and reporting official's affidavit. Arr. chron. by
date of report. No index. Hdw. pr. hd. 317 pp. 16 x 14 x 3.

36. DISTRICT & COUNTY CLERK'S REPORTS FROM MAY 1899 TO, 1899-1937.
         300 reports in 1 f.d.
County clerk's reports of fines, fees, and other collections made monthly
or quarterly to commissioners court, 1899-1933, showing court term,
classes and amounts of fees, fines, or other collections, reporting officer's signature, notarization, clerk's filing certificate, and judge's
certificate of approval; and attached to each report, treasurer's receipts, showing number and date of receipt, name of payer, amount of payment, name of county fund, and treasurer's signature. Also contains:
Fee officials' annual reports, 1931-37, entry 32; district clerk's collection reports, 1899-1933, entry 37; justices' of peace collection reports, 1899-1933, entry 39. Arr. chron. by filing date. No index.
Typed pr. fm. 11 x 5 x 14.

37. (DISTRICT CLERK'S COLLECTION REPORTS), 1861-94, 1899-1933.
         1861-94 in (Miscellaneous Papers), entry 3; 1899-1933 in Dis-
         trict & County Clerk's Reports from May 1899 to, entry 36.
District clerk's reports of fines, fees, and other collections made
monthly or quarterly to commissioners court, with treasurer's receipts
attached, showing items of information as in entry 36.

38. REPORT FROM COUNTY OFFICIALS (County Judge's), 1892-1919,
        1932-35. 250 reports in 1 f.d.
County judge's reports of fines, fees, and other collections made monthly
or quarterly to commissioners court, 1892-1919, with treasurer's receipts
attached, showing items of information as in entry 36. Also contains:
County judge's annual reports, of fees received and office expenses incurred, made to commissioners court (and to State Auditor and district
court), 1932-35, showing items of information as in entry 32. Arr.
chron. by filing date. No index. Hdw. pr. fm. 11 x 5 x 14.

39. JUSTICE OF THE PEACE REPORTS, 1894, 1899-1920, 1932-35. 200
        reports in 1 f.d. 1870-80 in (Miscellaneous Papers), entry 3;
        1899-1933 also in District & County Clerk's Reports from May
        1899 to, entry 36; 1936-- in (Treasurer's Reports &C), entry 15.
Justices' of peace reports of fines, fees, and other collections, made
monthly or quarterly to commissioners court, 1894, 1899-1920, with treas-
urer's receipts attached, showing items of information as in entry 36.
Also contains: Justices' of peace annual reports, 1932-35, entry 33.
Arr. chron. by filing date. No index. Hdw. pr. fm. 11 x 5 x 14.

40. SHERIFF'S & SURVEYOR'S REPORTS, 1873, 1887-92, 1899-1919, 1933-
        35. 150 papers in 1 f.d.
Contains:
    i. Copies of reports of fees received and office expenses incurred,
        made annually by sheriff to commissioners court (and to State
        Auditor and district court), 1889, 1933-35, showing items of
        information as in entry 32.
    ii. Bills for prisoners' board submitted by sheriff to commission-
        ers court for payment, 1914-16.
    iii. Field notes (General Land Office copies certified Apr. 19, 1909)
        of county line-survey between Jasper and Orange Counties,
        made by Jefferson County surveyor, Nov. 20, 1873, and of
        county line survey between Jasper and Newton Counties, made
        by Jefferson County surveyor, Dec. 8, 1873.
    iv. Surveyor's field notes and plats of county roads, 1900-1906.
Also contains: Sheriff's collection reports, 1887-92, 1899-1919, entry
43. Arr. chron. by filing date. No index. Hdw. pr. fm. 11 x 5 x 14.
Annex va.

41. COUNTY ATTORNEY'S REPORTS, Aug. 14, 1899-Mar. 1, 1938. 100
        reports in 1 f.d. 1861-94 in (Miscellaneous Papers), entry 3.
County attorney's reports of fines, fees, and other collections, made
monthly or quarterly to commissioners court, 1899-1918, with treasurer's
receipts attached, showing items of information as in entry 36. Also
contains: County attorney's annual reports, 1932-38, entry 34. Arr.
chron. by filing date. No index. Hdw. and typed pr. fm. 11 x 5 x 14.

42. CONSTABLE'S REPORTS, 1899-1920, 1933-36. 100 reports in 1 f.d.
Constables' reports of fines, fees, and other collections, made monthly
or quarterly to commissioners court, 1899-1920, with treasurer's receipts

attached, showing items of information as in entry 36. Also contains:
Copies of reports of fees received and office expenses incurred, made
annually by constables to commissioners court (and to State Auditor and
district court), 1933-36, showing items of information as in entry 32.
Arr. chron. by filing date. No index. Hdw. pr. fm. 11 x 5 x 14.

43.   (SHERIFF'S COLLECTION REPORTS), 1861-94, 1899-1919. 1861-94
           in (Miscellaneous Papers), entry 3; 1887-92, 1899-1919 in
           Sheriff's & Surveyor's Reports, entry 40.
Sheriff's reports of fines, fees, and other collections, made monthly or
quarterly to commissioners court, with treasurer's receipts attached,
showing items of information as in entry 36.
       For sheriff's copies see entry 345.

Claims (See also entry 69)

·44.   MINUTES OF ACCOUNTS ALLOWED, Jan. 17, 1916-Nov. 3, 1923.
           3 vols. (2-4).
Register of claims against county presented to, and ordered paid by commissioners court, showing claim number, name of claimant, nature of claim,
amount and date acted on, amount allowed, fund credited, scrip number,
and volume and page reference to Commissioners Court Minutes, entry 1.
Arr. chron. by date allowed. No index. Hdw. pr. hd. 321 pp. 16 x 14
x 4. Bsmt.

45.   BILLS, Dec. 3, 1897-Jan. 18, 1931. 3,700 papers in 7 f.d.
           Title varies: Audited Accounts, Feb. 11, 1904-Jan. 21, 1913,
           1 f.d. 1852-1924 also in (Miscellaneous Papers), entry 3.
Paid bills or invoices which were presented as claims against county,
showing date and place, name of firm or individual, items and amounts
due for labor, supplies, or materials, total amount due, claim number,
and date of commissioners court approval. Arr. chron. by filing date.
No index. Hdw. and hdw. pr. fm. 11 x 5 x 14. 3 f.d., 1897-1931, annex
va.; 4 f.d., 1904-16, c.c. va.

46.   REPORTS CLAIMS REGISTERED, 1871-89, 1898-1900. 500 papers in
           1 f.d.
Reports of registered claims against county, made monthly by treasurer
to commissioners court, 1871-89, showing dates covered by report, treasurer's claim number, registration date, name of fund, amount of claim,
and total for month. Also contains: Treasurer's receipts, 1898-1900,
entry 54. Arr. in reports and receipts subdivisions and chron. thereunder. No index. Hdw. pr. fm. 11 x 5 x 14. Annex va.

Exhibits to Accompany Reports

47.   REGISTER OF COUNTY EXPENDITURES, Nov. 29, 1852-Nov. 20, 1876,
           Jan. 3; 1887-Dec. 30, 1893. 3 vols. (1 vol. unlabeled; 1, 2).
           Untitled, Nov. 29, 1852-Nov. 20, 1876, 1 vol.
Register of certificates and drafts issued for county bills, 1852-76,
showing certificate or draft number, date issued, to whom issued, amount,
date of delivery, purpose of payment; and of warrants issued, 1887-93,

showing warrant number, date and to whom issued, purpose and amount of
warrant, on what fund drawn, and date of cancelation. Arr. chron. by
date issued, 1852-76; arr. numer. by warrant no., 1887-93. No index.
Hdw. 1852-76; hdw. pr. hd. 1887-93. 145 pp. 15 x 12 x 1.

48. WARRANTS (Stubs), Nov. 13, 1900-July 25, 1911, Sept. 8, 1933--.
    6 vols.
Stubs of time warrants issued by county clerk for county indebtedness,
showing warrant number, amount, date, to whom issued, what fund, purpose
of issue, term of commissioners court at which allowed, rate of interest,
and payee's receipt. Arr. numer. by warrant no. No index. Hdw. pr. fm.
200 pp. 16 x 14 x 1. 3 vols., 1900-1909, annex va.; 3 vols., 1908-1911,
1933--, c.c. va.

49. CANCELED VOUCHERS (Warrants), May 12, 1912-May 12, 1913. 500
    warrants in 1 f.d. 1861-74, 1914-29, 1937 in (Miscellaneous
    Papers), entry 3.
Canceled warrants which were issued by county clerk, authorizing payment
of claims by county treasurer, showing number and date of warrant, to
whom payable, amount, name of fund, purpose of payment, date issued,
clerk's signature, and treasurer's notation of number and date of check
issued in payment. Arr. chron. No index. Hdw. pr. fm. 11 x 5 x 14.

50. (COUNTY COURT JURY CERTIFICATES), Oct. 21, 1909--. 4 vols.
Stubs of certificates issued to county court jurors by county clerk,
authorizing payment by treasurer, showing number, amount, date, term of
court, name of juror, and number of days served. Arr. numer. by certificate no. No index. Hdw. pr. fm. 150 pp. 16 x 12 x 1.

51. (JUSTICE COURT JURY CERTIFICATES), Sept. 4, 1908-May 5, 1925.
    1 vol.
Stubs of certificates issued to justice court jurors by county clerk,
authorizing payment by treasurer, showing number, date, and amount of
certificate, name of juror, number of days served, term of court, by
whom received, and clerk's signature. Arr. numer. by certificate no.
No index. Hdw. pr. fm. Torn and faded. 500 pp. 8 x 14 x 2.

52. SPECIAL ROAD FUND WARRANTS ORANGE COUNTY (Stubs), May 25, 1912-
    Apr. 13, 1914. 2 vols.
Stubs of county warrants issued against special road funds, showing number, amount, and date of warrant, to whom issued, on what fund drawn,
purpose of payment, and term of court. Arr. numer. by warrant no. No
index. Hdw. pr. fm. Torn and faded. 250 pp. 16 x 14 x 1. Annex va.

53. CANCELLED SCHOOL VOUCHERS, Feb. 22, 1919-Mar. 25, 1926. 800
    vouchers in 1 f.d.
Canceled vouchers for teachers' salaries and school maintenance, showing amount, voucher number, school district number, date, and name of
teacher or purpose of payment, with signatures of county superintendent,
trustees, and payee. No obvious arr. No index. Hdw. pr. fm. 11 x 5
x 14. Annex va.

54. TREASURER RECEIPTS, Aug. 14, 1917-Aug. 3, 1928. 500 receipts
        in 1 f.d. 1898-1900 in Reports Claims Registered, entry 46.
Duplicates of receipts issued by county treasurer to county officials
for money deposited, showing date, number, and amount of receipt, from
whom deposit had, and treasurer's signature. Arr. chron. by date of
receipt. No index. Hdw. pr. fm. 11 x 5 x 14.

55. DUPLICATE DEPOSIT TICKETS, Jan. 18, 1934-Nov. 27, 1936. 23
        vols. 1933-37 also in (Miscellaneous Papers), entry 3.
Duplicates of deposit slips for money put in county depository, showing
county, bank, fund credited, date and amount of deposit, slip number,
and bank teller's signature. Arr. numer. by slip no. No index. Hdw.
pr. fm. 50 pp. 8 x 4 x 1.

56. THE ORANGE NATIONAL BANK ORANGE TEXAS, Mar. 1, 1930-Mar. 5,
        1937. 3 vols. Title varies: The First National Bank Orange
        Tex., 1930-35, 1 vol. 1927-37 also in (Miscellaneous Papers),
        entry 3.
Stubs of checks drawn on county funds by county clerk for payment of bills,
showing check number, to whom issued, for what purpose, date, and amount
of check. Arr. numer. by check stub no. No index. Hdw. pr. fm. Torn
and faded. 250 pp. 10 x 14 x 1. Annex va.

57. BANK STATEMENTS AND CANCELED CHECKS, Apr. 30, 1930-Jan. 31,
        1933, Jan. 1, 1934-Dec. 31, 1935, Jan. 15, 1937--. 4 f.d. and
        1 package (dated). Title varies slightly.
Bank statements and canceled checks; statements show name of bank, name
of fund, date of statement, balance from previous statement, dates and
amounts of deposits and withdrawals, and balance; checks show name of
bank, number, date, amount, name of payer, and signature of payee. No
obvious arr. No index. Typed pr. fm. F.d. 11 x 5 x 14; package 12 x
12 x 1. 2 f.d., 1930-33, c.c. va.; 2 f.d., 1930-32, 1937--, c.c. off.;
1 package, 1934-35, 2d fl. witness room.

Bids & Contracts
(See also entry 68)

58. INSURANCE POLICIES, Jan. 15, 1899-Dec. 26, 1916, Nov. 4, 1928--.
        3 f.d. Title varies: Insurance Policies & Official Bonds,
        Jan. 15, 1899-Dec. 26, 1916, 1 f.d. 1886-1922 also in (Miscel-
        laneous Papers), entry 3.
Insurance policies on county property, showing name of insurance company,
address, policy number, name of property insured, date issued, terms of
contract, date of expiration, description and location of property, and
signature of insurance company official. Also contains: County officials'
bonds and oaths, 1899-1916, entry 159. Arr. chron. No index. Hdw. pr.
fm. and typed. 11 x 5 x 14.

County Commissioners Court -
    Quarantine; Highways
    and Waterways
(59-63)

59. COURTHOUSE PROJECT PAPERS, Feb. 19-Nov. 2, 1936. 250 papers
      in 1 f.d.
Bids and specifications for construction of present courthouse, built
with PWA aid. No obvious arr. No index. Typed pr. fm. 11 x 5 x 14.
C.c. off.

Quarantine

60. (YELLOW FEVER BOARD MINUTES), Aug. 2-Dec. 31, 1878. 1 vol.
Minutes of the board of health appointed by commissioners court, showing
county, date of meeting, names of members present, name of health officer, copy of order establishing quarantine until abatement of yellow
fever epidemic, providing for establishment of quarantine stations, for
compensation of guards, and penalties for violation of quarantine, and
recommending disinfectants (chloride of lime, copperas, carbolic acid,
and nitrate of lead), and signatures of president and secretary of board.
Arr. chron. by date of meeting. No index. Hdw. 96 pp. (23 used) 8 x
14 x 1.

61. (QUARANTINE SUBSCRIPTIONS), Aug. 2-Oct. 1878. 1 vol.
Record of monthly subscriptions donated to defray the expense of quarantine until abatement of yellow fever epidemic, showing name of subscri-
ber, county, date and amount donated, and chairman's signature. Arr.
chron. by date subscribed. No index. Hdw. 130 pp. (5 used) 14 x 10 x 1.

Highways & Waterways
(See also entries 3-xii, 40-iv, 52)

62. ROAD MINUTES COMMISSIONERS CT. (Road Overseers' Appointments),
      Feb. term 1888-Feb. term 1914. 1 vol. (1).
Recorded copies of commissioners court orders appointing road overseers,
showing court term, name of overseer, expiration date of appointment,
road precinct number, beginning and ending points of precinct, and names
of persons designated as road hands. Arr. chron. by court term. No
index. Hdw. pr. fm. 296 pp. 18 x 14 x 2.

63. ROAD OVERSEERS' COMMISSIONS, Feb. 12, 1887-Oct. 13, 1914. 100
      booklets in 1 f.d. 1876-90 also in (Miscellaneous Papers),
      entry 3.
Road overseers' commissions, showing citations to road laws, name of
appointee, date of issuance and date of expiration of commission, name
and number of road precinct, description of boundaries of precinct, designation of road hands, and county clerk's signature. Arr. chron. by
date issued. No index. Hdw. pr. fm. 11 x 5 x 14. Annex va.

(64-68)

64. ROAD SUPERVISORS' REPORTS, Feb. 11, 1878-Feb. 14, 1893, Feb.
12, 1901-Feb. 19, 1921. 200 reports in 2 f.d. Title varies:
Miscellaneous Reports, 1878-93, 1 f.d. 1852-1924 also in
(Miscellaneous Papers), entry 3.
Road overseers' reports to commissioners court on the condition of roads,
bridges, and culverts in their road precincts, showing State and county,
court term, name of reporting overseer, precinct number, condition of
roads, culverts, and bridges, amount of money in hands of overseer, number of mile-posts and finger boards defaced or torn down; new roads,
bridges, culverts, and other improvements required, and estimated cost;
names of road overseers who have been neglectful of their duties, road
overseer's affidavit, and clerk's attest. No obvious arr. No index.
Hdw. and hdw. pr. fm. 11 x 5 x 14.

65. ROAD MINUTES (Juries of View), Nov. 13, 1905-Nov. 10, 1913.
1 vol.
Recorded copies of orders for jury to view roads and assess damages,
June 14, 1909-Nov. 10, 1913, showing name of landowner, description of
land, court term, judge's approval, and clerk's attest; and of reports
of juries of view, Nov. 13, 1905-Nov. 17, 1911, showing information as
in entry 66. Arr. in separate sections for orders and reports and thereunder chron. by court term. No index. Hdw. pr. fm. 140 pp. 18 x 14 x 1.

66. REPORT OF JURY OF VIEW, Sept. 8, 1893-May 10, 1918. 150 reports
in 1 f.d.
Reports of freeholders appointed as jurors to view roads and assess damages, showing court term, name of principal petitioner, date of appointment of jury, date road laid out, metes and bounds of survey, names of
landowners awarded damages, amounts due each, total damages, and juror's
signatures. Arr. chron. by filing date. No index. Hdw. pr. fm. 11 x
5 x 14.

67. ENGINEER'S ESTIMATES OF ROAD WORK, Dec. 2, 1912-Nov. 17, 1913,
Apr. 15, 1922. 200 papers in 1 f.d.
County engineer's estimates for road work, 1912-13, showing date, items
and cost of material, kind of work to be done, cost of labor, time required, location of road, and engineer's signature. Also contains: Copy
of $700,000 Orange County special road bond, Apr. 15, 1922. Arr. chron.
by filing date. No index. Typed. 11 x 5 x 14. Annex va.

68. BIDS AND CONTRACTS, Jan. 17, 1862-Feb. 11, 1927. 2 f.d. and
12 loose bids. 1927-- in (Miscellaneous Papers), entry 3.
Bids, bonds, contracts, proposals, and specifications for road work,
variously for grading, grubbing, and dredging, laying pipe, removing old
bridge over Caney Creek and building new one, constructing road drainage,
and surfacing road with concrete. Arr. chron. by filing date. No index.
Hdw., hdw. pr. fm., and typed. F.d. 11 x 5 x 14; bids 8 x 12. 1 f.d.
and 12 bids, 1862-1927, annex va.; 1 f.d., 1912-23, c.c. va.

69. ROAD FILE, Aug. 11, 1913-Mar. 23, 1914. 300 papers in 1 f.d.
Paid claims against county for road work, showing date, type of service
(team hire, labor, materials, etc.), name of claimant, amount due, date
allowed, and clerk's filing certificate. Also contains: Road precinct
and road engineering department payrolls. Arr. chron. by filing date.
No index. Hdw. pr. fm. 11 x 5 x 14.

70. APPLICATION FOR FRANCHISE, Oct. 15, 1927. 1 application in
1 f.d.
Application for franchise to construct and operate pipelines for transportation of gas, water, and oil across, along, on, and under public
roads and highways, showing county, date, name of applicant, filing date,
applicant's signature, and clerk's filing certificate. No obvious arr.
No index. Typed. 11 x 5 x 14.

71. ORANGE NAVIGATION DISTRICT, May 1, 1909-Aug. 14, 1911. 75
papers in 1 f.d.
Navigation district papers, including petition for establishing district,
petition for election for $43,000 bond issue, notices of election, and
copy of court order authorizing sale, bonds of navigation and canal commissioners and of W. H. Stark, board chairman, and commissioners' report
of work on district. Arr. chron. by filing date. No index. Hdw. 11 x
5 x 14.

Elections

72. RECORD OF ELECTION RETURNS, Aug. 2, 1852-Nov. 3, 1868, Nov. 8,
1886--. 5 vols. (1 vol. unlabeled; A-D). Title varies: Election Returns, Aug. 2, 1852-Nov. 3, 1868, 1 vol.
Tabulations of results of general and special elections. 1852-68 consists of recorded copies of election returns made by judges and clerks
of election precincts, showing date of election, precinct number, kind
of election, titles of officers and under each title list of names of
candidates and number of votes received by each, affidavits of presiding
officer, judges, and clerks, and chief justice's or county judge's certification; from 1886 consists of commissioners court canvass of returns,
showing kind and date of election, titles of State and county offices and
names of electors, abstract of proposition on amendments to State Constitution, names of candidates for State and county offices, names and numbers of election precincts, number of votes cast for each elector or candidate or for or against amendment in each election precinct, total number of votes received by each elector and candidate, totals for and
against amendment, and county judge's and commissioners' certification.
Arr. chron. by date of election. No index. Hdw. pr. hd. Pages torn,
1852-68, 1 vol. 83 to 100 pp. 10 x 14 x 1 to 18 x 12 x 1.

(73-78)

73. (ELECTION PAPERS), Sept. 24, 1883-Nov. 15, 1929. 600 papers
in 2 f.d. 1852-1939 also in (Miscellaneous Papers), entry 3.
Election papers, including petitions, copies of election notices posted
by sheriff, orders calling elections, returns, orders declaring results,
and certificates of nomination of candidates. Arr. chron. by filing date.
No index. Hdw., hdw. pr. fm., and typed. 11 x 5 x 14.

74. CANVASS BOOK BY ELECTION PRECINCTS, Nov. 2, 1920-Nov. 4, 1926.
2 vols. and 2 loose tally sheets.
Tally sheets kept by election judges, showing State and county, names of
candidates and office sought, date of election, name and number of precinct, number of votes for each candidate, total number of votes cast,
and election judge's affidavit. Arr. alph. by first letter of voter's
surname. No index. Hdw. pr. fm. 21 pp. 12 x 20 x 1. Annex va.

75. RECORD BALLOTS AND BALLOT BOX NO. 4, Nov. 2, 1904-Aug. 6, 1907.
1 vol. (1).
Clerk's record of ballots delivered to election precincts, showing precinct number, number of ballots delivered, clerk's notation "election
supplies as required by law," date delivered, signature of person to whom
delivered, and clerk's affidavit to delivery of sealed package to each
precinct containing 2½ times as many ballots as were cast for Governor
in last general election. Arr. one election to a page and thereunder
numer. by precinct no. No index. Hdw. pr. hd. 160 pp. (10 used) 18 x
14 x 1. Annex va.

76. GENERAL REGISTRATION BOOK OF ORANGE COUNTY, Sept. 5, 1871-73.
1 vol. Jan. 3, 1870 also in Jury Book, entry 86.
List of registered voters in all precincts of the county as filed with
district clerk, Sept. 5, 1871, with subsequent registrations to Apr. 1,
1873, on pp. 1-11, showing registration number, date of registration,
name, age, and State or county of birth of voter, voter's signature, and
remarks (dead, removed, colored); on pp. 13-18, list of voters in precinct 1, July 28-Aug. 1, 1873, showing precinct number, name of voter,
registration date, and voter's signature; on pp. 20, 25, names of voters
in precincts 2 and 3, undated; on pp. 30, 31, names of voters in precinct
4, 1873. Arr. in 4 sections as indicated above and thereunder numer. by
registration no. No index. Hdw. 160 pp. (21 used) 20 x 14 x 2.

77. REGISTRATION LIST PRECINCT NO. 1, Jan. 13, 1872. 1 vol.
List of voters registered in precinct 1 by justice of the peace, showing
number and name of voter, and justice's certification to correctness of
list. Arr. numer. by registration no. No index. Hdw. 165 pp. 14 x 8 x 1.

78. REGISTRATION LIST PRECINCT NO. 4, Nov. 22, 1873. 1 vol.
List of voters registered in precinct 4 by justice of peace, showing number and name of voter and certification of justices of peace of precincts
1, 3, and 4, that list is true and correct as revised Nov. 22, 1873.
Also contains, on flyleaf: "First annual registration commenced July
28, 1873"; and on p. 2, copy of article 3, section 1, Constitution of

1869. Arr. numer. by registration no. No index. Hdw. 165 pp. (4
used) 14 x 8 x 1.

79. CAMPAIGN EXPENDITURES, June 28, 1920-Sept. 6, 1932, July 18,
    1934-July 23, 1938. 650 reports in 2 f.d.
Reports made by candidates for office to county judge of amounts of campaign expenditures, showing name of candidate, items of expenses, total
amount, date of report, candidate's affidavit, notarization, filing date,
and clerk's signature. Arr. chron. by filing date. No index. Typed
1920-32; hdw. pr. fm. 1934-38. 11 x 5 x 14. 1 f.d., 1920-32, annex va.;
1 f.d., 1934-38, c.c. va.

Butchers' Reports

80. REPORT OF ANIMALS SLAUGHTERED, Feb. 16-Nov. 10, 1916. 7 re-
    ports in 1 f.d.
Reports of animals slaughtered, made quarterly by butchers to commissioners court, showing county, name of butcher, ending date of report, classes
or kinds of animals and ages, marks and brands of each class, name of
person from whom purchased, butcher's affidavit, and clerk's filing certificate. Arr. chron. by date of report. No index. Hdw. pr. fm. 11 x
5 x 14.

81. RECORD OF BUTCHERS REPORTS, July 31, 1887-Feb. 13, 1888.
    1 vol. (1).
Recorded copies of reports of animals slaughtered, made quarterly by
butchers to commissioners court, showing information as in entry 80.
Arr. chron. by recording date. No index. Hdw. pr. hd. 640 pp. (31
used) 18 x 12 x 3. D.c. off.

Convict Labor

82. RECORD OF CONVICT LABOR, June 7, 1899-June 21, 1926. 2 vols.
    (2, 3).
Minutes of commissioners court hiring county convicts to bonded individ-
uals or firms to work out fines and court costs due the county, showing
case number, name of convict, in what court convicted, description of
convict, name of employer, amounts due clerk, county attorney, jury,
sheriff, and county judge, total amount, dates of payments, date of bond,
amount due monthly, amount and date paid to county judge, date and amount
paid by county judge to treasurer, treasurer's receipt number, date paid
in full, and treasurer's signature; or, in cases where prisoner worked
on road or served time out in jail, this fact is noted under column for
treasurer's receipt and amount of fine, and costs are shown, but there
is no recording under amount of bond. Arr. chron. by date of bond. Indexed alph. by first letter of convict's surname and chron. thereunder,
1899-1911; no index, 1912-26. Hdw. pr. hd. 200 dbl. pp. 17 x 14 x 3.
1 vol., 1899-1911, c.c. va.; 1 vol., 1912-26, annex va.
    For convict bonds, see entry 3-ii.

83.   SCHOOL FUND REGISTER (Convict Fine Account), Dec. 8, 1902-
         Feb. 24, 1905. 1 vol.
Accounts of receipt and disposition of convict fines, showing name of
convict, date of entry, amounts of fines, amounts due sheriff, clerk
and county attorney, and trial fees, total fines and costs, dates and
amounts of receipts, and treasurer's receipt numbers. Arr. one case to
a page and thereunder chron. by date of entry. No index. Hdw. 300 pp.
(189 used) 16 x 10 x 2.

84.   (CONVICT HIRE RECEIPT BOOK), Jan. 17, 1925-Mar. 2, 1927.
         1 vol.
Duplicates of receipts issued by county judge upon payment of fines,
costs, and payments on convict bonds, showing amount, date of receipt,
from whom received, nature of payment, case number, and judge's signature. Arr. chron. by date of receipt. No index. Hdw. pr. fm. 100 pp.
12 x 10 x 1. Annex va.

85.   QUARTERLY REPORTS COUNTY JUDGE (Convict Hire), Aug. term 1911-
         Feb. term 1919. 1 vol.
Register of reports of convict hire made quarterly by county judge to
commissioners court, showing court term, case number, name of convict,
in what court convicted, description of convict, nature of employment,
name of employer, amount and date of bond, when paid to county judge,
amount paid to county treasurer, and treasurer's receipt; or, in cases
where no bond made and convict served time out in jail or worked on
county roads, amount of fines and costs entered under column for amount
of bond. Arr. chron. by court term. No index. Hdw. pr. hd. 189 pp.
18 x 14 x 2.
       For reports, see entry 3-iii.

                              Jury Selection

86.   JURY BOOK, 1867, 1868, Jan. 3, 1870, Jan. 31, 1872. 2 vols.
         Untitled, Jan. 31, 1872, 1 vol. Discontinued; since 1876
         selections by jury commissioners (Acts 1876, Gam. Laws, VIII,
         915).
Record of persons selected by district clerk, county clerk, and justice
of peace to serve as jurors in district court and county court for years
1867, 1868, and 1872, showing court term for which jurors to serve,
names of officers in whose presence lists were drawn, numbers and names
of persons selected, and certification of county clerk, district clerk,
and justice of peace that list was drawn according to law. Also contains: Lists of registered voters, all precincts, Jan. 3, 1870, entry
76. Jury lists arr. chron. by court term, 1867, 1868, and alph. by
first letter of juror's surname, with names numbered consecutively,
1872; registration lists arr. numer. by registration number. No index.
Hdw. 80 pp. 14 x 8 x 1. 1 vol., 1867, 1868, 1870, annex va.; 1 vol.,
1872, c.c. va.

II. COUNTY CLERK AS RECORDER

A county clerk was one of the group of officers who composed Orange County's first governmental organization.[1] For a period of about 6 years, when the office of county clerk was discontinued by the Constitution of 1869, the district clerks were the recorders of Texas counties;[2] with this exception, the county clerk has always served as recorder.[3] The clerk is elected from the county at large at each biennial general election.[4].

All of the records of the county clerk are in his vault except as otherwise indicated in the entries.

Registration

General

87. REGISTER OF INSTRUMENTS FILED FOR RECORD, Feb. 23, 1891--.
     16 vols. (A; 1 vol. unlabeled; B, C, 3-14).
Register of instruments filed with county clerk for recording, showing names of grantor, grantee, and person filing, kind and date of instrument, filing date, fees charged, to whom delivered, and date delivered. Arr. alph. by first letter of grantor's surname and thereunder chron. by filing date. No index. Hdw. pr. hd. 200 pp. 16 x 14 x 2.

88. ORANGE COUNTY (Abstracts), 1852-73. 2 vols.
Numerical abstract-register of transfers of title to real property recorded in Deed Record, entry 93; page heading shows abstract number, county and State, certificate or patent number, original grantee, and number of acres; each entry shows names of grantor and grantee, number of acres, kind and date of instrument, date of acknowledgment, filing date, and volume and page reference. Arr. numer. by abstract no. Indexed alph. by first letter of original grantee's surname and chron. thereunder. Hdw. under hdw. hd. and hdw. pr. hd. 136 to 445 pp. 14 x 8 x 1 to 16 x 12 x 3.

89. (ACREAGE OWNERSHIP RECORD), approx. 1939--. 1 vol.
Acreage ownership record; page headings on left and right pages show original grantee, patent number, date patent issued (from 1835), number

---

1. Acts 1846, Gam. Laws, II, 1542; Comr's. Ct. (1852-60), vol. A, p. 1, in Commissioners Court Minutes, see entry 1.
2. Const. 1869, art. V, sec. 9, Gam. Laws, VII, 412.
3. Acts 1846, Gam. Laws, II, 1542; Const. 1866, art. IV, sec. 18, Gam. Laws, V, 869; Const. 1876, art. V, sec. 20.
4. Ibid.

of acres in grant, and abstract number; map of original grant, on left
page, shows scale, and for each tract, number of acres and tract number;
right page gives numerical list of tracts within grant. Arr. numer. by
abstract no. Indexed alph. by original grantee's name, with reference
to abstract no. Hdw. pr. hd.; maps handdrawn. 1,200 pp. 18 x 16 x 5.

90. (CITY LOT OWNERSHIP RECORD), approx. 1939--. 1 vol.
City lot ownership record; page headings on left and right pages show
abstract number, block numbers, name of subdivision or survey, and name
of town; maps of subdivision or survey, on left pages, show scale and
numbered lots and blocks; right pages give numerical list of blocks within each tract. Arr. alph. by first letter of name of subdivision or survey. No index. Hdw. pr. hd.; maps handdrawn. 1,200 pp. 18 x 16 x 5.

91. MAP RECORD, May 16, 1914--. 2 vols. (1, 2).
Recorded copies of maps and plats of cities and towns, subdivisions, additions, canals, railroad rights-of-way, and surveys of tracts of lands,
showing title of map, scale, metes and bounds, roads, names of surveys,
block numbers, number of acres, filing date, and clerk's recording certificate. Arr. chron. by filing date. For index, see entry 92. Blue-
prints; handdrawn; rights-of-way photostats. 55 pp. 24 x 30 x 2.

92. INDEX TO MAP RECORD, May 16, 1914--. 2 vols. (1, 2). Untitled,
         May 16, 1914-Oct. 20, 1926, 1 vol.
Index by title of map to Map Record, entry 91, showing page reference.
Arr. alph. by first letter in first word of map title and chron. there-
under. Hdw. 70 pp. 18 x 10 x 1.

93. DEED RECORD, Apr. 19, 1852--. 90 vols. (A-Z, 1-64).
General registration books of the county used for recording instruments
filed to establish property titles and interests, including recorded
copies of deeds, patents, powers of attorney, wills and codicils, maps,
surveys, leases, transfers, agreements, assignments, and releases. Arr.
chron. by recording date. For index, see entries 94-96. Hdw. 1852-1911;
typed 1911--. 600 pp. 18 x 12 x 3.

94. GENERAL INDEX TO DEEDS, Apr. 19, 1852--. 10 vols. (1-10).
Grantor-grantee index (with exception of certain instruments indexed in
special volumes, see entries 95, 96) to Deed Record, entry 93; each entry
shows name of opposite party, kind and date of instrument, filing date,
and volume and page reference; and also, 1852-88, name of original grantee; and from 1903, printed alphabetical key table at top of each page
giving beginning page numbers of alphabetical sections. Arr. in separate
grantor and grantee sections, thereunder alph. by first letter of surname,
and chron. thereunder, 1852-88, 1936--; arr. alph., by first letter of
grantor's surname on left pages and by first letter of grantee's on right;
and chron. thereunder, 1888-1936.. Hdw. pr. hd. 500 pp. 18 x 12 x 2.

95. INDEX NEW ADDITION (Beaumont Land Corporation), Aug. 19, 1911-
        July 1, 1920. 1 vol.
Grantor (Beaumont Land Corporation) index to Deed Record, entry 93, showing name of grantee, date of instrument, filing date, and volume and page
reference -- made to prevent overcrowding the "B" grantor section of
General Index to Deeds, entry 94, which indexes these entries by grantee
only. Arr. chron. by filing date. Hdw. pr. hd. 88 pp. 16 x 12 x 1.

96. INDEX NEW ADDITION (Gratis Townsite Company), Oct. 25, 1909-
        Jan. 30, 1925. 1 vol.
Grantor (Gratis Townsite Company) and grantee index to Deed Record, entry
93; each entry shows name of opposite party, date of instrument, filing
date, and volume and page reference -- made to prevent overcrowding "G"
grantor section of General Index to Deeds, entry 94, which does not index
these entries. Arr. in 27 sections: One for grantee ("G"), thereunder
chron. by filing date; 26 (A-Z) for grantees, thereunder chron. by filing date. Hdw. pr. hd. 100 pp. 16 x 10 x 1.

97. TAX SALE DEED RECORD, May 17, 1897. 1 vol. (Q). No entries
        except on May 17, 1897.
Recorded copies of deeds given by sheriff on land sold in satisfaction
of district court judgments for delinquent taxes, showing county, date
order of sale issued, date of judgment, name of person against whom judgment rendered, and amount of judgment; name of sheriff, date property
levied upon, date advertised, and statement granting title; name of owner, abstract, certificate, and survey numbers, original grantee of acreage or city or town and lot and block numbers of city lot; sheriff's signature, notarization, and clerk's recording certificate. Arr. chron. by
filing date. No index. Hdw. pr. fm. 640 pp. (1 used) 18 x 14 x 4.

98. (INSTRUMENTS UNCLAIMED), Dec. 6, 1852-June 9, 1894, May 7,
        1908-Dec. 11, 1923. 700 papers in 2 f.d. 1852-1934 in (Mis-
        cellaneous Papers), entry 3.
Instruments filed for record and unclaimed by owners, including deeds,
deeds of trust and releases, chattel mortgages, redemption receipts,
bills of sale, powers of attorney, contracts, and leases. Arr. chron.
by filing date. No index. Hdw., hdw. and typed pr. fm., and typed.
11 x 5 x 14.

99. OLD DEEDS, Sept. 24, 1853-Sept. 23, 1902. 100 deeds in 1 f.d.
Deeds filed for record and unclaimed by owners, showing State and county,
date of instrument, names of grantor, grantee, and original grantee,
kind and description of land, consideration, date executed, filing date,
grantor's signature, notarization, and clerk's recording certificate.
Arr. chron. by filing date. No index. Hdw. 11 x 5 x 14.

100. COUNTY RIGHT-OF-WAY DEEDS, Mar. 15, 1884-Oct. 1, 1937. 530
        papers in 4 f.d.
Deeds to land granted to Orange County for roads and other public purposes, showing items of information as in entry 99. Also contains:

County depository bonds, 1905-June 4, 1935, showing name of bank, date
and amount of bond, conditions of obligation, signatures of principal and
sureties, county judge's approval, and clerk's recording certificate. Arr.
chron. by filing date. No index. Hdw. and typed pr. fm. 11 x 5 x 14.

101. TAX RECEIPT RECORD, July 22, 1915--. 1 vol.
Recorded copies of receipts issued upon payment of real and personal
property taxes, showing information as in entry 359, adding clerk's recording certificate. Arr. chron. by recording date. Indexed alph. by
first letter of taxpayer's surname and chron. thereunder. Hdw. pr. fm.
640 pp. 18 x 14 x 4.

102. RECORD OF REDEMPTION CERTIFICATES, Feb. 23, 1915--. 3 vols.
        (1-3).
Recorded copies of certificates issued by State Comptroller upon redemption of land by payment of delinquent taxes, showing number, date, and
amount of certificate, date and place of execution, year of sale, abstract, certificate, and survey numbers, original grantee, number of
acres, county, statement that parties against whom taxes were assessed
have exhibited evidence of payment, Comptroller's signature, and clerk's
recording certificate. Arr. chron. by recording date. Indexed alph. by
first letter of taxpayer's surname and chron. thereunder. Hdw. pr. fm.
640 pp. 18 x 14 x 4.

103. RECORD OF ALIEN OWNED LANDS, Dec. 22, 1922-Dec. 29, 1927,
        Jan. 18, 1937--. 2 vols. (1, 1). Last entry Jan. 18, 1937.
Recorded copies of affidavits filed by aliens to report land ownership,
showing State, county, name and address of alien, occupation, personal
description, birthplace, last foreign residence and allegiance, date
and port of arrival in United States, length of residence in State, name
of country alien now owes allegiance to, number of acres owned, name of
survey, abstract and certificate numbers, from whom land acquired, date
purchased, description of land, filing date, alien's signature, notarization, and clerk's recording certificate. Arr. chron. by filing date.
Indexed alph. by first letter of alien's surname and thereunder chron.
by filing date. Hdw. pr. fm. 1922-27; typed pr. fm. 1937. 160 pp. 18 x
14 x 2.

104. CONTRACT LIEN RECORD, May 6, 1919--. 19 vols. (1-19). Title
        varies: Contract Record, May 6, 1919-May 13, 1927, 7 vols.
Recorded copies of oil and gas leases, and leases on farm land, service
stations, and other real property, showing names of contracting parties,
file number, description of property, amount of consideration, period of
lease, filing date, lessor's signature, notarization, and clerk's recording certificate. Also contains: Recorded copies of applications to
prospect for oil, gas, and other minerals on public school lands, showing date and place of application, name and address of applicant, description of land (river bed mostly), applicant's signature, and clerk's

recording certificate. Arr. chron. by recording date. For index, see
entry 105. Typed. 640 pp. 18 x 14 x 4.

105. INDEX TO CONTRACT RECORD DIRECT AND REVERSE, May 6, 1919--.
    2 vols. (1, 2).
Grantor-grantee index to Contract Lien Record, entry 104; page heading
shows printed alphabetical key, beginning page numbers of surnames and
of 2-letter combinations of given names; each entry shows name of opposite party, kind and date of instrument, filing date, and volume and
page reference. Arr. alph., by first letter of grantor's surname on
left pages and by first letter of grantee's on right, thereunder by first
two letters of given name, and thereunder chron. by filing date, 1919-31;
arr. in separate grantor and grantee sections, thereunder alph. by first
letter of surname, thereunder alph. by first two letters of given name,
and thereunder chron. by filing date, 1931--. Hdw. pr. hd. 320 pp. 18 x
14 x 4.

106. POWER OF ATTORNEY RECORD, Sept. 17, 1853-Dec. 28, 1877, Feb.
    23, 1898--. 5 vols. (A-E). Title varies: P/A, Feb. 23,
    1898-May 26, 1909, 1 vol.
Recorded copies of powers of attorney, authorizing one person to repre-
sent another in business and legal matters, showing date and place of
execution, names of principal and agent, general and special powers
granted, principal's signature, notarization, and clerk's recording certificate. Arr. chron. by recording date. Indexed alph. by first letter
of grantor's surname and chron. thereunder, 1853-77; indexed alph., by
first letter of grantor's surname and by first letter of grantee's, and
chron. thereunder, 1906--; for index 1898-1909, see entry 107. Hdw.
1853-77, 1898-1909; typed 1909--. 300 pp. 16 x 12 x 2.

107. POWER OF ATTORNEY BOOK (Index), 1898-1909. 1 vol. (B).
Grantor index to Power of Attorney Record, vol. B, entry 106, showing name
of grantee and page reference. Arr. alph. by first letter of grantor's
surname and chron. thereunder. Hdw. 25 pp. 14 x 4 x 1.

108. RECORD OF BILLS OF SALE, Apr. 19, 1852--. 5 vols. (A-E).
    Title varies: Personal Property, Apr. 19, 1852-Aug. 14, 1876,
    1 vol.; Record of Personal Property, Dec. 16, 1876-Sept. 29,
    1903, 1 vol.; Record of Sales Personal Property, Nov. 23, 1895-
    June 28, 1930, 2 vols.
Recorded copies of bills of sale to personal property, showing State and
county, date and place of execution, names of vendor and vendee, location
and description of property, amount of consideration, terms of contract,
vendor's signature, clerk's attest, and clerk's recording certificate.
Also contains, in vol. A, pp. 1-9; Recorded copies of oaths of office
of chief justice and county commissioners, Apr. 19, 1852. Arr. chron.
by recording date. Indexed alph., by first letter of vendor's surname
and by first letter of vendee's, and chron. thereunder. Hdw. 1852-1918;
typed 1918--. 346 pp. 16 x 10 x 4.

Public Domain (See also entry 104)

    109. (APPLICATIONS FOR PUBLIC SCHOOL LANDS), 1916-27. In (Miscel-
           laneous Papers), entry 3.
Applications to purchase public school lands, made by actual settlers to
Commissioner of General Land Office, showing date and place of application, county in which land is situate, number of miles and direction
from county seat, section and certificate numbers, original grantee, number of acres, price per acre, and applicant's address and signature; accompanied by promissory notes, showing principal and interest, dates payments due, date of note, and applicant's signature.

    110. SCHOOL LAND PAPERS, June 11, 1898-Apr. 3, 1909, Feb. 22, 1913-
           Sept. 28, 1928. 2 f.d. Title varies: Public Land Reports,
           June 11, 1898-Apr. 3, 1909, 1 f.d.
Notices of classification and appraisement of public school lands in the
county, from Commissioner of General Land Office to county clerk, showing section and block numbers, township, certificate number, original
grantee or for whom land surveyed, classification (watered or dry, agricultural, grazing, or timber), number of acres, appraised value, price
per acre, date placed on market, date of appraisal, and Commissioner's
signature. Arr. chron. by filing date. No index. Hdw. and typed pr.
fm. 11 x 5 x 14.

    111. CLASSIFICATION OF LANDS (and Notice of Sale), May 31, 1895-
           May 21, 1923. 1 vol. (1).
Record of classification and appraisement of public school lands in the
county, showing items of information as in entry 110; and of notices
of sale, sent to county clerk by Commissioner of General Land Office,
showing date of notice, section and certificate numbers, original grantee, price per acre, name of purchaser, date of sale, and Commissioner's
name. Arr. chron. by date of sale. No index. Hdw. pr. hd. 79 pp.
20 x 12 x 1.

    112. RECORD LANDS LEASED (and Purchased), Feb. 6, 1898-Dec. 24,
           1904. 1 vol. (1).
Contains:
    i. Leases of public school lands in the county, register of,
        made by Commissioner of General Land Office, Feb. 6, 1898-
        Dec. 27, 1899, on p. 1, showing metes and bounds of land,
        number of acres, name of lessee, date and duration of lease,
        filing date, and registration date.
    ii. Purchases of public school lands, recorded copies of applica-
        tions for, made to Commissioner of General Land Office by
        actual settlers, Apr. 30, 1901-Dec. 24, 1904, on pp. 15-45,
        showing information as in entry 109.
Arr. chron. by recording date. Indexed alph. by first letter of lessee's
or applicant's surname and chron. thereunder. Hdw. 79 pp. (32 used)
18 x 14 x 1.

113. IRRIGATION RECORD, Apr. 28, 1914-Mar. 26, 1926. 1 vol. (1).
Recorded copies of applications to State Board of Water Engineers for
permits to appropriate water from public streams for irrigation, to operate power or pumping plants, or to construct dams, lakes, reservoirs, or
canals for the manufacture of power, showing county, name and address of
landowner, number of acres to be irrigated, name of irrigation ditch or
canal, location of pumping plant, length, width, depth, and carrying capacity of canal, stream from which water is to be taken, date work to
commence installing pump, scale of accompanying map, applicant's affidavit, and clerk's recording certificate. Arr. chron. by recording date.
Indexed alph. by first letter of applicant's surname and chron. thereunder. Hdw. 132 pp. 20 x 14 x 2.

Liens

114. ABSTRACT OF JUDGMENT RECORD, Mar. 13, 1882--. 7 vols. (B-H).
Recorded copies of abstracts of judgments, showing court and county, court
term, number and style of case, date and amount of judgment, amount of
costs, rate of interest, amount of credits, and amount due, sometimes
recorded copy of certificate of authentication of copy by clerk of court
issuing judgment, and clerk's recording and indexing certificate; and
also, from 1907, recorded copies of releases of judgments, showing date
of judgment, court and county, number and style of case, amount of judgment, amount of interest, volume and page of judgment record, statement
of release, grantor's signature, notarization, and clerk's recording certificate. Arr. chron. by recording date. Indexed alph., by first letter
of plaintiff's surname and by first letter of defendant's, and chron.
thereunder. Abstracts hdw. pr. hd. and hdw. pr. fm.; releases typed.
320 pp. 16 x 14 x 2.

115. ATTACHMENT RECORD, Aug. 14, 1889--. 1 vol. (A). Last entry
          Dec. 4, 1935.
Register of attachment liens operating against real and personal property,
pending settlement of civil suits, showing county, names of plaintiff and
defendant, amount of debt, from what court issued, and date of attachment;
recorded copy of officer's return, showing date writ received, date executed, description of property levied upon, officer's signature; and
clerk's recording certificate. Arr. chron. by filing date. Indexed
alph., by first letter of plaintiff's surname and by first letter of defendant's, and chron. thereunder. Register hdw. pr. hd.; returns hdw.
and typed. 68 pp. 18 x 14 x 2.

116. LIS PENDENS RECORD, Feb. 11, 1906--. 2 vols. (1, 2).
Recorded copies of notices filed by plaintiffs in civil actions to prevent sale or disposal of real property during litigation, showing county,
names of plaintiff and defendant, case number, filing date, court in
which trial pending, nature of suit, location and description of property,
plaintiff's signature, notarization, and clerk's recording certificate.
Arr. chron. by recording date. Indexed alph., by first letter of plaintiff's surname and by first letter of defendant's, and chron. thereunder.
Hdw. pr. fm. 1906-37; typed 1937--. 132 pp. 18 x 14 x 2.

(117-120)

117. NOTICE OF TAX LIEN & DISCHARGE OF TAX LIEN, June 29, 1936-
       May 9, 1938. 3 notices in 1 f.d.
Federal tax lien notices, showing district number, date of notice, name
and residence of tax payer, nature of taxes due, inclusive dates of taxable period, amount of tax assessed, amount of additional penalty if any,
date assessment list received, U. S. Internal Revenue Collector's signature, notarization, and clerk's recording certificate; and certificates
of discharge of tax liens, showing district number, date and place of
execution, certification that taxes have been paid in full and lien is
discharged, name and residence of taxpayer, nature and amount of tax,
dates of taxable period, Collector's signature, and clerk's recording
certificate. Arr. chron. by filing date. No index. Typed pr. fm. 11 x
5 x 14.

118. FEDERAL LIEN RECORD & INDEX, Apr. 27, 1923--. 1 vol.
Recorded copies of Federal tax lien notices and certificates of discharge,
showing information as in entry 117. Arr. chron. by recording date. Indexed alph. by first letter of taxpayer's surname and chron. thereunder.
Hdw. pr. fm. 268 pp. 14 x 16 x 2.

119. MECHANICS & MATERIALMAN'S LIEN RECORD, Nov. 23, 1897--.
       4 vols. (1-4).
Recorded copies of instruments filed to establish mechanics' liens on
real estate: Contracts between property owners and mechanics or contrac-
tors, showing names of contracting parties, terms of contract specifying
improvement to be made and material to be furnished, description of property, amount and terms of consideration, signatures of contracting parties, notarization, and clerk's recording certificate; affidavits of material and labor, showing amounts due for each item, total amount due,
mechanic's signature, notarization, and clerk's recording certificate;
releases and transfers of liens, showing names of grantor and grantee,
description of property, statement of release or transfer, mechanic's
signature, notarization, and clerk's recording certificate. Arr. chron.
by recording date. Indexed alph. by first letter of grantor's and grantee's surnames on left- and right-hand sections of same pages, with approximately 50 percent of the grantor entries showing name of grantee
and kind of instrument, 1897-1916; for index 1916--, see entry 120. Hdw.
1897-1916; typed 1916--. 640 pp. 18 x 14 x 4.

120. INDEX TO MECHANICS & MATERIALMEN'S LIEN RECORD, Aug. 17,
       1916--. 2 vols. (2, 3 & 4).
Grantor-grantee index to Mechanics & Materialman's Lien Record, vols.
2-4, entry 119; each entry shows name of opposite party and page reference; and also, from 1923, kind and date of instrument, filing date, and
volume reference. Arr. alph., by first letter of grantor's surname and
by first letter of grantee's, and chron. thereunder. Hdw. 1916-23; hdw.
pr. hd. 1923--. 60 pp. 18 x 10 x 1.

121. EMPLOYEES LIEN RECORD, Dec. 19, 1899--. 2 vols. (1, 2).
Recorded copies of affidavits filed by laborers to establish liens against
real estate to insure payment for labor performed or material used in
construction of, or repairs to buildings, showing county, date, name of
employer, itemized statement of labor performed and material used, nature
of work done, filing date, laborer's signature, notarization, and clerk's
recording certificate. Arr. chron. by filing date. Indexed alph., by
first letter of employer's surname on left pages and by first letter of
laborer's on right, and chron. thereunder, each entry showing name of
opposite party, 1921--; for index 1899-1921, see entry 122. Hdw. 1899-
1921; typed 1921--. 154 pp. 18 x 14 x 2.

122. INDEX (to Employees' Lien Record), Dec. 19, 1899-Sept. 6, 1921.
    1 vol. (1).
Index by name of laborer to Employees Lien Record, vol. 1, entry 121,
showing name of opposite party and page reference. Arr. alph. by first
letter of laborer's surname and chron. thereunder. Hdw. 70 pp. 14 x 7
x 1.

Mortgages

123. DEED OF TRUST LIEN & MORTGAGE RECORD, Nov. 5, 1853--. 21
    vols. (A-U). Untitled, Nov. 5, 1853-Apr. 26, 1880, 1 vol.
Recorded copies of: Deeds of trust mortgaging real property, showing
names of contracting parties (grantor, grantee, and trustee), statement
of conveyance of title in consideration of the debt and trust and the
sum of $1, description of property, conditions of contract, interest
rates of promissory notes, agreement that contract is of no effect if
payments are made and that upon default trustee is authorized to sell it,
grantor's signature, notarization, and clerk's recording certificate; releases of deeds of trust, showing name of trustee as releasing agent,
name of grantor of trust deed, date of original instrument with volume
and page reference, description of property and of promissory notes,
statement acknowledging payment and releasing obligations, date of release, signature of trustee as grantor of releasing instrument, notarization, and clerk's recording certificate; transfers of deeds of trust,
showing name of owner of trust deed, name of person to whom transferred,
description of promissory notes with volume and page reference, description of property, statement transferring or conveying title, agent's signature, notarization, and clerk's recording certificate. Arr. chron. by
recording date. Indexed alph., by first letter of grantor's surname and
by first letter of grantee's, and chron. thereunder, 1853-1908; for index
1908--, see entry 124. Hdw. 1853-1904; typed 1904--. 640 pp. 18 x 14
x 4.

124. GENERAL INDEX TO LIENS & MORTGAGES, Nov. 14, 1908--. 5 vols.
    (G-I, 1, 2).
Grantor-grantee index to Deed of Trust Lien & Mortgage Record, vols.
G-U, entry 123; each entry shows name of opposite party and page reference;

and from 1917, kind and date of instrument, filing date, and volume reference, with printed alphabetical key at top of each page, showing beginning page numbers of sections for surnames and given names. Arr. alph.,
by first letter of grantor's surname on right pages and of grantee's on
left: thereunder chron., 1908-16; alph. by first letter of given name
and chron. thereunder, 1917--. Hdw. pr. hd. 320 pp. 20 x 14 x 4.

   125. CHATTEL MORTGAGES, 1893--. 25,200 mortgages in 42 f.d. (la-
          beling varies).
Chattel mortgages, showing mortgage number, names of mortgagor and mortgagee, date of instrument, amount secured, description of property, date
due, notarization, filing date, and clerk's filing certificate. Arr.
numer. by mortgage no. No index. Hdw. and hdw. pr. fm. 1893-1911; hdw.
and typed pr. fm. and typed 1911--. 11 x 5 x 14. 19 f.d., 1893-1926,
annex va.; 23 f.d., 1926--, c.c. va.

   126. CHATTEL MORTGAGE INDEX AND REGISTER, Aug. 13, 1879--. 23 vols.
          (1 vol. unlabeled; 3-24). Title varies: Register of Mortga-
          ges, Aug. 13, 1879-Apr. 9, 1901, 1 vol.
Register of chattel mortgages, showing mortgage number, date of recep-
tion, date of instrument, names of mortgagor and mortgagee, amount involved, due date, description of property, and date of release. Arr.
numer. by mortgage no., 1879-1939; arr. alph. by first letter of mortgagor's surname and chron. thereunder, 1939--. Indexed alph., by first
letter of mortgagor's surname and by first letter of mortgagee's, and
chron. thereunder, 1879-1938; no index, 1939--; also supplemental index,
1913-16, see entry 127. Hdw. pr. hd. 300 pp. 18 x 16 x 4. 22 vols.,
1879-1916, 1920--, c.c. va.; 1 vol., 1916-20, annex va.

   127. INDEX TO CHATTEL MORTGAGE REGISTER, Nov. 12, 1913-Dec. 1,
          1916. 1 vol. (6).
Mortgagor-mortgagee index, supplemental to Chattel Mortgage Index and
Register, vol. 6, entry 126, showing names of mortgagor and mortgagee,
mortgage number, and page reference. Arr. alph., by first letter of
mortgagor's surname on left pages and by first letter of mortgagee's on
right, and chron. thereunder. Hdw. 50 pp. 18 x 12 x 1.

   128. CHATTEL MORTGAGE RECORD OF MACHINERY ON REALTY, Jan. 12,
          1918--. 1 vol. (2).
Register of chattel mortgages on machinery and other manufactured articles situated on realty, showing mortgage number, date and hour of recep-
tion, names of mortgagor and mortgagee, date of instrument, amount secured, date due, description of property mortgaged, and description of
real estate on which chattel is situated. Arr. numer. by mortgage no.
Indexed alph. by first letter of mortgagor's surname and chron. thereunder. Hdw. pr. hd. 293 pp. 18 x 14 x 4.

Livestock

129. (MARKS AND BRANDS), 1852-84. 1 vol.
Register of livestock marks and brands, showing registration date, name
of owner, location of mark on animal, facsimile of brand, and clerk's
signature. Arr. chron. by registration date. No index. Hdw. Torn,
faded, illegible, and mouldy. 80 pp. 14 x 8 x 1. Annex va.

130. RECORD OF MARKS AND BRANDS, 1852--. 2 vols. (1; 1 vol. un-
       labeled).
Register of livestock marks and brands, being a re-recording of brands
registered 1852-84, and original registrations from 1884, showing items
of information as in entry 129, adding registration number, owner's address, and purchaser's name. Arr. chron. by registration date, with registrations numbered consecutively. Indexed alph. by first letter of
owner's surname and chron. thereunder. Hdw. pr. hd. 200 pp. 16 x 14 x 2.

Vital Statistics

Marriages

131. DOCTOR'S CERTIFICATES, June 19, 1929--. 4 f.d. Untitled,
       Jan. 1, 1938-July 7, 1939, 1 f.d.
Health certificates issued to male applicants for marriage licenses by
physicians, showing county, name of applicant, name of physician, date
and result of examination, and applicant's and physician's signatures.
Arr. chron. by filing date. No index. Hdw. pr. fm. 11 x 5 x 14. 2 f.d.,
1929-37, annex va.; 2 f.d., 1933--, c.c. va.

132. NOTICE OF INTENTION TO MARRY, June 13, 1929-Mar. 31, 1933.
       1 vol. (1). Discontinued; law repealed 1933 (43d Leg., p. 284).
Recorded copies of applications for marriage licenses, giving 3 days'
notice of intention to marry, showing file number, filing date, names,
addresses, and ages of contracting parties, applicant's signature, and
clerk's attest. Arr. numer. by file no. Indexed alph., by first letter
of male's surname and by first letter of female's, and chron. thereunder.
Hdw. pr. fm. 400 pp. 16 x 14 x 3. Annex va.

133. MARRIAGE LICENSES (Stubs), Dec. 18, 1900--. 35 vols.
Stubs of marriage licenses issued by county clerk, showing license number,
names of contracting parties, date license issued, and clerk's signature;
and also, from 1933, affidavits to ages made by contracting parties, showing names and ages of contracting parties, statement that no legal objec-
tion exists, signatures of contracting parties, and clerk's attest. Arr.
numer. by license no. No index. Hdw. pr. fm. 300 pp. 14 x 14 x 2.
29 vols., 1900-1935, annex va.; 6 vols., 1935--, c.c. va.

134. MARRIAGE LICENSES, Oct. 13, 1855--. 22 f.d. Untitled, Oct.
      7, 1938-Apr. 20, 1939, 1 f.d.
Marriage licenses returned after performance of ceremony, showing State
and county, clerk's authorization to clergyman or magistrate to perform
rites of matrimony and make due return in 60 days, license number, names
of contracting parties, date and place of issuance, and clerk's signature; officiating party's return, showing date and place of ceremony,
signature and title, and clerk's filing certificate. No index. Hdw. pr.
fm. 11 x 5 x 14. 11 f.d., 1855-1937, annex va.; 11 f.d., 1925--, c.c. va.

135. MARRIAGE RECORD, Apr. 21, 1852--. 12 vols. (A, B, 3-12).
      Untitled, Apr. 21, 1852-60, 1 vol.
Recorded copies of marriage licenses, showing information as in entry
134. Arr. chron. by recording date. No index, 1852-60; indexed alph.
by first letter of male's surname, showing name of female, 1860-97; indexed alph., by first letter of male's surname and by first letter of
female's, each entry showing name of opposite party, 1906-- (1915-18,
1920-22 partial); for index 1897-1906, and supplemental index, 1915-18,
1920-22, see entry 136. Hdw. 1852-81; hdw. pr. fm. 1881--. 640 pp. 16
x 14 x 4.

136. SUP.(plemental) INDEX MARRIAGE RECORD, Apr. 9, 1897-May 17,
      1906, 1915-18, 1920-22. 3 vols. (4, 6, 7).
Index by names of male and female to Marriage Record, vol. 4, and those
alphabetical sections of volumes 6 and 7 which became overcrowded, entry
135; each entry shows name of opposite party and volume and page reference. Arr. alph., by first letter of male's surname on left pages and
by first letter of female's on right, and chron. thereunder. Hdw. 50 pp.
18 x 12 x 1.

Births & Deaths

137. REGISTER OF BIRTHS, 1903--. 2 vols. (1, 2).
Clerk's register of births, showing certificate number, place of birth,
name of child, sex, color, date of birth, name and address of father
and of mother, name of physician or other person reporting birth, and
filing date of certificate. Arr. alph. by first letter of child's surname and thereunder chron. by filing date. No index. Hdw. pr. hd.
319 pp. 20 x 16 x 2.

138. REGISTER OF DEATHS, Oct. 1, 1903--. 2 vols. (1, 2).
Clerk's register of deaths, showing certificate number, filing date,
place of death, name of deceased person, sex, race, marital status, names
of parents, date and cause of death, name and address of physician, date
and place of burial, and name and address of undertaker. Arr. alph. by
first letter of deceased person's surname and thereunder chron. by filing date. No index. Hdw. pr. hd. 319 pp. 20 x 16 x 2.

139.   BIRTH & DEATH CERTIFICATES, Jan. 9, 1929--. 500 certificates
        in 2 f.d. Untitled, Feb. 9, 1933--, 1 f.d.
Standard State Bureau of Vital Statistics birth and death certificates
filed for record by local registrars:
    i. Birth certificates show place of birth, full name of child
        and residence of mother, sex of child, if multiple birth,
        number in order of birth, legitimacy, and date of birth;
        for father and mother, name (mother's maiden), Social Se-
        curity number, post office address, color or race, age,
        birthplace, and occupation; number of children born to
        mother including this birth and number still living; signa-
        ture and address of informant; certification to medical
        attendance signed by physician or midwife; file number, fil-
        ing date, and signature and post office address of local
        registrar; on reverse, military ex-service record of father,
        and medical particulars as to delivery for statistical pur-
        poses. For justice's of peace copies, see entry 332.
   ii. Death certificates show place of death, full name of deceased
        person, length of residence where death occurred, residence
        address, Social Security number, color or race, whether
        single, married, widowed, or divorced, date of birth, age,
        trade or profession, place of birth, names and birthplaces
        of father and mother (mother's maiden name), signature and
        address of informant; place and date of burial or removal
        and signature and address of undertaker; certificate to
        date of death and medical particulars signed by physician
        or coroner; file number, filing date, and signature and
        post office address of local registrar; on reverse, items
        of military service record of deceased person, personal de-
        scription if deceased person unknown non-resident, name and
        age of husband or wife, and findings as to cause of death.
        For justice's of peace copies, see entry 333.
Arr. numer. by certificate no. No index. Hdw. pr. fm. 1929-38; typed
pr. fm. 1938--. 11 x 5 x 14.

Business Records

140. ASSUMED NAME FILE, June 14, 1921--. 300 affidavits in 1 f.d.
Affidavits filed by owners of unincorporated business firms to record
names assumed for business purposes and to designate real names of owners
who may be held responsible for operation of business, showing State and
county, date, name and address of firm, location and nature of business,
names and addresses of persons owning or operating firm, certificate number, filing date, owner's signature, notarization, and clerk's filing
certificate. Arr. numer. by certificate no. No index. Hdw. pr. fm.
11 x 5 x 14.

141. REGISTER OF ASSUMED NAMES, June 14, 1921--. 1 vol. (1).
Register of certificates filed by owners of unincorporated business firms,
showing file number, name and address of firm, names and addresses of

owners, filing date; and notations of withdrawals, showing filing date of notice. Arr. numer. by file no. Indexed alph. by first letter of assumed name and chron. thereunder. Hdw. pr. hd. 400 pp. 18 x 14 x 2.

142. RECORD OF SPECIAL PARTNERSHIP, Oct. 28, 1904-Aug. 3, 1910.
        1 vol. (1).
Recorded copies of partnership and limited partnership agreements, show-ing State and county, date of instrument, names and addresses of contract-ing parties, location of business, name of firm, general nature of busi-ness, amounts invested by each partner (and in case of limited partner-ship, amounts invested by general and special partners), duration of partnership, signatures of contracting parties, notarization, and clerk's recording certificate. Arr. chron. by recording date. No index. Hdw. 150 pp. (9 used) 14 x 8 x 1.

143. (OCCUPATION TAX REGISTER), June 12, 1852-Aug. 21, 1857, Jan.
        20-Nov. 9, 1859. 1 vol.
Occupation tax license record; in register form, June 12, 1852-Nov. 17, 1856, shows date of treasurer's receipt, to whom issued, kind of license, term of license, date issued, expiration date, amount of State tax, and amount of county tax; recorded copies of treasurer's and assessor-collec-tor's receipts, Jan. 20-Nov. 9, 1859, showing filing date, date of re-ceipt, name of party to whom issued, kind of occupation, term of license, and treasurer's or assessor-collector's signature. Also contains: Un-conditional headright certificates, Feb. 1, 1853-Aug. 21, 1857, entry 452. Arr. in 3 sections as indicated and chron. thereunder. No index. Hdw. 40 pp. (6 used) 14 x 8 x 1.

144. (DRUMMERS' LICENSES), Apr. 25, 1881-June 28, 1882. 1 vol.
Record of drummers' special $50 occupation tax receipts issued by the State Comptroller as licenses, kept as recorded copies, Apr. 25-May 31, 1881, and as register, June 1, 1881-June 28, 1882, showing receipt num-ber, name of drummer or commercial traveler, beginning and ending dates of license, date issued, Comptroller's signature, and clerk's recording certificate. Arr. chron. by recording date. No index. Hdw. 220 pp. 14 x 8 x 1. D.c. off.

145. (OCCUPATION BONDS AND LICENSES), Apr. 10, 1862-June 7, 1873.
        1 vol. (A).
Occupation bond and license record:
   i.   Ferrymen's bonds, recorded copies of, show names of princi-
        pal and sureties, date and amount of bond, conditions of
        contract, location of ferry, and date of approval.
   ii. License register shows date license issued, name of licensee,
        character of occupation, duration of license, and amount of
        tax paid; included are licenses to distill vinous and spir-
        ituous liquors, to practice medicine, and to practice law,
        and license to J. Goldstein, two-horse peddler, for 3 months
        beginning June 7, 1873, $13.22½ State tax paid; to J. F.
        Griffin, dentist, for 3 months beginning Mar. 11, 1872,

> State tax, $2.62 paid; to J. T. Allen to operate a billiard
> table for 3 months beginning Aug. 1, 1871; to W. B. Reynolds
> for sleight-of-hand exhibitions from May 11-Aug. 11, 1863;
> and to R. B. Russell to operate a hotel, from Jan. 13, 1863
> to Jan. 13, 1864.

Arr. chron. by recording date. No index. Hdw. Torn and mouldy. 150 pp.
(30 used) 14 x 8 x 1.

146. LOG BRANDS 1879, Jan. 26, 1878-Aug. 27, 1920. 1 vol. (1).
Register of log brands filed by owners of timber or sawmills, showing
date of registration, name of person or company, and description or
facsimile of brand. Arr. chron. by registration date. No index. Hdw.
Torn and faded. 120 pp. 14 x 8 x 1. Annex va.

147. (CIGARETTE DEALERS' LICENSE STUBS), Oct. 15, 1897-Nov. 25,
    1898. 1 vol.
Stubs of licenses to sell cigarettes issued to dealers by county clerk,
showing license number, county, name and address of dealer, inclusive
dates of license, amount of State tax, and amount of county tax. Arr.
numer. by license no. No index. Hdw. pr. fm. 50 pp. (5 used) 8 x 14
x 1.

148. LIQUOR DEALER'S BONDS, Sept. 19, 1898-Mar. 12, 1918. 500
    papers in 2 f.d.
Bonds made by retail malt and spirituous liquor dealers, showing State
and county, date, name of dealer, location of business, names of sureties, amount of bond, conditions of obligation, signatures of principal
and sureties, notarization, county judge's approval, and clerk's recording certificate. Also contains: Annual occupation tax receipts issued
to retail malt and liquor dealers by tax collector, 1907-8, showing receipt number, kind of occupation, dealer's name, amounts of State and
county tax, and State Comptroller's and tax collector's signatures. Arr.
chron. by filing date, 1898-1918, 1 f.d.; no obvious arr., 1907-11, 1 f.d.
No index. Hdw. pr. fm. 11 x 5 x 14.

149. LIQUOR DEALERS BOND RECORD, Dec. 23, 1893-Dec. 27, 1917.
    4 vols. (1, 1, 2; 1 vol. unlabeled).
Recorded copies of bonds made by retail malt and spirituous liquor dealers,
showing information as in entry 148. Arr. chron. by recording date. Indexed alph. by first letter of dealer's surname and chron. thereunder. Hdw.
pr. fm. 136 pp. 18 x 14 x 2. 1 vol., 1893-1907, annex va.; 3 vols., 1905-
17, c.c. va.

150. (RETAIL & MALT DEALERS' LIQUOR LICENSE STUBS), July 28, 1917-
    Mar. 12, 1918. 1 vol.
Stubs of licenses issued to retail malt and liquor dealers by county clerk,
showing kind of license, county, license number, to whom issued, location
of business, date issued, and amount of tax paid. Arr. numer. by license
no. No index. Hdw. pr. fm. 150 pp. (6 used) 8 x 14 x 1. Annex va.

151. LIVESTOCK KILLED T.&N.O.R.R. (Reports), Dec. 4,
      1914-Aug. 7, 1934. 500 reports in 3 f.d. Title varies:
      Livestock Killed Tex. & Ft. S. RR., Dec. 4, 1915-May 19, 1921,
      1 f.d.; Livestock Killed T. & F.S. R.R. Co., K.C.S., May 12,
      1922-July 8, 1933, 1 f.d.
Reports made by railroad section foremen to county clerk, of animals
killed or found dead on railroad rights-of-way, showing name of railroad, date animal killed or found dead, kind of animal, marks, brand,
color, apparent age, remarks, foreman's affidavit, and clerk's filing
certificate. Arr. chron. by date of report. No index. Hdw. pr. fm.
11 x 5 x 14.

152. PUBLIC UTILITY REPORT, Mar. 3, 1930-Mar. 1, 1934. 15 reports
      in 1 f.d.
Copies of annual reports made by public utility companies to Secretary
of State in compliance with franchise tax laws, showing name of corporation, date of report, amount of authorized capital stock, amount of
bonded indebtedness, amount of mortgages on property, value of tangible
property, annual cost of operation, amount of annual gross earnings,
rates charged public, rates charged city or town under contract, filing
date, signature of assistant treasurer of corporation, notarization, and
clerk's filing certificate. Arr. chron. by filing date. No index.
Typed pr. fm. 11 x 5 x 14.

153. GUARANTY BANK, Dec. 14, 1925-Dec. 13, 1929. 1 f.d.
Papers concerning liquidation of assets of Guaranty Bond Bank and Trust
Company (now defunct), including depository bond, Dec. 14, 1925; copy
of appointment of special agent in charge of liquidation, issued by State
Banking Commissioner, June 9, 1927; copy of inventory of assets made to
Banking Commissioner by special agent, June 18, 1927; and report to
county clerk from State Banking Commissioner of claims of depositors and
creditors approved for payment, Dec. 13, 1929. Arr. chron. by filing
date. No index. Typed. 11 x 5 x 14.

Professional Records

154. RECORD EMBALMER'S (&C), June 26, 1854-61, May 16, 1873--.
      1 vol. (1). Last entry June 14, 1938.
Contains:
    i. Dentists' licenses to practice, recorded copies of, issued by
        State Board of Dental Examiners, 1901-36, showing certifi-
        cate number, name of dentist, college of graduation, recital
        of examination and authorization to practice, date issued,
        signatures of members of examining board, and clerk's re-
        cording certificate.
   ii. Embalmer's certificates, recorded copies of, issued by State
        Board of Embalming, 1931-38, showing certificate number,
        name and address of embalmer or mortician, recital of exam-
        ination, authorization to practice, date certificate issued,

signatures of board members, and clerk's recording certificate.
Also contains: Physicians' licenses, 1873-1914, entry 254; actual settlers' certificates, 1854-61, entry 451. Arr. chron. by recording date.
Professional licenses and certificates indexed alph. by first letter of
applicant's surname and chron. thereunder; no index to actual settlers'
certificates. Hdw. 300 pp. 10 x 14 x 1.

155. OPTOMETRY REGISTER, Feb. 7, 1922--. 1 vol. (1). Last entry
        May 18, 1934.
Record of optometrists authorized to practice in the county; recorded
copies of declarations of intention to continue practice, Feb. 22-Oct.
5, 1922, and of intention to take subsequent examination, and grant of
authority to practice under declaration as license to Jan. 1, 1923, showing certificate number, name and address of optometrist, signatures of
members of State Board of Examiners in Optometry, and notarization, and
clerk's recording certificate; and from Jan. 1, 1923, recorded copies of
licenses, showing citation to statutes under which issued, name and address of optometrist, grant of authority to practice, definition of practice, signatures of board members, and clerk's recording certificate.
Arr. chron. by recording date. Indexed alph. by first letter of optometrist's surname and chron. thereunder. Hdw. pr. fm. 1922; typed 1923-34.
248 pp. (10 used) 16 x 10 x 2.

156. REGISTER OF NURSES, June 26, 1923--. 1 vol. (1). Last entry
        Feb. 11, 1933.
Clerk's record of registered nurses, consisting of recorded copies of
certificates issued to nurses by State Board of Nurse Examiners, showing
date certificate issued, name of nurse, and signatures of board members;
recorded copies of affidavits of two character witnesses, showing name
and address of nurse, school of graduation, and certificate number; and
clerk's recording certificate. Arr. chron. by recording date. Indexed
alph. by first letter of nurse's surname and chron. thereunder. Hdw.
pr. fm. 132 pp. 18 x 14 x 2.

Official Bonds & Deputations
(See also entries 100, 108)

157. RECORD OF OFFICIAL BONDS, May 15, 1852--. 6 vols. (A-C, 2-4).
        Title varies: Record, 1874-1910, 1 vol.
Recorded copies of county officials' bonds and oaths, except as recorded
separately from 1923, entry 158, showing information as in entry 159.
Arr. chron. by recording date. Indexed alph. by first letter of official's surname and chron. thereunder. Hdw. 1852-1910; hdw. pr. fm.
1892--. 450 pp. 18 x 12 x 2.

158. OFFICIAL BONDS, CO. CLERK CO. JUDGE, SHERIFF & COMMISSIONER,
        Mar. 12, 1923--. 1 vol. (1).
Recorded copies of bonds and oaths of county clerk, county judge, sheriff,
and county commissioners, showing information as in entry 159. Arr.

chron. by recording date. Indexed alph. by first letter of official's
surname and chron. thereunder. Hdw. pr. fm. 450 pp. 18 x 12 x 2.

    159.   BONDS, OFFICIALS, WAREHOUSEMAN, STEVEDORES, Jan. 10, 1899--.
        7 f.d. Title varies: Deputations, Bonds & Oaths, Jan. 10,
        1899-Dec. 31, 1934, 2 f.d.; County Deputies & Bonds, Dec. 31,
        1926-Aug. 10, 1937, 1 f.d.; untitled, June 1, 1909-Feb. 19,
        1921, 1 f.d. 1899-1916 also in Insurance Policies, entry 58;
        1936-37 also in (Miscellaneous Papers), entry 3.
County officials' bonds and oaths, showing State and county, name of official as principal, names of sureties, name of obligee, amount and conditions of bond, signatures of principal and sureties, and notarization;
oath endorsed on bond, shows name of official, title of office to which
elected or appointed, official's signature, and notarization; county
judge's approval; and clerk's recording certificate. Also contains:
    i. Applications to county clerk for certificate to operate as
          public warehouse, July 30, 1937-Nov. 6, 1938, showing loca-
          tion and name of warehouse and names of owners.
    ii. Bonds made by stevedores contracting to load or unload ves-
          sels, Jan. 9, 1937-Jan. 5, 1939, payable to county judge,
          and conditioned upon payment of wages promptly upon Saturday
          of each week and otherwise fulfilling terms of contract,
          with county clerk's approval, and recording certificate.
Deputations, 1899-1934, entry 160. Arr. chron. by filing date. No index.
Hdw. and typed pr. fm. 11 x 5 x 14. 2 f.d., 1899-1934, annex va.; 5 f.d.,
1909--, c.c. va.

    160.   DEPUTATIONS, Sept. 12, 1906--. 300 deputations in 2 f.d.
        1899-1934 in Bonds, Officials, Warehouseman, Stevedores,
          entry 159.
Deputations and oaths of office of deputy county officials, showing State
and county, date of appointment, name of appointing officer, name of deputy, recital of authority to perform duties of office, statement of oath,
signature of appointing official, notarization, and clerk's recording
certificate. Arr. chron. by filing date. No index. Hdw. and typed pr.
fm. 11 x 5 x 14.

    161.   DEPUTATION RECORD, Dec. 4, 1912--. 6 vols. (1-6).
Recorded copies of deputations and oaths of office of deputy county officials, showing information as in entry 160. Arr. chron. by recording
date. Indexed alph. by first letter of deputy's surname and chron. thereunder. Hdw. pr. fm. 400 pp. 18 x 12 x 2.

    162.   NOTARY PUBLIC BONDS, June 1, 1937--. 1 f.d.
Notaries' public bonds and oaths, showing State and county, name of notary
as principal, names of sureties, name of obligee, amount and conditions
of bond, signatures of principal and sureties, and notarization; oath
endorsed on bond and signed by notary; clerk's approval; and clerk's
recording certificate. Arr. chron. by filing date. No index. Typed pr.
fm. 11 x 5 x 14.

County Clerk as Recorder -
    Acknowledgments and Fees;
    Miscellaneous

                                                                     (163-166)

163. NOTARY BOND RECORD, June 2, 1913--. 4 vols. (1-4).
Recorded copies of notaries' public bonds and oaths, showing information
as in entry 162. Arr. chron. by recording date. Indexed alph. by first
letter of notary's surname and chron. thereunder. Hdw. pr. fm. and
typed. 320 pp. 18 x 12 x 2.

Acknowledgments & Fees

164. ACKNOWLEDGMENT RECORD, May 31, 1847-Sept. 21, 1850, May 12,
          1883-Apr. 10, 1905, Dec. 18, 1908-Oct. 15, 1909, June 15,
          1911-Aug. 3, 1926. 6 vols. Untitled, May 31, 1847-Sept. 21,
          1850, 1 vol.
Record of acknowledgments or proofs of instruments taken by notaries
public (1847-50 by Benjamin P. Gates and other notaries of Jefferson
County), showing date and kind of instrument, description and location
of land, names and addresses of grantor and grantee, amount of fees,
date of acknowledgment, and notary's signature. Includes, in untitled
vol.: Copy of protest against liability for damages, May 22, 1848,
signed by Claiborn Hugh, master of Flatboat Jenny, stating that on
way to Sabine Pass, May 17, 1848, boat ran on a snag and in order to
save boat and cargo, he was compelled to throw overboard 14 bales of
cotton; and protest by Samuel Steedem, Master, and by William Burns and
F. C. Steedem, hands, that Flatboat Sabine, loaded with 340 bales of cotton bound for Sabine Pass, struck a snag and sank. Arr. chron. by date
of acknowledgment. No index, 1847-50; indexed alph. by first letter of
grantor's surname and chron. thereunder, 1883-1905, 1908-9, 1911-26.
Hdw. 1847-50; hdw. pr. hd. 1883-1905, 1908-9, 1911-26. 25 to 140 pp.
8 x 8 x 1 to 18 x 14 x 1. 4 vols., 1847-50, 1891-99, 1908-9, 1911-17,
annex va.; 2 vols., 1883-1905, 1913-26, c.c. va.

165. (CLERK'S DAY BOOK), May 3, 1927-Dec. 23, 1935. 4 vols.
Clerk's open accounts of fees charged for recording instruments, showing
date of entry, name of payer or names of grantor and grantee, kind of
instrument, amount of fee, and date of payment. Arr. one account to a
page and thereunder chron. by date of entry. Indexed alph. by first
letter of surname of person filing and chron. thereunder, 1927-29, 1933-
35; no index, 1930-33. Hdw. 283 pp. 14 x 8 x 1. Annex va.

Miscellaneous

166. RECORD OF SCHOOL DISTRICTS, May 5, 1919--. 1 vol. (1). Last
          entry Sept. 14, 1931.
Recorded certified transcripts of orders of the county board of school
trustees defining or redefining boundaries of school districts, showing
names and numbers of districts affected, descriptions of boundary lines,
numbers and names of surveys included in district, number of acres in
each survey, total number of acres in district, signature of county
school superintendent to certificate of authentication, and clerk's recording certificate. Arr. chron. by recording date. Indexed alph. by

first letter of name of school district and chron. thereunder. Typed.
300 pp. (57 used) 18 x 12 x 2.

167. SOLDIERS & SAILORS DISCHARGE RECORD, Apr. 15, 1919--.
1 vol. (1).
Recorded copies of official military discharge certificates of soldiers,
sailors, and other residents of the county who served in the U.S. Army
or Navy. Arr. in separate Army and Navy sections and thereunder chron.
by recording date. Indexed alph. by first letter of surname and chron.
thereunder. Hdw., hdw. pr. fm., and typed. 592 pp. 18 x 14 x 4.

168. RECORD OF HUNTERS & TRAPPERS, Sept. 2, 1925-Nov. 21, 1926.
1 vol. (1).
Record of licenses issued to hunters and trappers, showing license number, date issued, name and address of licensee, age, height, weight,
color of hair and eyes, fee paid, and clerk's commission. Arr. in separate trapper and hunter sections and thereunder numer. by license no.
No index. Typed pr. fm. 100 pp. 20 x 14 x 2. Annex va.

169. AUTO REGISTER RECEIPTS (Stubs), Mar. 31, 1916-June 15, 1917.
1 vol. (labeled by contained receipt nos.).
Stubs of receipts issued by county clerk upon payment of automobile registration fees, showing number and date of receipt, name and address of
owner, and make of car. Arr. chron. by date issued, with receipts numbered consecutively. No index. Hdw. pr. fm. 500 pp. (300 used) 16 x
12 x 1.

170. AUTOMOBILE REGISTER, Feb. 9, 1909-Apr. 18, 1916. 1 vol. (1).
Clerk's register of automobile and motorcycle owners, showing registration number, name of owner, make of vehicle, and registration date. Arr.
chron. by registration date. Indexed alph. by first letter of owner's
surname and chron. thereunder. Hdw. pr. fm. 132 pp. 16 x 12 x 1.

171. LETTERS, Sept. 1, 1913-July 6, 1935. 300 letters in 5 f.d.
Clerk's official correspondence. Arr. alph. by subject and chron. thereunder. No index. Typed. 11 x 5 x 14. Annex va.

III. DISTRICT COURT

A district court was established in Orange County upon its organization in 1852,[1] and ever since has been the county's superior court of
general original jurisdiction. From the spring of 1870 to the spring of
1876 the district court was the court of original probate jurisdiction.[2]

----

1. Const. 1845, art. IV, sec. 10, Gam. Laws, II, 1286; Acts 1852, Gam.
    Laws, III, 966; and see entry 187.
2. Const. 1869, art. V, sec. 7, Gam. Laws, VII, 411.

From the fall of 1866 to the spring of 1876 it had appellate jurisdiction in all cases originating in the inferior courts of the county,[3] but at all other times in its history its appellate jurisdiction over the trial courts has been confined to probate cases.[4]

At present Orange County is in the 1st judicial district, and its district court is presided over by a district judge elected for a term of 4 years by the voters of Orange, Jasper, Newton, Sabine, and San Augustine Counties, of which the district is composed.[5] Other officers of the court are the district clerk, who is elected by the voters of the county at each biennial general election,[6] the sheriff,[7] and the district attorney of the 1st district.[8]

All of the records of the court are in the district clerk's office except as otherwise indicated in the entries.

General Civil

Case Papers

172. CIVIL CASES DISPOSED OF IN DISTRICT COURT, Oct. 10, 1858--. 7,000 cases in 155 f.d. Untitled, Oct. 10, 1858-Oct. 29, 1917, 74 f.d. Scattered papers, 1852-1911, in (Miscellaneous Papers), entry 3, and 1920-37, in (Civil and Criminal Cases), entry 180.
Papers of civil cases disposed of in district court, including plaintiffs' petitions, defendants' answers, citations, motions, writs, depositions; bonds, except as filed separately from 1923, see entries 175, 176; and verdicts, orders, and judgments, except as filed separately from 1910, see entries 177-179. Arr. numer. by case no. No index. Hdw., hdw. and typed pr. fm., and typed. 11 x 5 x 14.

173. (CIVIL CASES PENDING), 1933--. 2 f.d.
Papers of civil cases pending in district court, as partially listed in entry 172. Arr. chron. by filing date. No index. Hdw., hdw. and typed pr. fm., and typed. 11 x 5 x 14.

174. ON APPEAL, May 29, 1928--. 900 papers in 3 f.d.
Papers of civil cases in district court on appeal. Arr. chron. by filing date. No index. Typed pr. fm. and typed. 11 x 5 x 14.

---

3. Const. 1866, art. IV, sec. 6, Gam. Laws, V, 866; Const. 1869, art. V, sec. 7, Gam. Laws, VII, 411.
4. Const. 1845, art. IV, sec. 15, Gam. Laws, II, 1287; Const. 1876, art. V, sec. 8; Titus v. Latimer, 5 Tex. 433 (1849).
5. Const. 1876, art. V, sec. 7; Vernon's Texas St. 1936, RCS, art. 199, sub. 1.
6. Const. 1876, art. V, sec. 9.
7. Ibid., sec. 23; Vernon's Texas St. 1936, RCS, arts. 2022, 2333, 6873.
8. Const. 1876, art. V, sec. 21; Vernon's Texas St. 1936, RCS, art. 322.

175. COST BONDS AND INJUNCTION RECEIVERS, Sept. 23, 1931--. 300
     bonds in 1 f.d.
Bonds of civil cases disposed of in district court, including cost, injunction, and receivers' bonds. Arr. numer. by case no. No index. Hdw.
pr. fm. 11 x 5 x 14.

176. BONDS: APPEAL, REMOVAL, WRIT OF ERROR, SEQUESTRATION, SUPER-
     SEDEAS, Jan. 4, 1923--. 800 bonds in 2 f.d. Title varies:
     Bonds: Indemnifying, Replevy, Attachment, Garnishment,
     Guardian, 1923--, 1 f.d.
Bonds of civil cases disposed of in district court, including sequestration, writ of error, appeal, removal, supersedeas, replevy, attachment,
trustees', indemnity, and garnishment bonds. Arr. by kind of bond and
thereunder chron. by filing date. No index. Hdw. pr. fm. 11 x 5 x 14.

177. COURT ORDERS FELONY AND CIVIL, Sept. 29, 1931--. 500 orders
     in 2 f.d.
Court orders in civil and criminal cases disposed of in district court,
consisting of all orders in civil cases except judgments, see entries
178, 179, and all orders and judgments in criminal cases. Arr. chron.
by filing date. No index. Hdw. pr. fm. and typed. 11 x 5 x 14.

178. JUDGMENTS (Recorded), Oct. 31, 1910--. 3,000 judgments in
     5 f.d.
Judgments in civil cases disposed of in district court, recorded in Civil
Minutes Dist. Court, entry 187. Arr. chron. by filing date. No index.
Typed. 11 x 5 x 14.

179. JUDGMENTS TO BE RECORDED, Sept. 1934--. 40 judgments in 1 f.d.
Judgments in civil cases disposed of in district court, to be recorded
in Civil Minutes Dist. Court, entry 187. Arr. chron. by court term. No
index. Typed pr. fm. 11 x 5 x 14.

180. (CIVIL AND CRIMINAL CASES), 1920-37. 1,185 papers in 4 f.d.
Contains scattered papers of: Civil cases disposed of, entry 172; and
criminal cases disposed of, entry 214. No obvious arr. No index. Hdw.,
hdw. and typed pr. fm., and typed. 11 x 5 x 14. Annex va.

181. ATTORNEY'S RECEIPT FOR PAPERS, May 21, 1898-Oct. 3, 1908.
     1 vol.
Register of case papers withdrawn from and returned to custody of district clerk, showing number and style of case, quantity and kind of papers,
signature of person taking papers, date withdrawn, and date returned.
Arr. chron. by date withdrawn. No index. Hdw. pr. hd. 292 pp. 16 x
14 x 2.

182. SPECIAL ORDERS, RESOLUTIONS, GRAND JURY REPORTS ETC., May 30,
     1925--. 500 papers in 1 f.d.
Contains:
    i. Grand jury reports to district judge, made by grand jury fore-
       man, of felony cases investigated, showing date of report,

court term, number of days jury was in session, number of
witnesses questioned, number of indictments returned; and
of condition of county buildings inspected, of examination
of county finances, and recommendations relative to enforcement of criminal laws. For copies filed with commissioners
court, see entry 5.
  ii. Orders of the court extending court terms, designating special
judges, calling for special venires, and for grand jury to
reassemble.
Arr. chron. by court term. No index. Typed. 11 x 5 x 14.

Dockets & Fees

183. DISTRICT CLERK'S CIVIL FILE DOCKET AND FEE BOOK, Apr. 16,
      1883-Sept. 22, 1903, May 6, 1905--. 10 vols. (1 vol. unla-
      beled; 2-10).
Original entry docket of civil cases filed in district court, and from
1905, account of fees due thereon; 1883-1903 shows case number, names of
attorneys, names of parties to suit, filing date, object of suit, and
notation of court action; 1905-13 shows case number, names of attorneys,
names of parties to suit, filing date, object of suit, and itemized account of fees due clerk, sheriff, and witnesses; from 1913 shows case
number, names of attorneys, names of parties to suit, filing date, cause
of action, itemized account of fees due clerk and sheriff, total amounts
due clerk and sheriff, amounts of witness fees, recapitulation of fees
due jury, clerk, sheriff, witnesses, and other miscellaneous fees, total
amount of fees, and receipts acknowledging payment. Arr. numer. by case
no. No index, 1883-1903; indexed alph. by first letter of plaintiff's
surname and chron. thereunder, 1905-24; indexed alph., by first letter
of plaintiff's surname and by first letter of defendant's, and chron.
thereunder, 1924--. Hdw. pr. hd. 1883-1903; docket hdw. pr. hd. and fee
accounts hdw. pr. fm. 1905--. 428 pp. 16 x 14 x 3.

184. WITNESS CERTIFICATE, May 19, 1923--. 1 vol.
Affidavits made by witnesses serving in civil cases in district court,
kept by district clerk to charge the correct amount of fees against party
assessed costs of suit, showing date and place of execution, number and
style of case, for whom witness summoned, number of days served, number
of miles traveled, amounts due witness for per diem and mileage, witness'
affidavit, and clerk's attest. Arr. chron. by filing date. No index.
Hdw. pr. fm. 150 pp. 8 x 8 x 2.

185. DISPOSED OF CIVIL DOCKET DISTRICT COURT, fall term 1852-Apr.
      term 1881, 1892--. 13 vols. Oct. term 1881-Oct. term 1892
      in Civil Docket County Court (Disposed), entry 284.
Court docket of civil cases in district court, showing county, court term,
case number, names of plaintiff, defendant, and attorneys, object of suit,
filing date, and abstracts of court orders. Arr. chron. by court term,
1852-81, 1892-1905; arr. chron. by date of final judgment, 1906--. No
index, 1852-81, 1892-1903, 1906--; indexed alph. by first letter of plaintiff's surname and chron. thereunder, 1903-5. Hdw. 1852-81; hdw. pr. hd.

1892--.   239 to 800 pp. 8 x 14 x 8 to 18 x 14 x 4.   11 vols., 1852-81,
1892-1903, 1906--, d.c. off.; 1 vol., 1903-5, c.c. va.

186.   MOTION DOCKET, Oct. term 1879--.   2 vols. (1 vol. unlabeled;
        2).
Docket of motions made in civil and criminal cases in district court,
showing case number, names of parties and attorneys, nature of motion,
filing date, and disposition of motion.   Arr. chron. by court term.   No
index.   Hdw. pr. hd.   250 pp. 16 x 14 x 3.

Minutes

187.   CIVIL MINUTES DIST. COURT, July 26, 1852-Mar. 21, 1865, spring
        term 1866--.   20 vols. (A, A½, B-S).   Title varies: Records
        District Court, July 26, 1852-Mar. 21, 1865, 1 vol.; Minutes
        District Court, spring term 1866, 1871-81, 1885-1936, 16 vols.;
        untitled, fall term 1866-Apr. term 1871, 1 vol.
Minutes of district court in civil cases resulting in judgments, and of
all other acts and proceedings, except as recorded in separate volumes
from time to time; minutes for each term show court term, names of officers present, nature of business before the court and proceedings therein, judge's approval, and clerk's attest.   Also contains: Execution
docket, May 11, 1868-May 27, 1870, entry 191; minutes of divorce suits
contested, orders refusing divorce, orders dismissing divorce cases for
lack of prosecution; and divorce proceedings in which decree is granted
on judge's hearing, 1852-1906, entry 200; general criminal minutes, 1852-
1931, entry 224; probate minutes, 1870-76, entry 271.   Arr. chron. by
court term.   No index to criminal cases, 1852-1931; civil cases indexed
alph., by first letter of plaintiff's surname and by first letter of defendant's, and chron. thereunder, 1929--; for index to civil cases, 1852-
1929, see entry 188; for index to probate cases, 1870-76, see entry 272.
Hdw. 1852-1913; typed 1913--.   640 pp. 18 x 14 x 4.

188.   INDEX TO DISTRICT COURT MINUTES, July 26, 1852-Mar. 20, 1929.
        4 vols. (1, M-O).
Index by name of plaintiff to civil cases in Civil Minutes Dist. Court,
vols. A, A½, B-O, entry 187; shows case number, name of defendant, and
volume and page reference.   Arr. alph. by first letter of plaintiff's
surname and chron. thereunder.   Hdw. pr. hd.   40 to 640 pp. 18 x 14 x 1
to 18 x 14 x 4.

189.   TRIAL DOCKET (Record of Disposed Cases), Oct. term 1887--.
        3 vols. (1-3).
Record of civil and criminal cases disposed of in district court, showing
date of jury verdict or judge's order, number and style of case, copy of
jury verdict or notation of judge's order, names of jurors in those cases
where jury trial had, name of party demanding jury, names of witnesses
for plaintiff, and names of witnesses for defense.   Arr. chron. by date
of verdict or order.   Civil cases indexed alph. by first letter of plaintiff's surname and chron. thereunder; criminal cases indexed alph. by
first letter of defendant's surname and chron. thereunder.   Hdw. pr. fm.
150 pp. 16 x 10 x 2.

Process

    190. ORDERS OF SALE - EXECUTIONS, Apr. 2, 1913--. 1 f.d. 1903-10
          in Execution & Orders of Sale, entry 292.
Executions issued to enforce civil judgments of district court, and orders
of sale issued to collect, showing number and style of case, date process
issued, description of land, date of judgment, amount of judgment and
costs, and clerk's signature; and sheriff's returns on executions, showing date process received, date executed, description of property seized,
and officer's signature; on orders of sale, showing date received, date
executed, description of property seized, date of sale, amount received,
disposition of proceeds of sale, and officer's signature. Arr. chron.
by filing date. No index. Hdw. and typed pr. fm. 11 x 5 x 14.

    191. EXECUTION DOCKET, Dec. 29, 1870-July 25, 1878, Mar. 3, 1884--.
          6 vols. (1, A, B, 2-4). May 11, 1868-May 27, 1870 in Civil
          Minutes Dist. Court, entry 187.
Register of executions issued to enforce collection of judgments rendered
in civil cases in district court, showing case number, names of parties,
date and amount of judgment, rate of interest, items of costs and total
costs, date of execution, to whom delivered; and recorded copy of officer's return, showing date received, date and manner of execution, and
officer's signature. Also contains in vol. A, pp. 60-62: Execution
docket county court, 1886-1906, entry 291. Arr. chron. by date of execution. No index, 1870-78, 1907-23; indexed alph. by first letter of plaintiff's surname and chron. thereunder, 1884-1906; indexed alph., by first
letter of plaintiff's surname and by first letter of defendant's, and
chron. thereunder, 1923--. Hdw. 1870-78; hdw. pr. hd. 1884-1930; typed
pr. hd. 1930--. 165 pp. 16 x 14 x 3.

    192. SUBPOENA CIVIL, Feb. 16, 1931--. 4 vols.
Duplicates of district court writs directing sheriff or constable to summon witnesses in civil cases, showing number and style of case, name of
witness, date issued, date returnable by sheriff, filing date, and clerk's
signature. Arr. chron. by date issued. No index. Hdw. pr. fm. 150 pp.
8 x 9 x 1.

    193. (STUBS OF WITNESS ATTACHMENTS), Nov. 9, 1922--. 1 vol.
Stubs of district court writs directing sheriff or constable to bring
before the court witnesses failing to answer subpoenas, showing number
and style of case, date writ issued, date returnable, name of witness,
date to appear, amount of bond required for release, and whether summoned
by sheriff or not found. Arr. chron. by date issued. No index. Hdw.
pr. fm. 85 pp. 9 x 12 x 1.

Divorce

    194. DIVORCE (Disposed Cases), scattered papers 1897-1919, com-
          plete file 1919--. 5,000 cases in 23 f.d. (labeled by con-
          tained case nos.).
Papers of divorce suits disposed of in district court, including plaintiffs' petitions, citations with returns, defendants' answers, motions;

and orders, decrees, and judgments as to division of property and custody
of children, except as filed separately from 1932, see entry 196. Arr.
numer. by case no. No index. Hdw., hdw. and typed pr. fm., and typed.
11 x 5 x 14.

195. DIVORCE CASES (Pending), 1936--. 100 papers in 1 f.d.
Papers in divorce cases pending in district court, as partially listed in
entry 194. Arr. chron. by filing date. No index. Typed pr. fm. 11 x 5
x 14.

196. DIVORCE JUDGMENT & DIVORCE ORDERS, Feb. 17, 1932--. 100 orders
     in 1 f.d.
Orders, decrees, and judgments in divorce cases disposed of in district
court. Arr. chron. by filing date. No index. Hdw. and typed pr. fm.,
and typed. 11 x 5 x 14.

197. CLERK'S FILE DOCKET & FEE BOOK DIVORCE CASES, July 10, 1930--.
     2 vols. (1 vol. unlabeled; 2).
Original entry docket of divorce cases filed in district court and account
of fees due thereon, showing county, case number, names of attorneys,
names of parties to suit, filing date, and cause of action; items of fees
due clerk and total clerk's fees, items of fees due sheriff and total
sheriff's fees, recapitulation of totals of fees due jury, clerk, sheriff,
and miscellaneous fees, grand total, and receipts. Arr. numer. by case
no. Indexed alph. by first letter of plaintiff's surname and chron. thereunder. Dockets hdw. pr. hd.; accounts hdw. pr. fm. 520 pp. 16 x 14 x 4.

198. DISPOSED OF DIVORCE DOCKET, 1933--. 2 loose-leaf vols. (1 vol.
     labeled by contained case nos.; 1 vol. unlabeled).
Court docket of divorce cases disposed of in district court, showing case
number, names of parties and attorneys, cause of action, filing date, notations of court orders, and volume and page reference to Civil Minutes
Dist. Court, entry 187, or Divorce Minutes, entry 200. Arr. chron. by
date of final order. No index. 30 pp. 9 x 14 x 2.

199. DIVORCE DOCKET, Aug. 30, 1935--. 1 loose-leaf vol.
Court docket of divorce cases pending in district court, showing items
of information as in entry 198. Arr. chron. by filing date. No index.
Hdw. pr. hd. 40 pp. 9 x 14 x 2.

200. DIVORCE MINUTES, Apr. 9, 1906--. 5 vols. (1, 2, 2-4). Title
     varies: Divorce Record, Apr. 9, 1906-Apr. 29, 1921, 2 vols.;
     Divorce Minutes Decree; Jan. 1, 1932--, 1 vol. 1852-1906 in
     Civil Minutes Dist. Court, entry 187.
Minutes of district court in divorce cases in which decree is granted on
judge's hearing, showing court term, names of officers present, recorded
copy of judgment showing number and style of case, order granting divorce,
if custody of children involved names and ages of children and to whom
custody given, and if property involved description of property and to
whom awarded, judge's approval, and clerk's attest. Arr. in 3 sections:
Decree of divorce, custody of children, division of property, and thereunder chron. by date of proceedings. Indexed alph. by first letter of

plaintiff's surname and chron. thereunder.   Hdw. pr. fm. 1906--, 4 vols.;
typed 1933--, 1 vol.   480 pp. 18 x 14 x 4.

Tax Suits

Case Papers

201. ORANGE COUNTY TAX SUITS CURRENT, Sept. 26, 1896, July 16,
      1900--.   3,000 cases in 31 f.d. (labeled by contained case
      nos.).
Papers of suits for delinquent State and county taxes in district court,
including plaintiffs' petitions for foreclosure of tax liens, tax notices,
citations, defendants' answers, schedules of property owned by taxpayers;
and judgments and orders of sale, except as filed separately, see entries
204, 205. Arr. numer. by case no. No index. Hdw. pr. fm. 11 x 5 x 14.

202. CITY TAX SUITS CURRENT, Oct. 30, 1909-Aug. 27, 1926, Dec. 7,
      1938--.   1,321 cases in 6 f.d. (5 f.d. labeled by contained
      nos.; 1 f.d. unlabeled).
Papers of suits for delinquent city taxes in district court, as partially
listed in entry 201. Arr. numer. by case no. No index. Hdw. and typed
pr. fm. 11 x 5 x 14.

203. ORANGE INDEPENDENT SCHOOL DISTRICT (Tax Suits), Jan. 31, 1927--.
      200 cases in 5 f.d. (labeled by contained case nos.).
Papers of suits in district court for delinquent taxes due Orange Independent School District, as partially listed in entry 201. Arr. chron.
by case no. No index. Typed and typed pr. fm. 11 x 5 x 14.

204. TAX JUDGMENTS, STATE OF TEXAS AND ORANGE COUNTY IND. SCHOOL
      DIST., Nov. 28, 1925--. 400 papers in 1 f.d.
Judgments rendered in district court cases for delinquent taxes due State
and county and Orange Independent School District. Arr. chron. by filing date. No index. Typed. 11 x 5 x 14.

205. ORDERS OF SALE FOR STATE, ORDERS OF SALE FOR CITY OF ORANGE,
      June 27, 1917-Feb. 1, 1918. 1 f.d.
Orders of sale issued to collect judgments issued for delinquent taxes
due State and county and city of Orange, showing items of information
as in entry 190. Arr. in 2 sections: State and county, city of Orange.
No index. Hdw. pr. fm. 11 x 5 x 14.

Dockets

206. CIVIL DOCKET DELINQUENT TAX SUITS, July 16, 1900--. 4 vols.
      (2 vols. unlabeled; 2, 3).
Docket of delinquent tax suits in district court, showing case number,
names of attorneys and parties, cause of action, filing date, and court
orders. Arr. numer. by case no. No index, 1900-1927; indexed alph. by
first letter of defendant's surname and chron. thereunder, 1928--. Hdw.
pr. hd. 200 pp. 16 x 14 x 4.

207. CIVIL DOCKET CITY TAX SUITS, Apr. 10, 1917--. 1 vol.
Docket of delinquent tax suits filed by the city of Orange in district
court, showing items of information as in entry 206. Arr. numer. by case
no. No index. Hdw. pr. hd. 201 pp. 16 x 14 x 4.

208. DELINQUENT TAX DOCKET ORANGE IND. SCHOOL DIST., Jan. 14, 1927--.
      1 vol. (1).
Docket of delinquent tax suits filed by Orange Independent School District
in district court, showing items of information as in entry 206. Arr.
numer. by case.no. Indexed alph. by first letter of defendant's surname
and chron. thereunder. Hdw. pr. hd. 201 pp. 16 x 14 x 4.

Minutes

209. JUDGMENT RECORD DELINQUENT TAX SUITS STATE & COUNTY ORANGE
      IND. SCHOOL DIST., Apr. term 1917--. 2 vols.
Minutes of district court judgments in suits for delinquent taxes due
State and county, and from 1923, due local taxing agencies of the county,
including navigation, draihage, and independent school districts. Shows
court term, number and style of case, names of attorneys, amount of taxes
due, interest, penalty, and costs, location and description of property,
years delinquent, amount of judgment, judge's approval, and clerk's attest.
Also contains: City of Orange tax minutes, 1927--, entry 211. Arr. chron.
by date of proceedings. No index, 1917-23; for index 1923--, see entry 210.
Hdw. pr. fm. 1917-23; hdw. pr. fm. and typed 1923--. Aver. 690 pp. 18 x
12 x 3.

210. INDEX TAX JUDGMENTS STATE & COUNTY CITY SCHOOL, 1923--. 1 vol.
Index by name of defendant to Judgment Record Delinquent Tax Suits State
& County Orange Ind. School Dist., entry 209, showing case number, name
of plaintiff, and reference to page. Arr. alph. by first letter of defendant's surname and chron. thereunder. Hdw. 100 pp. 16 x 10 x 1.

211. MINUTES TAX JUDGMENTS (City of Orange), Apr. 1915-Apr. 1927.
      2 vols. Title varies: Minutes Dist. Court, Orange County
      Tax Suits, Apr.-May 1915, 1 vol. 1927-- in Judgment Record
      Delinquent Tax Suits State & County Orange Ind. School Dist.,
      entry 209.
Minutes of district court judgments in suits for delinquent taxes due
city of Orange, showing items of information as in entry 209. Arr.
chron. by date of proceedings. No index. Typed 1915; hdw. pr. fm.
1916-27. 500 pp. 18 x 11 x 3.

Naturalization

212. DECLARATION OF INTENTION, Oct. 8, 1903-Sept. 22, 1906.
      1 vol. (1).
Recorded copies of declarations of intention to become citizens, showing
State, county, and court, name, age, sex, personal description, and
nationality of declarant, date and place of birth, date and place of
arrival in United States, oath of allegiance, date of declaration, alien's

affidavit, and clerk's attest. Arr. chron. by date of declaration. No
index. Hdw. pr. fm. 160 pp. 14 x 10 x 2.

Criminal

Guide to Cases

213. CRIMINAL INDEX, 1925--. 1 vol.
Alphabetical list of defendants in criminal cases filed in district court,
giving case number for each, compiled by clerk as a means of locating
case papers and docket entries. Arr. alph. by first letter of defendant's
surname and chron. thereunder. No index. Hdw. 75 pp. 16 x 10 x 1.

Case Papers

214. FELONY, scattered cases 1852-75, complete file 1875--. 48 f.d.
        Title varies: District Court Old Papers, 1852-1922, 1 f.d.
        Scattered papers, 1854-96, in (Miscellaneous Papers), entry
        3, and 1920-37 in (Civil and Criminal Cases), entry 180.
Papers of criminal cases disposed of in district court, including complaints, indictments, warrants of arrest, capias, witness subpoenas and
attachments, bonds, verdicts; and orders and judgments except as filed
separately from 1931, see entry 177. Arr. numer. by case no. No index.
Hdw., hdw. and typed pr. fm., and typed. 11 x 5 x 14. 22 f.d., 1852-
1922, bsmt.; 26 f.d., 1908--, d.c. off.

215. CURRENT FELONY CAUSES, 1938--. 1 f.d.
Papers of criminal cases pending in district court, as partially listed
in entry 214. Arr. chron. by filing date. No index. Hdw., hdw. and
typed pr. fm., and typed. 11 x 5 x 14.

216. MANDATES, Jan. 1, 1939--. 400 papers in 1 f.d.
Mandates issued by Court of Criminal Appeals to district court, showing
number and style of case, orders with date issued, volume and page reference to Criminal Minutes Dist. Court Plain, entry 224, and signature
of clerk of court of appeals. Arr. chron. by filing date. No index.
Hdw. pr. fm. 11 x 5 x 14.

217. COPIES OF INDICTMENTS, Nov. 2, 1923--. 1,200 papers in 2 f.d.
        Title varies: Certified Copies of Indictments and Bail Bonds,
        Nov. 2, 1923-June 14, 1932, 1 f.d.
Original and certified copies of indictments returned by grand jury, showing number and style of case, names of witnesses, filing date, and signatures of district clerk and grand jury foreman. Also contains: Bail
bonds, May 29, 1929-June 14, 1932. Arr. in separate sections for indictments and bonds and thereunder chron. by filing date, 1923-32; arr. chron.
by filing date, 1931--. No index. Typed pr. fm. 11 x 5 x 14.

218. EXAMINING TRIALS, 1902-7, 1924-31, 1933--. 7 f.d. (1 f.d. un-
        labeled; 6 f.d. labeled by contained justice precinct nos.).
        Title varies: Justice Criminal, 1924-31, 1 f.d.
Papers of examining trials held in justice of peace and county courts, including complaints, testimony of witnesses, appearance bonds, subpoenas,
and warrants of arrest. Arr. chron. by filing date. No index. Typed pr.
fm. 11 x 5 x 14. 1 f.d., 1902-7, c.c. va.; 1 f.d., 1924-31, bsmt.; 5
f.d., 1933--, d.c. off.

219. INQUEST PROCEEDINGS, Nov. 1, 1896-May 19, 1907, Jan. 26,
        1929--. 1,050 papers in 4 f.d. (labeled by justice precinct
        nos.).
Reports of inquest proceedings held by justices of the peace, showing precinct number, by whom held, filing date, date and place of inquest, date
and place of death, name and description of deceased person, and signatures
of justice of peace and district clerk. Arr. chron. by filing date. No
index. Hdw. and typed pr. fm. 11 x 5 x 14. 1 f.d., 1896-1907, c.c. va.;
3 f.d., 1929--, d.c. off.

Dockets (See also entry 186)

220. DISPOSED OF CRIMINAL DOCKET DISTRICT COURT, spring term 1859-
        June term 1876, Apr. term 1891-Apr. term 1894, Apr. term
        1900--. 6 vols. Untitled, spring term 1859-Dec. term 1870,
        1 vol. Apr. term 1882-Apr. term 1888 in Criminal Docket County
        Court (Disposed), entry 298.
Docket of criminal cases disposed of in district court, showing case number, names of defendant and attorneys, filing date, offense, notations
and dates of court orders, and from 1905, volume and page reference to
judgment. Arr. chron. by court term, 1859-76, 1891-94, 1900-1905; arr.
chron. by date of final judgment, 1905--. No index. Hdw. 1859-76; hdw.
pr. hd. 1891-94, 1900--. 110 to 500 pp. 10 x 16 x 6 to 16 x 11 x 2.

221. CURRENT CRIMINAL DOCKET DISTRICT COURT, Sept. 23, 1938--.
        1 vol.
Docket of criminal cases pending in district court, showing items of information as in entry 220. Arr. chron. by filing date. No index. Hdw.
pr. hd. 25 pp. 12 x 8 x 1.

222. CRIMINAL BAR DOCKET, Apr. term 1888-Apr. term 1891. 1 vol.
Docket of criminal cases in district court, made for the convenience of
attorneys, showing case number, names of defendant and attorneys, and
court orders. Arr. chron. by court term. No index. Hdw. pr. hd. 400 pp.
(55 used) 16 x 14 x 3.

Minutes

223. INDEX TO CRIMINAL CASES WHERE THE DEFENDANT HAS RECEIVED A
        TERM IN THE STATE PENITENTIARY - SUSPENDED SENTENCES NOT
        INCLUDED, Jan. 1, 1931--. 1 vol.
Index by name of defendant to judgments as per title in Criminal Minutes
Dist. Court Plain, entry 224; in Criminal Minute Book (Final Judgments),

entry 225; and in Criminal Minute Book (Conviction Plea Guilty), entry 226; each entry shows number and style of case, length of sentence, and volume and page reference. Arr. alph. by first letter of defendant's surname and chron. thereunder. Hdw. 150 pp. 16 x 10 x 1.

224. CRIMINAL MINUTES DIST. COURT PLAIN, June 1, 1931--. 1 vol.
(1). 1852-1931 in Civil Minutes Dist. Court, entry 187.
Minutes of district court in all proceedings in criminal cases prior to final judgments, including grand jury actions in bringing defendants into court, setting bonds, releasing defendants on bond or remanding them to jail; and also, of such final judgments as not adapted to printed forms, see entries 225-227. Shows court term, date and place of meeting, names and titles of court officers present, proceedings and orders of the court, judge's approval, and clerk's attest. Arr. chron. by court term. Indexed alph., by first letter of plaintiff's surname on left pages and by first letter of defendant's on right, and chron. thereunder, each entry showing name of opposite party; for index to judgments resulting in penitentiary sentences, 1931--, see entry 223. Typed. 540 pp. 18 x 12 x 2.

225. CRIMINAL MINUTE BOOK (Final Judgments), Apr. 16, 1894--.
5 vols. (1 vol. unlabeled; B-E).
Minutes of the following final judgments in criminal cases in district court: Judgment plea not guilty; judgment plea guilty-misdemeanor; sentence; judgment on verdict of not guilty; judgment of conviction on plea of not guilty, judgment of acquittal on plea of not guilty; judgment on application for writ of habeas corpus; judgment on motion for new trial and sentence; judgment and sentence plea of guilty suspended sentence; plea not guilty - judgment order overruling motion - sentence. Shows court term, date and place of proceedings, names and titles of court officers present, recorded copy of judgment, judge's approval, and clerk's attest. Also contains: Judgment of conviction on plea of guilty, 1913-1931, entry 226; criminal minutes dismissals, 1914-31, entry 227. Arr. in sections by types of judgments as shown above and thereunder chron. by court term. No index, 1894-1931, 3 vols.; indexed alph. by first letter of defendant's surname and chron. thereunder, 1923--, 2 vols.; for index to judgments resulting in penitentiary sentences, 1931--, see entry 223. Hdw. pr. fm. 1894-1931; typed pr. fm. 1931--. 500 pp. 18 x 12 x 2.

226. CRIMINAL MINUTE BOOK (Conviction Plea Guilty), Feb. 1,
1932--. 1 vol. (F). 1913-31 in Criminal Minute Book
(Final Judgments), entry 225.
Minutes of district court in final judgments of conviction by the court on plea of guilty, showing court term, date and place of proceedings, names and titles of officers present; copy of judgment reciting defendant's appearance, plea of guilty, and waiver of jury trial; amount of fine and sentence; judge's approval, and clerk's attest. Arr. chron. by court term. Indexed alph. by first letter of defendant's surname and chron. thereunder; for index to judgments resulting in penitentiary sentences, see entry 223. Typed pr. fm. 400 pp. 18 x 12 x 2.

227. CRIMINAL MINUTES DISMISSALS (Nolle Prosequi), May 30, 1932--.
        1 vol. 1914-31 in Criminal Minute Book (Final Judgments),
        entry 225.
Minutes of district court in final judgments dismissing cases upon motion
of prosecuting attorney, showing court term, date and place of proceedings, names and titles of officers present, copy of order dismissing
case, judge's approval, and clerk's attest. Arr. chron. by court term.
No index. Hdw. pr. fm. 300 pp. 18 x 12 x 2.

228. RECOGNIZANCE RECORD, Oct. 27, 1924-June 2, 1930, Sept. term
        1939--. 2 vols. (1 vol. unlabeled; 1). Title varies: Scire
        Facias Minutes, Oct. 27, 1924-June 2, 1930, Jan. 29, 1940,
        1 vol.
Minutes of the following district court proceedings:
    i. Bonds, recognizance, to insure appearance of defendants in
        criminal cases, show date and place of court term, names of
        officers present; copy of court order, showing date of or-
        der, case number, names of defendant and sureties, amount
        of acknowledged indebtedness to State conditioned upon sub-
        sequent appearance in court, and judge's approval.
   ii. Judgments nisi by State against defendants or defendants and
        their sureties, for non-appearance, Apr. 26, 1926, Oct. 25,
        1926, and Jan. 29, 1940, showing date and place of court
        term, names of officers present; copy of judgment, showing
        case number, names of defendant and sureties, date of judg-
        ment, statement of non-appearance and default of recogni-
        zance or bail bond, statement that bond will be forfeited
        unless cause be shown at next term of court, and judge's
        approval.
Arr. in separate sections for bonds and judgments and thereunder chron.
by court term. No index. Hdw. pr. fm. 160 pp. (20 used) and 348 pp.
(1 used) 18 x 14 x 2 and 18 x 12 x 2.

229. MINUTES OF GRAND JURY, May 4, 1908-Oct. 31, 1910, Apr. 23,
        1928--. 3 vols. (1 vol. unlabeled; 11, 12). Untitled, May
        4, 1908-Oct. 31, 1910, 1 vol.
Minutes of grand jury investigations, showing court term, name of accused,
date of offense, charge, names and residences of witnesses, and whether
no bill or true bill. Arr. chron. by court term. No index. Hdw. 1908-
10; hdw. pr. hd. 1928--. 60 to 200 pp. 8 x 10 x 1 to 14 x 12 x 3. 1 vol.,
1908-10, c.c. va.; 2 vols., 1928--, d.c. off.

230. MINUTES OF TRANSCRIPT TO LOWER COURT, Oct. 17, 1900-May 21,
        1914, May 17, 1923--. 2 vols. (A, 2).
Minutes of district court in transfer of misdemeanor cases to county
court, showing county, place and date of beginning of term, date of ad-
journment, name of presiding judge, name of defendant, case number, date
of delivery of indictment by grand jury foreman; order finding district
court has no jurisdiction, case having been proved a misdemeanor, and
transferring case to county court; and recorded copy of bill of costs,
showing number and style of case, items and amounts of fees due, and

totals; and district clerk's certificate. Arr. chron. by date of clerk's certificate. No index. Hdw. pr. fm. 155 pp. 14 x 10 x 1.

Process

231. CAPIAS DISTRICT COURT, Sept. 21, 1931--. 3 vols. Title
        varies: Alias Capias D.C., Feb. 2, 1938--. 1 vol.
Duplicates of district court writs directing sheriff or constable to arrest defendants in criminal cases and bring them before the court at specified time, showing State and county, number and style of case, date capias issued, date prisoner is to appear in court, and signature of district clerk; the alias capias adding recital that a capias has previously issued for the same person in the same cause. Arr. chron. by date issued. No index. Hdw. pr. fm. 175 pp. 6 x 8 x 2.

232. CAPIAS INSTANTER, Sept. 22, 1937--. 2 vols.
Duplicates of district court writs directing sheriff or constable to arrest defendants in criminal cases and to bring them before the court forthwith, showing items of information as in entry 231. Arr. chron. by date issued. No index. Hdw. pr. fm. 175 pp. 6 x 8 x 2.

233. SUBPOENA FELONY, Oct. 2, 1935--. 5 vols.
Duplicates of district court writs directing sheriff or constable to summon in-county witnesses in criminal cases to appear at specified time, showing State and county, number and style of case, name and address of witness, date and place of appearance, date subpoena issued, and district clerk's signature. Arr. chron. by date issued. No index. Hdw. pr. fm. 165 pp. 8 x 8 x 2.

234. SUBPOENA FELONY INSTANTER, Apr. 7-18, 1900, June 5, 1920--:
        3 vols.
Stubs of district court writs directing sheriff or constable to summon witnesses in criminal cases to appear forthwith, showing items of information as in entry 233. Arr. chron. by date issued. No index. Hdw. pr. fm. 200 pp. 8 x 8 x 2.

235. SUBPOENAS NON-RESIDENT FELONY, May 6, 1913--. 2 vols.
Duplicates of district court writs directing sheriff or constable to summon out-county witnesses in criminal cases to appear at specified time, showing number and style of case, date issued, to whom delivered, date returnable, name and address of witness, from what county summoned, date and place of appearance, and district clerk's signature. Arr. chron. by date issued. No index. Hdw. pr. fm. 250 pp. 8 x 12 x 3.

236. SUBPOENAS FELONY NON RESIDENT INSTANTER, May 31, 1939--.
        1 vol.
Duplicates of district court writs directing sheriff or constable to summon out-county witnesses in criminal cases to appear before court forthwith, showing items of information as in entry 235. Arr. chron. by date issued. No index. Hdw. pr. fm. 150 pp. 8 x 12 x 2.

237. GRAND JURY PROCEEDS, 1897, 1903-4. 60 papers in 1 f.d.
Duplicates of grand jury writs directing sheriff or constable to subpoena
witnesses, showing items of information as in entry 233. Also contains:
Mayor's report to grand jury of misdemeanor cases on docket, June 1-Oct.
1, 1897. No obvious arr. No index. Hdw., and hdw. pr. fm. 11 x 5 x 14.
C.c. va.

238. SUBPOENA - GRAND JURY (Out-County), Sept. 22, 1939--. 1 vol.
Stubs of grand jury writs directing sheriff or constable to subpoena out-
county witnesses, showing items of information as in entry 235. Arr.
chron. by date issued. No index. Hdw. pr. fm. Faded. 350 pp. 8 x 16
x 4.

239. WITNESS ATTACHMENT FELONY INSTANTER (Stubs); May 10, 1915--.
        1 vol.
Stubs of district court writs directing sheriff or constable to bring
before the court forthwith witnesses in criminal cases failing to answer
subpoenas, showing State and county, number and style of case, name and
address of witness, court term, amount of bail, amount of fine, date
issued, and district clerk's signature. Arr. chron. by date issued. No
index. Hdw. pr. fm. 150 pp. (50 used) 9 x 12 x 1.

240. WITNESS ATTACHMENT BEFORE THE GRAND JURY, Nov. 19, 1906-May
        4, 1919, June 24, 1936. 2 vols.
Duplicates of district court and grand jury writs directing sheriff or
constable to produce witnesses failing to answer subpoenas, showing State
and county, court term, name and address of witness, date writ issued,
and district clerk's signature. Arr. chron. by date issued. No index.
Hdw. pr. fm. 125 pp. 8 x 12 x 1. 1 vol., 1906-19, annex va.; 1 vol.,
1936, d.c. off.

241. JUROR ATTACHMENT, Oct. 23, 1922--. 1 vol. Last entry June
        19, 1933.
Duplicates of district court writs directing sheriff or constable to
produce jurors failing to appear, showing State and county, name of
juror, court term, kind of service (petit or special venire), date of
appearance, place and date writ issued, and district clerk's signature.
Arr. chron. by date issued. No index. Hdw. pr. fm. 200 pp. (40 used)
8 x 10 x 1.

Fees & Costs Payable by State

242. RECORD DISTRICT CLERK'S ACCOUNTS FELONY CASES, Oct. 27, 1913-
        Oct. 18, 1920, Feb. 1925--. 2 vols. (2, 2).
Minutes of the district court allowing district clerk's accounts of fees
in criminal cases, in form of duplicate fee bills from 1925, showing
court term, number and style of case, date of account, offense charged,
verdict, itemized account of fees, clerk's affidavit, and judge's approval. Arr. chron. by court term. No index. Hdw. pr. fm. 220 pp. 14 x
12 x 3.

243. MINUTES OF WITNESS AND SHERIFF'S ACCOUNTS, Oct. 15, 1883-Oct.
        3, 1902. 2 vols.
Minutes of district court allowing in-county sheriff's accounts of fees
in criminal cases, Oct. 15, 1883-Oct. 15, 1900, showing date of account,
county, number and style of case, offense charged, itemized account of
fees, sheriff's affidavit, clerk's attest, and judge's approval. Also
contains: Minutes of out-county sheriffs' accounts, Oct. 14, 1889-Apr.
16, 1894, entry 244; minutes of witness accounts, Apr. 14, 1890-Oct. 3,
1902, entry 248. Arr. chron. by court term. No index. Hdw. pr. fm.
150 pp. 16 x 14 x 2. Shff. off.

244. CLERK'S CERTIFICATE OF SHERIFF'S PAY FOR ADVANCES & SUMMONING
        NON-RESIDENT WITNESSES, Oct. 16, 1899-May 31, 1911, May 1,
        1913--. 5 vols. Title varies: Minutes Clerk's Certificate
        Sheriff's Pay, Oct. 16, 1899-May 31, 1911, 1 vol. Oct. 14,
        1889-Apr. 16, 1894 in Minutes of Witness and Sheriff's Accounts,
        entry 243.
Minutes of district court allowing out-county sheriffs' fees for attach-
ing or conveying non-resident witnesses to criminal trials in district
court, on State Comptroller's standard certificates (recorded copies,
1899-1911; duplicates, 1913--), showing court term, number and style of
case, offense, names of witnesses, items of fees, mileage, per diem, total due sheriff, sheriff's affidavit, clerk's attest, and judge's approval. Arr. chron. by date of approval. No index. Hdw. pr. fm. 40 to
300 pp. 14 x 12 x 1 to 18 x 14 x 1.

245. CLERK'S CERTIFICATES SHERIFF'S PAY FOR ADVANCING SUMMONING
        NON-RESIDENT WITNESS BEFORE GRAND JURY, Feb. 11, 1936--.
        1 vol.
Minutes of district court allowing of out-county sheriffs' for fees summoning of and advances to out-county witnesses for appearance before
grand jury, on State Comptroller's standard certificates, showing items
of information as in entry 244. Arr. chron. by court term. No index.
Hdw. pr. fm. 100 pp. 14 x 12 x 1.

246. MINUTES DIST. ATTY'S OR DIST. JUDGE'S EXPENSE ACCTS. (D.A.
        only), May 12, 1916-Dec. 28, 1938. 3 vols. Title varies:
        Record of Dist. Atty's. Per Diem, May 12, 1916-Mar. 4, 1933,
        1 vol.; District Attorney's Fee Bill, June 23, 1933-Oct. 17,
        1935, 1 vol.
Minutes of district court allowing district attorney's fees and expenses,
showing judicial district, name of attorney, dates and items of expense,
grand total, attorney's affidavit, judge's approval, and clerk's attest.
Arr. chron. by recording date. No index. Hdw. pr. fm. 190 pp. 15 x 12
x 2.

247. COURT REPORTER'S EXPENSE ACCOUNT RECORD, May 30, 1929-Oct. 13,
        1933. 1 vol. (1).
Minutes of district court allowing court reporter's expense accounts,
showing county, judicial district number, number of counties in district,

reporter's name, term of court, mileage and hotel expenses, reporter's
affidavit, clerk's attest, and judge's approval. Arr. chron. by date
of approval. No index. Hdw. pr. fm. 50 pp. 14 x 10 x 1.

248. WITNESS ACCOUNT AND CERTIFICATE BEFORE COURT, Feb. 22, 1937--.
        2 vols. (2, 1 vol. unlabeled). Apr. 14, 1890-Oct. 3, 1902 in
        Minutes of Witness and Sheriff's Accounts, entry 243.
Duplicates of certificates issued by district clerk to witnesses for services in criminal cases in district court, showing certificate number, case
number, name of witness, name of defendant, offense charged, address of
witness, itemized account of mileage and per diem, date reported, witness'
affidavit, to clerk's attest, and judge's approval. Arr. numer. by certificate no. No index. Hdw. pr. fm. 129 pp. 14 x 12 x 2.

249. WITNESS CERTIFICATE BEFORE GRAND JURY, May 9, 1912-May 3,
        1921, Jan. 18, 1934--. 2 vols. (1, 2).
Duplicates of certificates issued by district clerk to out-county witnesses for services before grand jury, showing items of information as
in entry 248, adding grand jury foreman's signature. Arr. chron. by
date of clerk's certification. No index. Hdw. pr. fm. 107 pp. 14 x
10 x 1.

Jury Service

250. PETIT JURORS, GRAND JURORS AND SPECIAL VENIRES, BEGINNING FEB.
        TERM 1935, Feb. 3, 1932--. 500 in 1 f.d.
Lists of persons selected as petit and grand jurors and special veniremen in civil and criminal cases in district court, showing week and term
of court, number and style of case, cause of action or offense charged,
kind of juror, date of service, sheriff's return, and signatures of district clerk and sheriff. Arr. chron. by court term. No index. Typed
pr. fm. 11 x 5 x 14.
        For county clerk's copies, see entry 3-vii.

251. JURORS TIME BOOK, Oct. term 1879-Oct. term 1884, Jan. term
        1891-Jan. term 1907, May term 1911--. 5 vols.
Clerk's record of time served by jurors in district court, 1879-84,
1911, 1917--, showing court term, kind of jury, name of juror, number
of days served, days of week served, number of scrip in which paid, total amount of fees, list of bailiffs, and amounts due. Also contains:
Jurors' time book, county court, Apr. term 1895-Jan. term 1905, Oct.
term 1912-Oct. term 1926, entry 312; jurors' time book, justice court,
Jan. term 1891-Jan. term 1907, entry 329. Arr. chron. by court term.
No index. Hdw. pr. hd. 318 pp. 14 x 8 x 2. 2 vols., 1879-84, 1891-
1907, 1911-26, c.c. va.; 3 vols., 1917--, d.c. off.

252. JURY CERTIFICATES (Stubs), Oct. 1902-Nov. 1905, Feb. 1932-Feb.
        9, 1934, June 22, 1936--. 4 vols.
Stubs of certificates for pay issued to grand and petit jurors, bailiffs,
riding bailiffs, and jury commissioners, showing number, date, and amount
of certificate, name of payee, number of days served, kind of service,

and date of court term. Arr. numer. by certificate no. No index. Hdw.
pr. fm. 120 pp. 16 x 14 x 1. 1 vol., 1902-5, annex va.; 3 vols., 1932-
34, 1936--, d.c. off.

253. SPECIAL VENIRE WARRANTS (Stubs), June 15, 1931--. 1 vol.
Stubs of certificates issued to special veniremen serving district court
and grand jury, showing items of information as in entry 252. Arr. numer.
by certificate no. No index. Hdw. pr. fm. 150 pp. 16 x 14 x 1.

District Clerk Ex Officio

254. RECORD OF MEDICAL CERTIFICATES, Feb. 2, 1908--. 2 vols. (1,
       1). 1873-1914 also in Record Embalmer's (&C), entry 154.
Recorded copies of licenses issued to physicians by State Board of Medical Examiners, showing clerk's file number, name and address of physician,
whether license granted upon examination or reciprocity with another
State, date issued, and board members' signatures; affidavits by physicians applying for registration of license, showing applicant's age, date
and place of birth, post office address, school of medicine, date license
issued, physician's signature, and clerk's attest; and clerk's certificate of authentication and recording. Arr. chron. by recording date.
Indexed alph. by first letter of physician's surname and chron. thereunder. Hdw. pr. fm. and typed. 132 pp. 16 x 12 x 1.

255. (NOTICES TO INDUSTRIAL ACCIDENT BOARD), Oct. 15, 1937--. 2 vols.
Clerk's copies of notices to State Industrial Accident Board of suits filed
in district court to set aside decisions previously made by the board, showing place and date of notice, number and style of case, filing date,
board's case number, date of injury, name of employer, date copy of judgment mailed to board, and signature of district clerk. Arr. chron. by
date of notice. No index. Hdw. pr. fm. 30 pp. 5 x 8 x 1.

256. RECORD OF PROOFS ACKNOWLEDGMENTS BY DISTRICT CLERK, July 3,
       1874-Dec. 21, 1876. 1 vol.
Record of instruments acknowledged by district clerk, showing number of
acknowledgment, names and addresses of grantor and grantee, date of instrument, location and description of property, date of acknowledgment,
and clerk's signature. Arr. numer. by acknowledgment no. No index.
Hdw. Torn and faded. 290 pp. 16 x 12 x 2.

257. GENERAL FEE BOOK, Jan. 2, 1931--. 1 vol.
Clerk's daily account of fees accrued and office expenses, from which is
compiled annual report to State Auditor; on left pages shows date of
accrual, name of payer, purpose of payment, classification (State fees,
such as felony, habeas corpus, or other, filing and recording certificates and copies, misdemeanor, civil, and delinquent tax), totals of each
class, and page totals; on right pages shows deductible expenses, giving
date of payment, name of payee, explanation of payment (salary, bond pre-
mium, and stamps), amount of payment, totals of each class, and grand
total for page. Arr. chron. No index. Hdw. pr. fm. 200 pp. 16 x 16 x 2.

258. CLERK'S CASH RECORD, Jan. 1, 1931--. 4 vols.
Clerk's daily account of cash collections (including trust funds deposited
with clerk to pay judgment or costs), from all sources and disbursements
thereof, showing date of collection, amount, from what source, explanation,
case number, and classification of collections; date of disbursement, to
whom paid, for what purpose, check number, and classification of disbursements. Arr. chron. No index. Hdw. 76 pp. 18 x 18 x 1.

IV. COUNTY COURT

An inferior trial court called the county court was established in
Orange County upon its organization in 1852,[1] and with the exception of
a period of about 6 years, from the spring of 1870 to the spring of 1876,
when this tribunal was discontinued by general law,[2] has had uninterrupted existence and has always been the court of original probate jurisdiction.[3] Limited original civil and criminal jurisdiction and appellate
jurisdiction over cases brought up from the justice of peace courts,
granted the county courts by general law, was taken from the county court
of Orange by special law in 1879.[4] Full criminal jurisdiction, original
and appellate, was restored in 1879;[5] civil in 1903.[6]

The county judge is the judge of the county court.[7] Other officers
are the county clerk,[8] the sheriff,[9] and the county attorney.[10]

All of the records of the county court are in the county clerk's
vault except as otherwise indicated in the entries.

Probate

Case Papers

259. PROBATE, May 27, 1852--. 40 f.d. (35 f.d. labeled by contained
      case nos.; 5 f.d. labeled by contained first letters of princi-
      pals' surnames). Scattered papers, 1915-21, in (Miscellaneous
      Papers), entry 3.
Papers of probate cases disposed of, including wills except as filed separately, see entry 262; applications to probate wills, for letters testamen-
tary, letters of administration, and letters of guardianship; judgments of

---

1. Acts 1848, Gam. Laws, III, 113.
2. Const. 1869, art. V, secs. 1-26; Acts 1870, Gam. Laws, VI; 282.
3. Acts 1848, Gam. Laws, III, 113; Const. 1866, art. IV, sec. 16, Gam.
    Laws, V, 868; Const. 1876, art. V, sec. 16; and see entries 259, 271.
4. Acts 1879, Gam. Laws, VIII, 1368; Acts 1881, Gam. Laws, IX, 95; Acts
    1885, Gam. Laws, IX, 697; Acts 1887, Gam. Laws, IX, 852.
5. Acts 1897, Gam. Laws, X, 1146.
6. Acts 1903, 28th Leg., p. 41.
7. Const. 1876, art. V, sec. 15.
8. Ibid., sec. 20; Vernon's Texas St. 1936, RCS, art. 1935.
9. Const. 1876, art. V, sec. 23; 38 Texas Jurisprudence 431.
10. Const. 1876, art. V, sec. 21; Vernon's Texas St. 1936, CCP, art. 26.

heirship; appraisals for inheritance tax; inventories of estates; letters of administration; administrators', executors', and guardians' bonds and reports. Arr. numer. by case no., 1852--, 35 f.d.; arr. alph. by first letter of principal's surname and thereunder chron. by filing date, 1852-1902, 5 f.d. No index. Hdw., hdw. and typed pr. fm., and typed. 11 x 5 x 14.

260. UNFINISHED PROBATE, Dec. 18, 1939--. 150 papers in 1 f.d. Papers of probate cases pending in county court, as partially listed in entry 259. Arr. numer. by case no. No index. Hdw. pr. fm. 11 x 5 x 14.

261. UNFINISHED INACTIVE, May 19, 1937-Apr. 30, 1938. 60 papers
          in 1 f.d.
Papers of inactive probate cases, as partially listed in entry 259. No obvious arr. No index. Typed pr. fm. 11 x 5 x 14.

262. (WILLS), 1873, 1898, 1907, 1924--. In (Miscellaneous Papers),
          entry 3.
Wills filed for probate, showing State and county, name of testator, provisions of will, names of heirs, description of property bequeathed, names of witnesses if any, testator's and witnesses' signatures, and clerk's filing certificates.

263. (WILL RECORD), Mar. 31, 1862-Jan. 2, 1880. 1 vol. (A). Recorded copies of wills filed for probate, showing information as in entry 262. Arr. chron. by recording date. Indexed alph. by first letter of deceased person's surname and thereunder chron. by filing date; also separate index see entry 272. Hdw. Torn and faded. 150 pp. 14 x 8 x 1.

264. (Probate) RECORDS, Apr. 1852-Apr. 28, 1882. 3 vols. (1 vol.
          unlabeled; B, C). Untitled, Apr. 1852-Jan. 23, 1869, 2 vols.
Recorded copies of papers of probate cases, as partially listed in entry 259. Arr. chron. by recording date. For index 1852-69, see entry 272; for index 1869-82, see entry 265. Hdw. Pages torn and writing faded. 500 pp. 13 x 8 x 3.

265. INDEX TO BOOK C; PROBATE RECORDS, Jan. 25, 1869-Apr. 28, 1882.
          1 vol.
Index by name of principal to (Probate) Records, vol. C, entry 264, showing name of principal, kind of instrument, and volume and page reference. Arr. alph. by first letter of principal's surname and chron. thereunder. Hdw. 50 pp. 16 x 16 x 1. Annex va.

Dockets & Fees

266. PROBATE DOCKET & FEE BOOK, Jan. 1853-Jan. 1855, Aug. 27, 1860-
          Feb. 1863, June 1866-Apr. 1879, Feb. 23, 1887--. 9 vols.
          (4 vols. unlabeled; A-E). Untitled, Jan. 1853-Jan. 1855, Aug.
          27, 1860-Feb. 1863, June 1866-Apr. 1879, 4 vols.
Account of fees in probate cases; 1853-55, 1860-63, 1876-77, fees due clerk, and 1866-79, 1887-1924 fees due clerk, judge, and sheriff, shows

names of administrator, executor, or guardian, date of clerk's entry,
and list of instruments issued or recorded and amount due for each; from
1925, consists of duplicates of bills of cost in probate cases, showing
case number, name of principal, name of guardian, and of administrator
or executor, items of fees due judge, sheriff, and clerk, recapitulation
of totals due judge, sheriff, and clerk, grand total, and clerk's affidavit. Arr. one case to each page and thereunder chron. by date of entry.
No index, 1853-55, 1860-63, 1887-1924; indexed alph. by first letter of
principal's surname and chron. thereunder, 1866-79, 1925--. Hdw. 1853-
55, 1860-63, 1866-79; hdw. pr. hd. 1887--. 20 to 640 pp. 12 x 8 x 1 to
16 x 14 x 4. 5 vols., 1853-55, 1866-79, 1929--, c.c. va.; 4 vols., 1860-
63, 1876-77, 1887-1929, annex va.

    267.   PROBATE DOCKET, June 2, 1852-Dec. 11, 1855, June 13-Sept. 10,
              1861, Dec. term 1870--. 8 vols. Untitled, June 2, 1852-Dec.
              11, 1855, June 13, 1861, Apr. term 1871-May term 1885, 2 vols.;
              title varies: Claim Docket District Court, June 13-Sept. 10,
              1861, Jan. 17-Apr. 4, 1871, 1 vol.; Probate Docket District
              Court, Dec. term 1870-Apr. term 1871, 1 vol.; Judge's Probate
              Docket, 1894-1904, 1 vol.; Probate Docket Disposed Cases,
              1903-23, 1 vol.
Docket of probate cases, showing case number, name of principal, name of
administrator, executor, or guardian, name of attorney, nature of application, petition, or exhibit, filing date, and notations of court orders
with dates thereof. Also contains: Claim docket, Jan. 17-Apr. 4, 1871,
entry 268. Arr. numer. by case no., 1852-55, June 13, 1861, 1914--; arr.
chron. by filing date, June 13-Sept. 10, 1861, Jan. 17-Apr. 4, 1871; arr.
chron. by court term, 1870-1904; arr. alph. by first letter of principal's
surname and thereunder chron. by date of final order, 1903-23. No index,
1852-55, 1861, 1870-85, 1903--; indexed alph. by first letter of principal's surname and chron. thereunder, 1884-1904. Hdw. 1852-55, 1861, 1870-
71; hdw. under hd. 1871-85; hdw. pr. hd. 1884--. 50 to 450 pp. 14 x 8 x 1
to 16 x 12 x 2. 3 vols., 1852-55, 1861, 1903--, c.c. va.; 1 vol., 1861,
1871, d.c. off.; 4 vols., 1870-1904, annex va.

    268.   CLAIM DOCKET, May 3, 1871--. 1 vol. Jan. 17-Apr. 4, 1871 in
              Probate Docket, entry 267.
Docket of claims filed by creditors against estates in probate cases,
showing case number, name of estate, name of claimant, date and amount of
claim, date due, rate of interest, when allowed, amount allowed, filing
date, date approved, amount approved, and class of claim. Arr. one case
to a page and thereunder chron. by filing date. No index. Hdw. pr. hd.
147 pp. 20 x 14 x 2.

    269.   (COUNTY JUDGE'S FEE BOOK), Jan. 3, 1885-June 1897. 1 vol.
Judge's account of fees earned and collected in probate and civil cases
in county court, and miscellaneous fees, such as for approving liquor
bonds and taking acknowledgments, showing date of entry, style of case
or name of person for whom service performed, classification of fee (kind
of court order or proceeding), amount of fee, and amount of cash payment.
Arr. chron. by date of entry. Indexed alph. by first letter of surname

of principal in case or person for whom service performed, and chron.
thereunder. Hdw. pr. hd. 136 pp. 14 x 10 x 1.

270. GENERAL FEE BOOK COUNTY CLERK, Dec. 1, 1919-Oct. 20, 1933.
        1 vol.
Clerk's account of fees, fines, and costs collected in probate, civil,
and criminal cases in county court, showing date of collection, name of
payer, amounts of fines and costs, volume and page reference to Probate
Docket & Fee Book, entry 266, Civil Docket & Fee Book, entry 282, or
Criminal File Docket & Fee Book, entry 297, and distribution of amounts
due sheriff, county attorney, judge, and treasurer. Arr. chron. by date
collected. No index. Hdw. pr. hd. 160 pp. 16 x 14 x 2.

Minutes

271. PROBATE MINUTES, Apr. 1852-Apr. 1870, July term 1876--.
        14 vols. (A, B, D-O). Untitled, Apr. 1852-67, 1 vol.
        1870-76 in Civil Minutes Dist. Court, entry 187.
Minutes of county court in probate cases, involving estates of decedents,
guardianship of minors and lunatics, and apprenticeships, showing court
term, names of officers present, subject of hearing, names of interested
parties, court orders, judge's approval, and clerk's attest. Also contains, in vol. D: Minutes of a few civil cases, 1879, entry 289; general
criminal minutes, July term 1876-Apr. term 1879, entry 303. Arr. chron.
by court term. For index, see entry 272. Hdw. 1852-70, 1876-1914; typed
1914--. 640 pp. 18 x 14 x 4.

272. INDEX TO PROBATE MINUTES, Apr. 1852--. 1 vol. (1).
Index by name of principal to probate minutes, 1870-76, in Civil Minutes
Dist. Court, entry 187; to (Will Record), 1862-80, entry 263; to (Probate)
Records, 1852-69, unlabeled vol. and vol. B, entry 264; and to Probate
Minutes, 1852-70, 1876--, entry 271; shows case number, filing date,
name of principal, name of administrator, executor, or guardian, kind of
instrument, and volume and page reference. Arr. alph. by first letter
of principal's surname and chron. thereunder. Hdw. pr. hd. 640 pp. 18 x
14 x 4.

Lunacy

273. LUNACY, Oct. 3, 1900--. 1,500 papers in 3 f.d. Scattered
        papers, 1867-93, in (Miscellaneous Papers), entry 3.
Papers of lunacy hearings in county court, including complaints, subpoenas, witness testimony, warrants of arrest, jury lists, and commitments.
Arr. alph. by first letter of defendant's surname and thereunder chron.
by filing date, 1900-1927; arr. numer. by case no., 1926--. No index.
Hdw. pr. fm. 11 x 5 x 14. 1 f.d., 1900-1927, annex va.; 2 f.d., 1926--,
c.c. va.

274. PROBATE LUNACY DOCKET (Commission Hearings), Aug. 23, 1913-
        June 14, 1916. 1 vol. (1).
Minutes in lunacy trials in county court conducted under commission form
of hearing, showing date of proceedings, names of respondent and county

judge; recorded copy of report of commissioners, showing name of respondent, case number, names of commissioners, findings and recommendations
as to mental condition, treatment, restraint, age, causes of mental condition, amount of property owned, commissioners' signatures, and judge's
affidavit; order discharging respondent, or adjudging a lunatic and ordering conveyance to State asylum; recorded copies of fee bills, showing
amounts due judge, clerk, attorney, sheriff, and commissioners, and total
amount of fees. Arr. chron. by date of proceedings. Indexed alph. by
first letter of defendant's surname and chron. thereunder. Hdw. pr. fm.
79 pp. (13 used) 18 x 14 x 2.

275. LUNACY RECORD, Dec. 3, 1918--. 1 vol.
Minutes of jury trials of lunacy cases in county court, showing date of
hearing, names of court officers present, case number, name of defendant,
recorded copy of jury verdict with answers to special issues, jurors'
signatures, judgment of the court, judge's approval, and clerk's attest.
Arr. chron. by date of hearing. Indexed alph. by first letter of defendant's surname and chron. thereunder. Hdw. pr. fm. 430 pp. 16 x 14 x 2.

Defectives

276. TUBERCULARS, Sept. 11, 1930--. 20 applications in 1 f.d.
Copies of applications (originals to sanatorium) made to county judge for
admission to State tuberculosis sanatoriums, showing county, date of
application, name, address, description, and occupation of applicant,
list of property owned if any, names of persons legally liable for support, names and addresses of parents and husband or wife, name, age, and
sex of each child; class of application, indigent or pay, and applicant's
signature; physician's affidavit to examination and results of examination; judge's order granting or denying petition, and ordering application and transcript sent to superintendent of State hospital; clerk's
certification of transcript of proceedings. Arr. numer. by case no. No
index. Typed pr. fm. 11 x 5 x 14.

277. CRIPPLED CHILDREN, Apr. 17, 1936-Feb. 1, 1938. 20 papers in
     1 f.d.
Applications filed in county juvenile court for admittance of crippled
children to State institutions, showing county, filing date, case number,
name of child, and notarization; order of commitment, showing name of
child, date of hearing, name of physician making examination and report,
name and location of hospital, and judge's signature, and on reverse,
examining physician's affidavit, showing result of diagnosis and recommendations as to necessary treatment, and parent's or guardian's affidavit of consent to treatment or operation. Arr. numer. by case no. No
index. Hdw. pr. fm. 11 x 5 x 14.

Civil
(Jurisdiction diminished 1879-1903, see essay, p. 96)

Case Papers

278. CIVIL CASES (Disposed), 1867-69, 1885-86, 1896--. 650 cases
      in 40 f.d. Untitled, Apr. 14, 1930-Oct. 24, 1931, 1 f.d.
      Scattered papers, 1886-1928, in (Miscellaneous Papers), entry 3.
Papers of civil cases disposed of in county court, including plaintiffs'
petitions, citations, defendants' answers, subpoenas, motions, writs, depositions, bonds, verdicts, and judgments. Arr. chron. by filing date,
1867-69, 1885-86, 1930-31, 3 f.b.; arr. numer. by case no.; 1896--, 37 f.b.
No index. Hdw., hdw. and typed pr. fm., and typed. 11 x 5 x 14.

279. CIVIL COUNTY COURT (Pending), Mar. 6, 1931--. 150 papers
      in 1 f.d.
Papers of civil cases pending in county court, as partially listed in
entry 278. Arr. numer. by case no. No index. Typed pr. fm. 11 x 5
x 14.

280. PAPERS ON APPEAL, June 3, 1913-Dec. 10, 1934. 600 papers in
      2 f.d.
Papers of civil cases appealed to higher courts, as partially listed in
entry 278. Arr. chron. by filing date. No index. Typed. 11 x 5 x 14.

281. COUNTY COURT MANDATES, Sept. 8, 1899-Aug. 20, 1925. 30 man-
      dates in 1 f.d.
Mandates issued by Court of Civil Appeals to county court reversing or
affirming judgments, showing county, date, names of appellant and appel-
lee, case number, judgment of court, filing date, and signatures of clerk
of Court of Civil Appeals and of county clerk. Arr. chron. by filing
date. No index. Typed pr. fm. 11 x 5 x 14.

Dockets & Fees (See also entries 269, 270)

282. CIVIL DOCKET & FEE BOOK, Feb. 10, 1902--. 5 vols. (1 vol.
      unlabeled; 2-5). Title varies: Clerk's File Docket County
      Court, Feb. 10, 1902-Sept. 15, 1919, 1 vol.; Clerk's File
      Docket and Fee Book, 1920-28, 2 vols.
Account of fees in civil cases in county court, consisting of duplicate
copies of bills of cost, showing case number, names of parties and attorneys, amount of judgment, amount of fees, date and amount paid, filing
date, cause of action, itemized statement of fees due clerk, sheriff,
notaries, and witnesses, recapitulation of fees, and clerk's affidavit.
Arr. numer. by case no. Indexed alph. by first letter of defendant's
surname and chron. thereunder. Hdw. pr. fm. 385 pp. 16 x 14 x 2.

283. FEE BOOK COUNTY COURT, Feb. 13-May 9, 1869. 1 vol.
Clerk's account of fees collected in civil cases in county court, showing number and style of case, date and from whom collected, for what purpose, and amount. Arr. chron. by date of entry. No index. Hdw. Torn
and faded. 100 pp. 14 x 9 x 1.

284. CIVIL DOCKET COUNTY COURT (Disposed), Oct. term 1867-June
            term 1870, Nov. term 1876-June term 1879, Oct. term 1881-Oct.
            term 1892, Aug. 1902--. 5 vols.
Court docket of civil cases disposed of in county court, Oct. term 1867-
June term 1870, Nov. term 1876-June term 1879, Aug. term 1885-May term
1887, Aug. 1902--, showing number and style of case, names of attorneys,
cause of action, filing date, notations of court orders with dates thereof, and volume and page reference to Civil Minutes, entry 289. Also contains: Civil docket district court, Oct. term 1881-Oct. term 1892, entry
185. Arr. chron. by court term, 1867-70; arr. numer. by case no., 1876-
79, 1881-92, 1903-7; arr. chron. by filing date, 1902--. No index. Hdw.
1867-70; hdw. pr. fm. 1876-79, 1881-92, 1902--. Torn and faded, 1867-70,
1 vol. 75 to 1,000 pp. 16 x 14 x 2 to 16 x 12 x 6. 4 vols., 1867-70,
1876-79, 1881-92, 1903-7, 1926--, c.c. va.; 1 vol., 1902-26, annex va.

285. CIVIL DOCKET COUNTY COURT (Pending), June 26, 1930--. 1 vol.
Docket of civil cases pending in county court, showing items of information as in entry 284. Arr. chron. by filing date. No index. Hdw. pr.
hd. 140 pp. 16 x 12 x 2.

286. BAR CIVIL DOCKET, Aug. term 1885-May term 1887, Aug. term
            1901-May term 1905. 1 vol.
Bar docket of civil cases, and of criminal cases, 1901-5, in county court,
made for use of attorneys, showing court term, case number, names of plaintiff, defendant, and attorneys, cause of action, filing date, and court orders. Arr. numer. by case no. No index. Hdw. pr. fm. 159 pp. 16 x 14 x 2.

287. MOTION DOCKET, Feb. 1, 1886-Feb. 19, 1887, Apr. 25, 1914-Feb. 15,
            1938. 2 vols. Title varies: Estray, Feb. 1, 1886-Feb. 19,
            1887, 1 vol.
Docket of motions filed in civil cases in county court, showing court term,
number and style of case, names of attorneys, nature of motion, filing date,
and disposition of motion. Arr. chron. by court term. Also contains:
Criminal motion docket, 1914-38, entry 300. No index, 1886-87; criminal
motions indexed alph. by first letter of defendant's surname, civil motions
alph. by first letter of plaintiff's, and chron. thereunder, 1914-38. Hdw.
pr. hd. 160 pp. 16 x 14 x 2.

288. (Jury) TRIAL DOCKET COUNTY COURT, Jan. term 1910. 1 vol. (1).
            No entries except 2 in Jan. 1910.
Docket of civil cases tried before jury in county court, showing case number, names of parties, names of jurors, names of witnesses for plaintiff
and for defendant, and copy of jury verdict. No obvious arr. No index.
Hdw. pr. fm. 160 pp. (1 used) 16 x 14 x 1. Annex va.

Minutes

    289. CIVIL MINUTES, Aug. 5, 1867-Apr. 5, 1870, Aug. term 1885-May
          term 1887, June term 1897--. 4 vols. (3 vols. unlabeled; D).
          Title varies: County Court Minutes, Aug. 5, 1867-Apr. 5,
          1870, 1 vol. A few civil cases, 1879, in Probate Minutes,
          entry 271.
Minutes of civil cases in county court, Aug. 5, 1867-Apr. 5, 1870, Aug.
term 1885-May term 1887, 1903--, showing court term, names of officers
present, number and style of case, cause of action, names of attorneys,
subject of proceedings, court orders, judgment, date of trial, judge's
approval, and clerk's attest. Also contains: General criminal minutes,
June term 1897-1915, entry 303. Arr. chron. by court term. No index,
1867-70, 1885-87, 1897-1907; for index 1907--, see entry 290. Hdw.
1867-70, 1885-87, 1897-1915; typed 1915--. 250 to 628 pp. 16 x 6 x 2
to 18 x 14 x 4.

    290. GENERAL INDEX TO MINUTES COUNTY COURT, Apr. 1, 1907--. 1 vol.
Plaintiff - defendant index to Civil Minutes, 3d unlabeled vol. (re-
ferred to as "C" in index) and vol. D, entry 289; shows case number,
names of plaintiff and defendant, and volume and page reference. Arr.
alph. by first letter of surname and chron. thereunder. Hdw. pr. hd.
150 pp. 18 x 14 x 2.

Process

    291. EXECUTION DOCKET (County Court), Dec. 1, 1906--. 2 vols. (1
          vol. unlabeled; C). 1886-1906 in Execution Docket, vol. A,
          pp. 60-62, entry 191.
Docket of executions issued to enforce collection of judgments in civil
cases in county court, showing number and style of case, date and amount
of judgment, amount due, rate of interest, amount of costs, date judgment issued, and to whom delivered; and copy of sheriff's return, showing date writ received, date, manner, and place of execution, and sheriff's signature. Arr. chron. by date issued. No index. Hdw. pr. hd.
160 pp. 18 x 12 x 1.

    292. EXECUTION & ORDERS OF SALE, 1901-13. 250 papers in 1 f.d.
Contains: County court bills of cost in civil and probate cases, and
capias pro fine, 1901-8; district court executions and orders of sale,
1903-10, entry 190. No obvious arr. No index. Hdw. pr. fm. 11 x 5
x 14.

    293. ATTORNEY'S ORDER BOOK COUNTY CT., Oct. 30, 1885-Mar. 6, 1886,
          Feb. 24, 1905. 1 vol.
Record of attorneys' orders to clerk for issuance of witness supoenas in
civil and criminal cases in county and district courts, showing county,
date of order, names of parties, names of witnesses subpoenaed, in whose
behalf ordered, date issued, clerk's fees, and signature of attorney.
Arr. chron. by date issued. No index. Hdw. pr. fm. Torn and faded.
136 pp. (6 used) 14 x 8 x 1. Annex va.

294. SUBPOENA CIVIL, July 22, 1907--. 3 vols. Untitled, Apr. 5,
        1929--, 1 vol.
Copies and stubs of subpoenas issued by county clerk to summon witnesses
in civil cases in county court, showing number and style of case, court
term, names of parties, names of witnesses, date issued, date delivered
to sheriff, and clerk's signature. Arr. chron. by date issued. No index. Hdw. pr. fm. 175 pp. 11 x 8 x 2. 1 vol., 1907-20, annex va.;
2 vols., 1920--, c.c. va.

Criminal
(Jurisdiction diminished 1879-97, see essay p. 96)

Case Papers

295. CRIMINAL, 1867-69, 1876, 1908, 1910--. 45 f.d. (17 f.d. un-
        labeled; 28 f.d. labeled by contained case nos.). Title
        varies: County Court, 1867-69, 1876, 1908, 17 f.d.; untitled,
        Aug. 31, 1937--, 1 f.d. Scattered papers, 1852-89, in (Miscel-
        laneous Papers), entry 3.
Papers of criminal cases disposed of in county court, including complaints,
indictments, warrants of arrest, capias, subpoenas, attachments, bonds,
verdicts, and judgments. Arr. numer. by case no. No index. Hdw., hdw.
and typed pr. fm., and typed. 11 x 5 x 14. 17 f.d., 1867-69, 1876,
1908, bsmt.; 28 f.d., 1910--, c.c. va.

296. PENDING CRIMINAL CASES, Sept. 25, 1937--. 1 f.d.
Papers of criminal cases pending in county court, as partially listed in
entry 295. Arr. numer. by case no. No index. Hdw. and typed pr. fm.,
and typed. 11 x 5 x 14.

Dockets & Fees (See also entries 270, 286)

297. CRIMINAL FILE DOCKET & FEE BOOK, June 14, 1897--. 12 vols.
        (1-12). Title varies: Criminal Fee Book County Court, June
        14, 1897-Oct. 12, 1927, 7 vols.
Clerk's original entry docket of criminal cases filed in county court
and account of fees due thereon, showing case number, name of defendant,
date judgment rendered, amount of fine, term of imprisonment, items of
fees due clerk, sheriff, and witnesses, recapitulation of fees due, and
receipts. Arr. numer. by case no. No index. Hdw. pr. fm. 200 pp. 16 x
14 x 4.

298. CRIMINAL DOCKET COUNTY COURT (Disposed), Jan. term 1877-Apr.
        term 1879, Apr. term 1882-Apr. term 1888, June term 1897-Aug.
        term 1901, 1907--. 5 vols. Title varies slightly.
Court docket of criminal cases disposed of in county court, 1877-79,
1897-1901, 1907--, showing court term, number and style of case, charge,
filing date, and abstracts of court orders; and also 1907--, volume and
page reference to Criminal Minutes (General), entry 303. Also contains:
Criminal docket district court, Apr. term 1882-Apr. term 1888, entry 220.
Arr. chron. by court term, 1877-79, 1882-38, 1897-1901; arr. chron. by

date of final judgment, 1907-40. No index. Hdw. pr. hd. 159 to 2,500 pp.
16 x 14 x 2 to 16 x 12 x 8. 2 vols., 1877-79, 1882-88, 1897-1901, c.c.
va.; 3 vols., 1907-40, annex va.

299. CRIMINAL DOCKET COUNTY COURT (Pending), Jan. 27, 1936--. 1 vol.
Court docket of criminal cases pending in county court, showing items of
information as in entry 298. Arr. chron. by filing date. No index. Hdw.
pr. hd. 75 pp. 16 x 18 x 2.

300. CRIMINAL DOCKET (Motions), Aug. term 1903-July term 1907.
          1 vol. 1914-38 in Motion Docket, entry 287.
Docket of motions filed in criminal cases in county court, showing number
and style of case, name of party filing, date and nature of motion, filing date, and notations of court orders. Arr. chron. by court term. No
index. Hdw. pr. hd. 159 pp. 18 x 14 x 2.

301. SCIRE FACIAS DOCKET, Jan. term 1911-Oct. term 1914. 1 vol. (1).
Docket of cases involving bond forfeitures in county court, showing court
term, number and style of case, names of attorneys, cause of action, filing date, and notations of court orders. Arr. chron. by court term. No
index. Hdw. pr. hd. 105 pp. 16 x 12 x 2.

302. EXAMINING TRIAL DOCKET, Mar. 4, 1919-Dec. 4, 1934. 1 vol.
Record of examining trials in criminal cases held by county judge to
determine probable guilt of defendant and to fix bond awaiting action of
grand jury, showing number and style of case, name of State's attorney,
date complaint filed, names of complainants, name of defendant, charge,
date warrant issued and name of officer to whom delivered, and judge's
order requiring defendant to answer at next term of district court and
setting bond in bailable offenses or discharging defendant if evidence
held insufficient, and judge's signature. Arr. numer. by case no. No
index. Hdw. pr. fm. 296 pp. 16 x 14 x 2. Annex va.

Minutes

303. CRIMINAL MINUTES (General), Oct. term 1915--. 1 vol. (3).
          July term 1876-Apr. term 1879 in Probate Minutes, entry 271;
          June term 1897-1915 in Civil Minutes, entry 289.
Minutes of proceedings in criminal cases in county court prior to judgment, and final judgments except as recorded separately 1897-1917, see
entry 304, showing court term, names of officers present, number and
style of case, names of witnesses and State's and defendant's attorneys,
offense, date of charge, plea, date of trial, verdict, judgment of court,
judge's approval, and clerk's attest. Arr. chron. by court term. No
index. Typed. 640 pp. 18 x 14 x 4.

304. CRIMINAL MINUTES (Final Judgments), June 14, 1897-Jan. term
          1917. 2 vols. (1, 2).
Minutes of county court in criminal cases in which final judgments are
rendered, showing court term, names of officers present, and recorded
copy of judgment: Of guilty by court without jury, June 14, 1897-June
16, 1907; of not guilty by court without jury, June 21, 1897-June 7, 1907;

of guilty on plea of not guilty by jury, June 21, 1897-Oct. term 1913;
on plea of guilty misdemeanor, July 1, 1907-Jan. term 1917; of guilty on
plea of not guilty by court, July 9, 1907-July term 1916; verdict not
guilty by jury, Oct. 21, 1907-Jan. term 1917; each shows number and style
of case, date of order, judge's approval, and clerk's attest. Arr. chron.
by court term. No index. Hdw. pr. fm. 400 pp. 18 x 12 x 2.

305. SCIRE FACIAS MINUTES COUNTY COURT, Nov. 5, 1900-Oct. 21, 1910.
     1 vol. (1).
Minutes of the county court in criminal cases in which bonds are taken
to insure appearance at trial, showing court term, names of officers present and recorded copies of judgments nisi on defendants' recognizance or
bail bonds; judgments nisi against defendants set aside; witness recognizance; forfeitures of witness bond or recognizance; judgments nisi against
subpoenaed witness; final judgments against defendant or attached witness;
each shows number and style of case, date of order, judge's approval, and
clerk's attest. Arr. in sections as above and thereunder chron. by court
term. No index. Hdw. pr. fm. 418 pp. 18 x 12 x 3.

Process

306. CAPIAS COUNTY COURT, Dec. 14, 1912--. 17 vols. Untitled,
     Jan. 1, 1923-Oct. 5, 1927, Apr. 4, 1938--, 6 vols.
Stubs of county court writs directing sheriff or constable to arrest defendants in criminal cases and bring them before the court, showing number and style of case, offense, date appearance reopened, date writ returnable, date issued, and clerk's signature, the alias capias adding
recital that a capias has previously issued for the same person in the
same cause. Arr. chron. by date issued. No index. Hdw. pr. fm 150 pp.
8 x 10 x 2. 15 vols., 1912--, c.c. va.; 2 vols., 1917-18, 1921-22, annex va.

307. SUBPOENA CRIMINAL COUNTY COURT, Oct. 5, 1908--. 55 vols. Un-
     titled, Jan. 9, 1911-Apr. 7, 1913, Jan. 21, 1925-Apr. 13, 1926,
     4 vols.
Duplicates and stubs of county court writs directing sheriff or constable
to summon witnesses in criminal cases, showing number and style of case,
date writ applied for and on whose behalf, name of witness, date returnable, date issued, to whom delivered, and clerk's signature. Arr. chron.
by date issued. No index. Hdw. pr. fm. 50 to 150 pp. 6 x 8 x 1 to 8 x
10 x 2. 51 vols., 1908--, c.c. va.; 4 vols., 1911-13, 1925-26, annex va.

308. WITNESS ATTACHMENTS CRIMINAL COUNTY COURT, Mar. 5, 1913-Jan.
     14, 1930. 1 vol.
Stubs of county court writs directing sheriff or constable to bring before the court witnesses in criminal cases failing to answer subpoenas,
showing number and style of case, name and address of witness, date writ
issued, date returnable, to whom delivered, and clerk's signature. Arr.
chron. by date issued. No index. Hdw. pr. fm. 150 pp. 8 x 10 x 1.

Juvenile Delinquency

309. JUVENILE, Apr. 15, 1910--. 2 f.d.
Papers of juvenile delinquency cases in county court, including complaints, information, warrants of arrest, capias, subpoenas, attachments, and judgments. Arr. numer. by case no. No index. Hdw. pr. fm. 11 x 5 x 14.

310. JUVENILE RECORD, Aug. 7, 1919--. 3 vols. (1-3).
Minutes of county court in juvenile delinquency cases, showing case number, name of defendant, filing date, date citation issued, date set for hearing, names of witnesses, disposition of case, and judge's signature. Arr. numer. by case no. Indexed alph. by first letter of defendant's surname and chron. thereunder. Hdw. pr. fm. 161 pp. 16 x 10 x 2.

Jury Service

311. LIST OF JURORS, July 1, 1915-Dec. 19, 1927, Jan. 24, 1931-
        July 16, 1935. 500 lists in 1 f.d. 1922-35 also in (Miscellaneous Papers), entry 3.
Lists of persons selected for jury service in county court, showing name, age, address, and occupation, date of service, and court term, and jury commissioners' signatures. Arr. chron. by filing date. No index. Hdw. pr. fm. 11 x 5 x 14.

312. (JURORS TIME BOOK), Apr. term 1895-Jan. term 1905, Oct. term
        1912-Oct. term 1926. In Jurors Time Book, entry 251.
Clerk's record of time served by jurors in county court, showing court term, kind of jury, name of juror, number of days served, days of week served, number of scrip in which paid, and total fees.

Liquor Hearings

313. COUNTY COURT, July 1-Aug. 8, 1907. 1 vol.
Record of court orders setting dates for hearings on applications for beer and liquor licenses, showing court term, names of officers present, and copies of orders. Arr. chron. by court term. No index. Hdw. 157 pp. 18 x 10 x 1.

314. LIQUOR DEALERS LICENSE RECORD, July 24, 1908-Mar. 9, 1918.
        1 vol. (1).
Recorded copies of judgments in hearings before county judge on applications for retail liquor licenses, showing county, date of hearing, license number, name of petitioner, address of place of business, court order granting or refusing license, judge's signature, and clerk's attest. Arr. chron. by date of judgment. No index. Hdw. pr. fm. 160 pp. 16 x 14 x 2.

315. WINE AND BEER CASES, 1934--. 250 petitions in 1 f.d. 1933-
      35 also in (Miscellaneous Papers), entry 3.
Applications for licenses to wholesale and retail beer and wine, showing
date of application, name of applicant, location of business; clerk's
certificate to posting notice of hearing on petition before county judge,
showing case number, address of place of business, date and place set for
hearing, and signatures of clerk, city secretary, applicant, and judge.
Arr. chron. by filing date. No index. Typed pr. fm. 11 x 5 x 14.

316. BEER & WINE DOCKET, Dec. 26, 1935--. 1 vol.
Docket and orders on applications for beer and wine licenses, showing file
number, name and address of petitioner, kind of license applied for, location of business, and filing date; recorded copy of court order granting or rejecting application with judge's signature; until Feb. 1938,
court order authorized assessor-collector to issue license upon payment
of fees; since then, license granted subject to approval of the State
Liquor Control Board and to payment of fees. Arr. chron. by filing date.
No index. Hdw. pr. fm. 80 pp. 10 x 14 x 1.

Trust Funds

317. TRUST FUND PAPERS, Dec. 16, 1938. 3 instruments in 1 f.d.
Application to county judge for authority to withdraw money held in trust,
signed by applicant and approved by county judge; bond of applicant withdrawing money; letter from insurance company relative to deposit of money
with clerk; applicant's receipt to county clerk for money withdrawn attached. No obvious arr. No index. Typed pr. fm. 11 x 5 x 14.

318. RECORD OF TRUST FUNDS, July 6, 1887--. 1 vol. (1).
Account of money deposited to be held in trust, showing case number, date
received, from whom received, items and amounts, on what account, dispo-
sition of funds, and clerk's signature. Arr. chron. by date received.
Indexed alph. by first letter of name of account and chron. thereunder.
Hdw. pr. hd. 65 pp. 16 x 14 x 1.

V. JUSTICES OF THE PEACE

Since the organization of Orange County in 1852, provision has
always been made for the establishment of justice precincts as subdivisions of the county and for the election of justices in the precincts.[1]
Justices of the peace were among the group of officers composing Orange
County's first governmental organization.[2] At present it is required

1. Const. 1845, art. IV, sec. 13, Gam. Laws, II, 1286; Const. 1866,
   art. IV, sec. 19, Gam. Laws, V, 869; Const. 1869, art. V, secs. 19,
   21, Gam. Laws, VII, 414; Const. 1876, art. V, sec. 18.
2. Comr's. Ct. (1852-60), vol. A, pp. 21, 23, 38, in Commissioners
   Court Minutes, see entry 1.

that each county be divided into at least four precincts and that a justice be elected in each; the maximum number of precincts and justices
permitted is eight. The justices are elected by the voters of their
respective precincts at each biennial general election.[3]

The justice courts are the tribunals for the trial of minor civil
cases and petty misdemeanors.[4] As committing magistrates, the justices
hold examining trials for the purpose of making inquiry into criminal
accusations to determine whether persons charged with crime should be
discharged or bailed.[5] They are also ex-officio coroners,[6] and primary
registrars of vital statistics in their precincts.[7]

All of the records of the justice of the peace of precinct 1 are in
his office, except as otherwise indicated in the entries.

                          Civil & Criminal

Case Papers

    319. (CIVIL CASES DISPOSED OF), Jan. 14, 1925-Nov. 4, 1932. 1,500
            papers in 1 f.d. Scattered papers, 1857-1929, in (Miscella-
            neous Papers), entry 3.
Papers of civil cases in justice court, including plaintiffs' petitions,
citations, defendants' answers, subpoenas, motions, writs, bonds, and
depositions. Arr. numer. by case no. No index. Hdw. and typed pr. fm.,
and typed. 8 x 14 x 24.

    320. PENDING (Civil Cases), Apr. 23, 1937--. 100 papers in 2 f.d.
Papers filed in civil cases pending in justice court, as partially listed
in entry 319. Arr. chron. by filing date. No index. Hdw. pr. fm. and
typed. 11 x 5 x 14.

    321. FORCIBLE DETAINER DISPOSED, July 16, 1937--. 1 f.d.
Papers in eviction cases disposed of in justice court, including complaints, citations, bonds, verdicts, and judgments. Arr. chron. by filing date. No index. Hdw. pr. fm. 11 x 5 x 14.

    322. FORCIBLE DETAINER PENDING, Mar. 14, 1939--. 1 f.d.
Papers of eviction cases pending in justice court, as partially listed in
entry 321. Arr. numer. by case no. No index. Hdw. pr. fm. 11 x 5 x 14.

_____

3. Const. 1876, art. V, sec. 18.
4. Ibid., sec. 19.
5. Vernon's Texas St. 1936, CCP, art. 35; Childers v. State, 16 SW 903
      (1891).
6. Vernon's Texas St. 1936, CCP, arts. 968, 990.
7. Ibid., RCS, art. 4477, rule 36a; Acts 1941, 47th Leg., H. B. 821.

323. DISPOSED (Criminal Cases), Feb. 25, 1889--. 41,000 papers
        in 48 f.d. Title varies: Justice, Jan. 6, 1919-Jan. 3, 1920,
        1 f.d. Justice Odds & Ends, June 10, 1919-Feb. 4, 1929, 2 f.d.
        Scattered papers, 1860-1912, in (Miscellaneous Papers), entry 3.
Papers of criminal cases in justice court, including complaints, warrants
of arrest, capias, witness subpoenas and attachments, bonds, verdicts,
and judgments. No obvious arr., 1889-1924, 17 f.d.; arr. numer. by case
no., 1913-1917, 1919--, 31 f.d. No index. Hdw., hdw. and typed pr. fm.,
and typed. 11 x 5 x 14. 34 f.d., 1889-1929, bsmt.; 14 f.d., 1926--,
j.p. off.

Dockets & Fees

324. J.P. CIVIL DOCKET, Sept. 19, 1856-Dec. 26, 1864, May 30, 1870-
        Jan. 25, 1874, Sept. 8, 1904-Jan. 2, 1907, Feb. 3, 1912--.
        11 vols. Untitled, Sept. 19, 1856-Dec. 26, 1864, 1 vol.
Record of civil cases in justice court; 1856-64, 1870-74, consists of
recorded copies of judgments, showing number and style of case, date of
order, judgment, and justice's signature; 1904-7, 1912--, consists of
docket of civil cases filed, judgments, and account of fees, showing case
number, names of plaintiff, defendant, and attorneys, court term, cause
of action, filing date, account of fees earned, judgment of court, disposition of case, and justice's signature. Also contains: Justice's
criminal docket, 1856-64, 1870-74, entry 325; examining trial docket,
1870-74, entry 327. Arr. chron. by filing date, with cases numbered consecutively. No index, 1856-64, 1870-74, 1912--; indexed alph., by first
letter of plaintiff's surname and by first letter of defendant's and chron.
thereunder, 1904-7. Hdw. 1856-64, 1870-74; hdw. pr. hd. 1904-7, 1912--.
150 pp. 18 x 12 x 2. 1 vol., 1856-64, annex va.; 2 vols., 1870-74, 1904-7,
c.c. va.; 8 vols., 1912--, j.p. off.

325. JUSTICE'S CRIMINAL DOCKET, June 11, 1878-Sept. 10, 1879, Oct.
        10, 1904-Oct. 28, 1907, Jan. 1912--. 29 vols. Untitled:
        June 11, 1878-Mar. 7, 1879, 1 vol.; title varies: Journal,
        Apr. 28-Sept. 10, 1879, 1 vol.; Criminal Docket, Dec. 15,
        1906-Sept. 17, 1907, 1 vol. 1856-64, 1870-74 in J.P. Civil
        Docket, entry 324.
Docket of criminal cases filed in justice court, judgments, and account
of fees due thereon, showing precinct number, county, name of justice,
number and style of case, offense, date complaint filed, by whom complaint
made, against whom, nature of charge, date warrant issued; judgment of
guilty or not guilty in cases wherein jury is waived, or copy of jury
verdict with judgment confirming verdict, and justice's signature; items
and amounts of fees due constable, amounts of trial, county attorney's,
and jury fees, amount of fine, and total costs. Arr. numer. by case no.
No index, 1878-79, 1925-26, 1928-30, 1932-33, 7 vols.; indexed alph. by
first letter of defendant's surname, 1904-7, 1912--, 22 vols. Hdw. 1878-
79; hdw. pr. fm. 1904-7, 1912--. Aver. 280 pp. 16 x 12 x 2. 2 vols.,
1878-79, c.c. va.; 3 vols. 1904-7, annex va.; 19 vols., 1912--, j.p. off.;
5 vols., 1916-17, 1925-26, 1928-30, 1932-33, 2d fl. witness rm.

326. DOCKET STATE HIGHWAY CASES, Apr. 1-Aug. 30, 1918. 1 vol.
Docket of highway traffic violation cases filed in justice court by State
Highway patrolmen, showing county, number and style of case, filing date,
offense, amount of fees earned, judgment of court, and justice's signature. Arr. numer. by case no. Indexed alph. by first letter of defendant's surname and chron. thereunder. Hdw. pr. hd. 160 pp. 12 x 14 x 1.

327. EXAMINING TRIAL DOCKET, July 24, 1903-Dec. 11, 1909, Feb. 23,
      1912--. 8 vols. (7 vols. unlabeled; 2). 1870-74 in J.P.
      Civil Docket, entry 324.
Docket of examining trials held in justice court and account of fees
thereon, showing number and style of case, name of State attorney, date
complaint filed and by whom, charge, dates warrants and subpoenas issued, dates returnable, and dates executed, date of hearing, and court
order granting and setting amount of bail, discharging defendant, or
committing defendant to jail. Arr. numer. by case no. No index. Hdw.
pr. fm. 280 pp. 16 x 14 x 1. 1 vol., 1903-9, annex va.; 6 vols.,
1912--, j.p. off.; 1 vol., 1928-31, 2d fl. witness rm.

328. JUSTICE PEACE GENERAL FEE BOOK PRECT. 1, Jan. 2, 1931--.
      1 vol. (1).
Justice's account of fees earned in civil and criminal cases in justice
court, showing number and style of case, amount of fees earned, for what
service, date of accrual, amount and date fee received, and justice's
signature. Arr. chron. No index. Hdw. pr. fm. 161 pp. 10 x 14 x 2.

329. (JURORS' TIME BOOK), Jan. term 1891-Jan. term 1907. In
      Jurors Time Book, entry 251.
Record of time served by justice court jurors, showing court term, kind
of jury, name of juror, number of days served, days of week served, number of scrip in which said, and total fees.

                                Inquests

330. INQUEST RECORDS, Feb. 14, 1912--. 3 vols.
Record of inquests held by justice of peace, showing date of inquest,
name and description of deceased person, if known, testimony heard, date,
place, and cause of death, place inquest held, and justice's signature.
Arr. chron. Indexed alph. by first letter of deceased person's surname
and chron. thereunder. Hdw. pr. fm. 82 pp. 16 x 12 x 1.

                            Vital Statistics

331. (MARRIAGE FEES), Aug. 6, 1936--. 1 vol.
Justice of peace account of fees received for marriages performed, showing date, names of parties married, and amount of fees received. Arr.
chron. by recording date. No index. Hdw. pr. fm. 80 pp. 14 x 16 x 1.

332. (BIRTH CERTIFICATES), Sept. 18, 1930--. 1 loose-leaf vol.
Copies of standard State Bureau of Vital Statistics birth certificates issued by justice of the peace as local registrar, showing information as in
entry 139-i. Arr. chron. by recording date. No index. Typed pr. fm. 300
pp. 6 x 8 x 3.

333. (DEATH CERTIFICATES), Aug. 5, 1930--. 1 loose-leaf vol.
Copies of standard State Bureau of Vital Statistics death certificates filed
with justice of peace as local registrar, showing information as in entry
139-ii. Arr. chron. by filing date. No index. Typed pr. fm. 300 pp. 6 x
8 x 3.

Acknowledgments

334. (ACKNOWLEDGMENT RECORD), Mar. 2-Dec. 7, 1917. 1 vol.
Record of instruments notarized by justice of the peace, showing date, number, and kind of instrument, description and location of land, names and
residences of grantor and grantee, names of witnesses, and amount of fees.
Arr. chron. by date of acknowledgment. No index. Hdw. pr. fm. 140 pp.
12 x 14 x 1.

VI. DISTRICT ATTORNEY

The office of district attorney has been provided for by each of the
constitutions of the State. Until the adoption of the present Constitution in 1876, it was required that the office be filled in each judicial
district,[1] but since its adoption, the legislature from time to time has
designated the districts in which district attorneys must be elected.[2]
The 1st judicial district, in which Orange County is situated, is one of
those in which the election of a district attorney is required.[3]

The district attorney serving in Orange County is elected at each
biennial general election by the voters of the 1st judicial district,[4]
which is composed of Orange, Jasper, Newton, Sabine, and San Augustine
Counties.[5] He represents the State in all criminal cases instituted in
the district court[6] and performs many other important duties.[7]

The district attorney keeps no public records in Orange County.

---

1. Const. 1845, art. IV, sec. 12, Gam. Laws, II, 1286; Const. 1866, art.
    IV, sec. 14, Gam. Laws, V, 868; Const. 1869, art. V, sec. 12, Gam.
    Laws, VII, 413.
2. Const. 1876, art. V, sec. 21; Vernon's Texas St. 1936, RCS, arts.
    321, 322.
3. Vernon's Texas St. 1936, RCS, art. 322.
4. Const. 1876, art. V, sec. 21.
5. Vernon's Texas St. 1936, RCS, art. 199, sub. 1.
6. Ibid., CCP, art. 25.
7. Ibid., RCS, arts. 334, 491, 1130, 1377, 3273, 3972, 4549, 4563, 4666,
    4668, 5157, 6380.

VII. COUNTY ATTORNEY

The office of county attorney was first provided for in 1866. Originally, the county attorney was the appointee of the governing court of the county.[1] The office was abolished in 1871,[2] but was reestablished as an elective one in 1876.[3]

In counties like Orange County, that have no criminal district attorney, a county attorney must be elected; he is elected from the county at large at each biennial general election.[4] He represents the State in criminal cases instituted in the county court and other inferior courts within the county[5] and performs other important duties.[6]

The county attorney keeps no public records.

VIII. SHERIFF

A sheriff was among the group of officers composing Orange County's first governmental organization,[7] and the office has had uninterrupted existence ever since.[8] The sheriff is the county's chief conservator of the peace[9] and process officer,[10] the custodian of the jail,[11] and, subject to certain powers of the commissioners court, of the courthouse.[12] He is elected from the county at large for a term of 2 years.[13]

All of the sheriff's records are in his office except as otherwise indicated in the entries.

1. Const. 1866, art. IV, sec. 16, Gam. Laws, V, 868.
2. Acts 1871, Gam. Laws, VI, 937.
3. Const. 1876, art. V, sec. 21.
4. Ibid.
5. Vernon's Texas St. 1936, CCP, art. 26.
6. Ibid., RCS, arts. 334, 491, 1130, 1377, 2333, 2747, 3273, 3654, 3660, 3972, 4549, 4551c, 4666, 4668, 6327, 6716.
7. Const. 1845, art. IV, sec. 13, Gam. Laws, II, 1286; Comr's. Ct. (1852-60), vol. A, p. 1, in Commissioners Court Minutes, see entry 1.
8. Const. 1866, art. IV, sec. 19, Gam. Laws, V, 869; Const. 1869, art. V, sec. 18, Gam. Laws, VII, 414; Const. 1876, art. V, sec. 23.
9. Vernon's Texas St. 1936, CCP, art. 41, and RCS, art. 6876.
10. Ibid., arts. 2022, 2333, 2346, 2400, 2401, 6873.
11. Ibid., art. 6871.
12. Ibid., art. 6872.
13. Const. 1876, art. V, sec. 23.

Service Records

335.   SHERIFF'S GENERAL DOCKET & FEE BOOK, Mar. 28, 1923-Feb. 28,
         1925, Dec. 31, 1930--. 3 vols. (1 vol. unlabeled; 3, 4).
Sheriff's record of process served in civil, probate, and criminal cases,
in all courts, and account of fees earned therein, showing number and
style of case, court of origin, kind of process, signature of court clerk
or justice, date received, and date executed; sheriff's return shows manner of service, signature of sheriff or deputy, and items and amounts of
fees. Arr. chron. by date process received. Indexed alph. by first letter of plaintiff's surname and chron. thereunder. Hdw. pr. hd. 240 pp.
16 x 14 x 2.

336.   SHERIFF'S EXECUTION DOCKET, Jan. 11, 1887-Aug. 2, 1927.
         2 vols. Untitled, Jan. 11, 1887-Feb. 2, 1898, 1 vol.
Sheriff's record of civil executions served for all in- and out-county
courts, and account of fees earned therein, showing number and style of
case, court of origin, nature of writ, name of defendant, name of attorney, amount of judgment, number of execution, date received, date of levy,
date of sale of property, amount received from sale, amounts due clerk,
sheriff, witnesses, and printer, jury tax, date executed, date returned,
manner of execution, net receipts from sale, and remarks. Arr. chron.
by date received. Indexed alph., by first letter of plaintiff's surname
and by first letter of defendant's and chron. thereunder. Hdw. pr. hd.
200 pp. 16 x 12 x 2. 1 vol., 1887-98, c.c. va.; 1 vol., 1897-1927, shff.
off.

337.   WARRANTS OF ARREST, Aug. 19, 1937--. 1 f.d.
Warrants of arrest issued by justices of the peace, showing case number,
court of origin, date issued, title of officer to whom addressed, name
of defendant, offense charged, date of appearance, sheriff's return, and
signatures of justice of peace and sheriff. No obvious arr. No index.
Typed pr. fm. 11 x 5 x 14.

338.   COMMITMENTS, May 1, 1939--. 1 f.d.
Commitments of prisoners convicted in justice court, showing number and
style of case, precinct number, date of judgment, amounts of fine and
costs, length of sentence, and signature of justice of peace. No obvious
arr. No index. Typed pr. fm. 11 x 5 x 14.

339.   NOTICE TO JUROR COUNTY COURT, Jan. 10, 1938--. 8 vols.
Duplicates of notices sent to jurors selected for service in county court,
showing court term, notice number, name of juror, appearance date, and
signature of sheriff. Arr. chron. by date of notice, with notices numbered consecutively. No index. Hdw. pr. fm. 25 pp. 3 x 9 x 1.

340.   NOTICE TO JUROR SPECIAL VENIRE, Sept. 1935--. 14 vols.
Duplicates of notices sent to special veniremen selected service in district court, showing number and style of case, notice number, juror's
name, term of court, date of trial, and signature of sheriff. Arr. chron.
by date of notice, with notices numbered consecutively. No index. Hdw.
pr. fm. 50 pp. 4 x 6 x 1.

341. SHERIFF'S NOTICE TO GRAND JUROR, Feb. 10, 1936--. 19 vols.
Duplicates of notices sent to persons selected as grand jurors, showing
court term, date, number of notice, juror's name and address, date service begins, and signature of sheriff. Arr. chron. by date of notice,
with notices numbered consecutively. No index. Hdw. pr. fm. 25 pp.
3 x 9 x 1.

342. SUBPOENAS NON-RESIDENT FELONY, May 6, 1911---. 2 vols.
Sheriff's copies of district court writs directing sheriff or constable
to summon out-county witnesses in criminal cases to appear at specified
time, made out by sheriff upon receipt of the subpoena from district
clerk, showing information as in entry 235. Arr. chron. No index. Hdw.
pr. fm. 250 pp. 8 x 12 x 3.

343. SUBPOENAS WITNESS BEFORE GRAND JURY, Dec. 18, 1937--. 1 vol.
Sheriff's copies of district court writs directing sheriff or constable
to summon witnesses to appear in criminal investigations before grand
jury, made out by sheriff upon receipt of subpoena from district clerk,
showing information as in entry 233. Arr. chron. by date issued. No
index. 150 pp. 8 x 12 x 1.

Prison Register

344. PRISON REGISTER, May 12, 1908--. 9 vols.
Sheriff's register of prisoners committed to county jail, showing case
number, name, age, address, and personal description of prisoner, nature
of offense, date committed, amount of fine, number of days spent in jail,
date of sentence, date discharged, and condition of discharge. Arr. chron.
by date of commitment. No index. Hdw. pr. hd. 160 pp. 16 x 14 x 2.
8 vols., 1908-39, j.p. off.; 1 vol., 1939--, shff. off.

Accounts

345. RECORD OF FINES, May 4, 1903-Nov. 29, 1924. 2 vols.
Recorded copies of quarterly reports of fines, fees, and other collections, made by sheriff to commissioners court, showing items of information as in entry 36. Arr. chron. by date of report. No index. Hdw.
pr. fm. 165 pp. 16 x 14 x 2.
    For originals, see entry 43.

346. (SHERIFF'S FEE AND EXPENSE RECORD), 1933-36. 1 vol.
Sheriff's itemized accounts of fees collected from justice, county,
and district courts, and other sources, and deductible expenses, as reported in sheriff's annual report to State Auditor, showing year date,
classification of fees (civil, criminal, probate, posting election notices, &c), and amounts due from each class (with numerical list of cases
under each court, giving amounts earned in each case and totals); credits
show items and amounts of deductible expenses (groceries for jail, automobile expense, and stenographer's salary) and total expenses; summarized

statement shows classification of fees, amount due from each class, and
total amount due. Arr. chron. by year and thereunder in sections by
class of fee. No index. Typed. 100 pp. 18 x 8 x 1. Annex va.

347. (VOUCHERS), 1938. 1,000 vouchers in 1 f.d.
Canceled vouchers covering purchases made by sheriff's department, showing voucher number, date and amount of purchase, from whom purchased,
date approved, and date paid. No obvious arr. No index. Hdw. 11 x 5
x 14.

IX. CONSTABLES

Since the organization of Orange County in 1852, the office of constable has had uninterrupted existence.[1] Constables are conservators of
the peace;[2] process officers of all the courts, with authority to serve
civil and criminal process throughout the county;[3] and the attendance
officers of the justice courts.[4]

It is required that each county be divided into at least four justice
precincts and that a constable be elected in each; the maximum number of
precincts and constables permitted is eight. The constable's term of office is 2 years.[5]

348. CONSTABLE'S FEE BOOK, June 8, 1905-Nov. 19, 1908. 1 vol. (1).
Constable's accounts of fees and fines collected in criminal cases in
justice court, showing number and style of case, offense, name of court,
date process received, dates of execution and return, amounts of justice's,
constable's, and county attorney's fees, total fees, and remarks (made
bond, committed to jail, paid to justice, &c). Arr. chron. by date of
service. Indexed alph. by first letter of defendant's surname and chron.
thereunder. Hdw. pr. fm. 132 pp. 14 x 10 x 1. Annex va.

X. TAX ASSESSOR-COLLECTOR

An assessor-collector was one of the group of officers forming Orange
County's first governmental organization.[6] The offices of assessor and

---

1. Const. 1845, art. IV, sec. 13, Gam. Laws, II, 1286; Const. 1866,
   art. IV, sec. 19, Gam. Laws, V, 869; Const. 1869, art. V, sec. 21,
   Gam. Laws, VII, 415; Const. 1876, art. V, sec. 18.
2. Vernon's Texas St. 1936, CCP, arts. 36, 95-103, and RCS, art. 6886.
3. Ibid., arts. 2346, 6885, 6889.
4. Ibid., art. 6885.
5. Const. 1876, art. V, sec. 18.
6. Const. 1845, art. VII, sec. 29, Gam. Laws, II, 1294; Acts 1846, Gam.
   Laws, II, 1653; Comr's. Ct. (1852-60), vol. A, p. 1, in Commissioners
   Court Minutes, see entry 1.

collector were separated in 1869,[7] and in Orange County remained as separate offices until 1934, when they were again combined. Orange County
elected an assessor-collector at the November general election in 1934.[8]
This officer is elected from the county at large and his term of office
is 2 years.[9]

Assessments

Guides

349. ABSTRACT LANDS, 1885--. 6 vols. (2 vols. unlabeled; 3-5; 1
        vol. unlabeled). Untitled, 1898-1911, 1 vol.
Abstracts of lands; page headings show abstract number, number and date
of patent, original grantee or patentee, class and character of certificate, and total acreage; rendition record shows date of rendition, name
of owner, number of acres, and valuation of each tract. Arr. numer. by
abstract no. Indexed alph. by original grantee's surname, 1885-1911; no
index, 1918-30, 1937--; for index 1912-17, 1930-36, see entry 350. Hdw.
pr. hd. 1885-1935; typed pr. hd. 1936--. 500 pp. 18 x 14 x 5. T.a.c. off.

350. (INDEX TO ABSTRACT LANDS), 1912-17, 1930-36. 2 vols.
Index by name of original grantee to Abstract Lands, entry 349, showing
abstract number and page reference. Arr. alph. by first letter of original grantee's surname and chron. thereunder. Hdw. 35 pp. 14 x 8 x 1.
T.a.c. off.

351. ABSTRACT OF LOTS, 1885--. 6 vols. (2 vols. unlabeled; 3-5; 1
        vol. unlabeled).
Abstracts of city lots; page headings show city or town, addition, and
block number; rendition record shows year rendered, name of owner of each
lot, lot number, and valuation. Arr. in separate sections for cities and
additions and numer. thereunder by block nos. For index 1885-1901, 1912-
17, 1930-38, see entry 352; no index, 1901-11, 1918-29, 1939--. Hdw. pr.
hd. Aver. 600 pp. 18 x 14 x 5. T.a.c. off.

352. (INDEX TO ABSTRACT OF LOTS), 1885-1901, 1912-17, 1930-38.
        3 vols.
Index by name of city or addition to Abstract of Lots, 1st unlabeled vol.
and vols. 3-5, entry 351, showing page reference. Arr. alph. by name of
city or addition. Hdw. Aver. 25 pp. 14 x 18 x 1. T.a.c. off.

---

7. Const. 1869, art. XII, sec. 28, Gam. Laws, VII, 424.
8. Record of Election Returns, vol. C, p. 48, see entry 72.
9. Const. 1876, art. VIII, secs. 14, 16.

353. (LISTS OF OIL LEASES & ROYALTY OWNERS), approx. 1940--.
        1 vol.
Record of royalty and working interests on oil leases kept for purpose
of determining valuations for ad valorem taxes (when oil from leases is
sold to pipeline companies or others, the figures are reported to the
State Railroad Commission, who in turn gives them to the State Comptroller,
who forwards them to the assessor-collectors), showing name of operator
of lease, name of lease, total number of barrels produced per quarter, daily average production, value per barrel; list of royalty owners showing
names and addresses, percentage of lease owned by each, daily average number of barrels received by each, total amount of valuation for ad valorem
tax for each owner; grand totals of daily averages and valuations. Arr.
one section for each lease. No index. Typed. 50 pp. 14 x 10 x 1. T.a.c.
off.

354. INFORMATION CHARTS, 1933-39. 6 charts.
Computation tables based on property valuations from $10 to $6,000, in $10
units, based on the tax levy for the year, showing amount of valuation,
amounts of State, county, drainage, and navigation district taxes for each
$10 multiple. Arr. chron. by years. No index. Typed under typed hd. 20
pp. 14 x 18. T.a.c. off.

Inventories

355. TAX INVENTORY, 1926, 1931--. 83 vols. and 1 f.d.
Renditions of real and personal property for taxation by owners or their
agents, showing name and address of owner, year of assessment, description of real estate by number of acres and valuation, itemized list of
personal property with valuation of each item, total value of real estate, total value of personal property, and grand total of all property,
signature of person making rendition, and assessor-collector's attest.
Arr. alph. by owner's name. No index. Hdw. pr. fm. Vols. 150 to 1,000
pp. 16 x 8 x 6; f.d. 12 x 12 x 24. T.a.c. va.

Rolls

356. PHOTOSTATIC COPY FIRST TAX ROLL ORANGE CO. COMPILED 1852
        ASA L. STARK ASSESSOR & COLLECTOR, 1852. 1 vol.
Photostatic copy of first assessment roll of property in Orange County
compiled in 1852 by Worthy Patridge, assessor-collector of Jefferson
County, showing signature of Asa L. Stark acknowledging receipt of rolls,
July 6, 1852, year date, name of Jefferson County assessor-collector,
name of property owner, under heading "real property," number of acres,
valuation, name of original grantee, from what tract taken (2,530, 4,428,
1,476, 640, or 320 acres), class of claim (1st, 2d, 3d), on what stream
(Neches, Cow Bayou, Sabine, Adams Bayou); under heading "town lots,"
name of town, block number, and valuation; under heading "personal property," number of Negroes, horses, cattle, and miscellaneous items, such
as wagons, oxen, schooner, sloop, money at interest, and merchandise on
hand, and valuation of each class of personal property; total valuation
of real and personal property; amount of poll tax; amount of State tax;

and amount of county tax. Arr. alph. by owner's name. No index. Photo-
stat. 7 pp. 16 x 20 x 1. T.a.c. off.

357. (TAX ROLLS), 1884--. 63 vols.
Annual assessment rolls of real and personal property, rendered (form B)
and unrendered (form D), including the property of railroads (form E, also
used for rolling stock and intangible assets), State and National banks
(form G), and all public utilities other than railroads (form H); showing
line number, name and post office address of owner; under heading "real
estate," abstract or lot number, certificate, tract, or block number, survey, division, or outlot, original grantee or city or town; under subhead
"acreage property," number of acres rendered, valuation, and valuation of
that portion designated as homestead; value of city property; value of
personal property; total value of real and personal property for county
tax and total value for State tax; amounts of State, county, road district, and district school taxes, and total amount of property taxes;
amount of State poll tax and of county poll tax; date payment received
and tax receipt number; and page totals for each column. Recapitulation
(form Z) shows tax roll page number, page totals of each page of rolls,
page totals of individual recapitulation sheets, grand total for each
subdivision of rolls, grand totals for all subdivisions, assessor-collector's affidavit that rolls are true and correct; and commissioners court
certificate to approval and examination of rolls and correction of valuations. Rolls bound by years and thereunder sometimes arr. alph. by owner's
name, sometimes in sections in accordance with character of owner as individual or corporation, and thereunder alph. by owner's name. No index.
Hdw. and typed pr. fm. 150 pp. 18 x 24 x 1. 34 vols., 1884-1910, t.a.c.
va.; 29 vols., 1911--, t.a.c. off.
        For county clerk's copies, see entry 407.

358. SUPPLEMENTAL ROLL (Form F), 1902-23. 4 vols. Untitled,
        1919-23, 1 vol. 1925-- in Collectors Copy General State-
        ment, entry 386.
Supplemental assessment rolls (form F), of real and personal property
not assessed on regular rolls, showing items of information as in entry
357. Arr. chron. by years and thereunder alph. by taxpayer's name. No
index. Hdw. pr. fm. 150 pp. 18 x 24 x 2. 3 vols., 1902-23, t.a.c. off.;
1 vol., 1915, annex va.
        For county clerk's copies, see entry 20-i.

                            Collections

Property Tax

359. TAX RECEIPTS, Oct. 11, 1902--. 220 vols. Untitled, Oct. 11,
        1902-17, 1936, 1939--, 115 vols.
Copies of receipts issued upon payment of real and personal property
taxes, showing date and place issued, receipt number, page and line of
tax roll, name and address of person assessed, abstract or lot number,
certificate or block number, survey or division, original grantee or city
or town, number of acres and value, value of personal property, total

valuation, distribution of taxes as to State ad valorem, county road, and
district school taxes; total amount of taxes; and signatures of assessor-
collector and deputy. Arr. numer. by receipt no. No index. Hdw. and
typed pr. fm. Aver. 250 pp. 18 x 14 x 2. T.a.c. va.
       For stubs and other copies, see entries 29, 101.

360. SUPPLEMENTAL TAX RECEIPTS, Oct. 4, 1921--. 29 vols.
Copies of receipts issued upon payment of real and personal property
taxes assessed on supplemental rolls, showing items of information as in
entry 359. Arr. numer. by receipt no. No index. Hdw. pr. fm. 50 pp.
18 x 14 x 1. T.a.c. off.

361. TAX RECEIPTS FIRST HALF 1939, Oct. 24-Nov. 30, 1939. 1 vol.
Copies of receipts issued upon payment of real and personal property
taxes for the first half of year, showing items of information as in
entry 359. Arr. numer by receipt no. No index. Hdw. pr. fm. 100 pp.
18 x 14 x 1. T.a.c. off.

362. TAX RECEIPTS ROAD DIST. NO. 1, 1916-18. 1 vol.
Copies of receipts issued upon payment of real and personal property taxes
for road district 1, showing items of information as in entry 359. Arr.
numer. by receipt no. No index. Hdw. pr. fm. 50 pp. 20 x 14 x 1.
T.a.c. off.

363. (TAX RECEIPTS ROAD DIST. NO. 2), Dec. 22, 1916-Jan. 29, 1919.
              1 vol.
Copies of receipts issued upon payment of real and personal property taxes
for road district 2, showing items of information as in entry 359. Arr.
numer. by receipt no. No index. Hdw. pr. fm. 100 pp. 20 x 14 x 1.
T.a.c. va.

364. TAX RECEIPTS ROAD DISTRICT NO. 3, 1918. 1 vol.
Copies of receipts issued upon payment of real and personal property taxes
for road district 3, showing items of information as in entry 359. Arr.
numer. by receipt no. No index. Hdw. pr. fm. 150 pp. 20 x 14 x 1.
T.a.c. va.

365. TAX RECEIPTS DRAINAGE DISTRICT NO. 1, 1918. 1 vol.
Copies of receipts issued upon payment of real and personal property taxes
for drainage district 1, showing items of information as in entry 359.
Arr. numer. by receipt no. No index. Hdw. pr. fm. 150 pp. 20 x 14 x 1.
T.a.c. va.

366. (RECEIPTS FIRST HALF SCHOOL TAXES), June 29, 1933-Jan. 31,
              1935. 1 vol.
Copies of receipts issued upon payment of real and personal property
school taxes for the first half of year, showing items of information as
in entry 359. Arr. numer. by receipt no. No index. 75 pp. 16 x 14 x 1.
T.a.c. off.

367. (MEMORANDUM RECEIPTS), Feb. 2, 1931--. 5 vols.
Copies of memorandum receipts issued upon payment of real and personal
property taxes to deputy collector sent to Vidor to handle collections in

that precinct, to be kept by taxpayer until issue of regular receipt,
showing date and amount of receipt, name and address of taxpayer, and signature of assessor-collector and deputy. Arr. chron. by date of receipt.
No index. Hdw. pr. fm. 25 pp. 14 x 6 x 1. T.a.c. off.

368. (CLAIMS FOR TAX EXEMPTION), 1932-36. 4 statements loose on
        shelf.
Claims filed for tax exemption on property owned by churches and school
districts, showing name of church or school district, abstract or lot
number, certificate, tract, or block number, survey, division or addition,
original grantee, number of acres and value, value of city property,
reason for exemption, owner's affidavit, and notarization. Arr. chron.
by date of claim. No index. Hdw. pr. fm. 14 x 8. T.a.c. va.

369. CANCELLATION CERTIFICATES, 1901-35. 5 vols. Untitled, 1921-
        25, 1 vol.
Copies of certificates of cancelation of delinquency of land erroneously
reported delinquent, submitted by commissioners court to State Comptroller for approval, showing State and county, Comptroller's and assessor-
collector's certificate numbers, years delinquent, page and line of roll
and of delinquent tax record, in whose name reported delinquent, abstract,
certificate, and survey numbers, original grantee or city or town, number
of acres, lot, block, and addition, total State tax, total county tax,
reason for cancelation, date of commissioners court order for cancelation,
court approval, and clerk's attest. Arr. numer. by certificate no. No
index. Hdw. pr. fm. 150 pp. 14 x 12 x 1. T.a.c. va.

370. REDEMPTION RECEIPTS, Apr. 24, 1899--. 44 vols. Untitled,
        July 3, 1937--, 9 vols.
Copies and stubs of receipts issued by assessor-collector for payments
made in redemption of lands sold or delinquent, showing State, name and
county of assessor-collector, name of person to whom issued, number,
date, and amount of receipt, page and line as shown on form 18, see entry 387, and DTR, see entry 389, name of person assessed, years sold or
delinquent, amounts of taxes, penalty, and interest due State and county;
description of property redeemed; amount of costs; grand total; date and
place of payment, and assessor-collector's signature. Arr. numer. by receipt no. No index. Hdw. pr. fm. Aver. 300 pp. 16 x 12 x 1. T.a.c. va.

371. JUDGMENT RECEIPT, Oct. 6, 1925-Feb. 7, 1928. 2 vols.
Copies of receipts issued by assessor-collector to sheriff for money re-
alized on sale of real property under execution of district court tax
judgments, showing receipt number, name and county of sheriff, name of
person to whom property sold, date of judgment, district court case number, date of sale, page and line of delinquent tax record, name of person
against whom delinquent taxes assessed, years sold or delinquent, amounts
distributed to State ad valorem, poll, interest and penalty, and to county ad valorem, district school, road district, interest and penalty; abstract or lot number, survey or block number, original grantee or city
or town, number of acres, date receipt issued, and assessor-collector's
signature. Arr. numer. by receipt no. No index. Hdw. pr. fm. 100 pp.
12 x 14 x 1. T.a.c. va.

372. TAX STATEMENTS, Apr. 24, 1937--. 1 f.d.
Original and duplicate annual statements of taxes due, showing from whom
due, abstract number, description of property, kinds and amounts of taxes,
and signature of assessor-collector. Arr. alph. by owner's name. No
index. Hdw. pr. fm. 12 x 12 x 24. T.a.c. off.

Poll Tax

373. POLL TAX RECEIPTS, Oct. 1, 1935--. 114 vols. and 24 packages.
Copies of poll tax receipts issued, showing State and county, precinct
number, page and line of tax roll, number and date of receipt, town where
issued, amount of poll tax paid, name and address of taxpayer, age, length
of residence in State, county, and city, whether native-born or naturalized citizen, birthplace, sex, race, and occupation; place receipt issued,
jurat, deputy's and assessor-collector's signatures. Arr. numer. by receipt no. No index. Hdw. pr. fm. Vols. aver. 205 pp. 16 x 14 x 1; packages aver. 200 sheets 4 x 6 x 3. T.a.c. va.
       For other copies, see entry 30.

374. COLORED POLLS, Jan. 15, 1936-Jan. 31, 1939. 4 vols. Title
              varies: Negroes and Negresses, 1938, 1 vol.
Duplicates of poll tax receipts issued to Negroes, showing items of information as in entry 373. Arr. numer. by receipt no. No index. Hdw.
pr. fm. Aver. 200 pp. 16 x 14 x 1. T.a.c. va.

375. POLL TAX EXEMPTIONS, Oct. 24, 1935--. 8 vols.
Copies of certificates issued to persons exempted by law from the payment of poll taxes, showing number and date of certificate, precinct number, name and address of person to whom issued, age, length of residence
in State and county, citizenship, birthplace, sex, race, reason for exemption, and assessor-collector's signature. Arr. numer. by certificate
no. No index. Hdw. pr. fm. 50 pp. 16 x 14 x 1. T.a.c. va.

376. (POLL ORDERS), 1936. 1 package.
Orders issued by taxpayers to assessor-collector for agent named therein
to make affidavit and pay poll tax, showing name of taxpayer, age, race,
birth place, residence, occupation, post office address, whether native-
born or naturalized citizen, date of order, and taxpayer's signature.
No obvious arr. No index. Hdw. and hdw. pr. fm. 300 pp. 6 x 8 x 2.
T.a.c. va.

377. ALPHABETICAL LIST POLL TAXPAYERS, 1918, 1927, 1935, 1937--.
              9 vols. and 1 unbound list. Untitled, 1927, 1935, 1937--, 2
              vols. and 1 list.
Certified lists of voters, prepared annually by assessor-collector from
poll tax receipts and certificates of exemption, showing precinct number,
year date, receipt number, name, post office address, and occupation of
voter, race, age, number of years residence in State and county, whether
native-born or naturalized, and assessor-collector's certification that
list is true and correct. Vols. arr. alph. by voter's name; list arr.

numer. by receipt no. No index. Typed. 20 pp. 16 x 18 x 1. 9
vols., 1918, 1935, 1937--, t.a.c. va.; 1 list, 1927, annex va.

Motor Vehicle Licenses

378. (MOTOR VEHICLE LICENSE RECEIPTS), 1930--. 15 vols., 2 f.d.,
      and 1 package.
Copies of receipts issued upon payment of fees for motor vehicle license
plates, showing, for passenger cars, old and new license numbers, receipt
number, date, weight of car, amount of license fee, year, make, model,
and engine number of car, name of person from whom purchased, name and
address of owner or licensee, and assessor-collector's signature; and
adding, for trucks, commercial vehicles, and trailers, weight empty,
carrying capacity, and gross weight. Arr. numer. by receipt no., with
licenses numbered consecutively. No index. Hdw. pr. fm. T.a.c. off.

379. (BILL OF SALE AND APPLICATION FOR TRANSFER), Oct. 25, 1937--.
      1,400 applications in 1 shelf section and 1 package.
Copies of bills of sale and applications for transfer of title to motor
vehicles, showing State and county, date of transfer, name and address
of purchaser, consideration, license and engine numbers, make, model,
and year of vehicle, full name and address of transferee, vendor's signature, and notarization. Arr. numer. by application no. No index.
Hdw. pr. fm. Section 12 x 14 x 16; package 5 x 8 x 4. 1 section,
1937--, t.a.c. off.; 1 package, 1938, t.a.c. va.

380. (APPLICATIONS FOR REGISTRATIONS), Apr. 4, 1939--. 800 appli-
      cations in 2 packages.
Applications for registration of motor vehicles, showing date of application, kind of vehicle, weight, name, model, year, make, and engine
number of car, name and address of person or firm from whom purchased,
and owner's signature; and, if car not previously registered, vendor's
certificate of sale and delivery of car and authority to sell car under
laws of the State. No arr. No index. Hdw. pr. fm. 12 x 8 x 14.
T.a.c. off.

381. (RECEIPTS FOR APPLICATION FOR TITLE CERTIFICATE), Oct. 2,
      1939--. 11 vols.
Copies of receipts issued as title certificates to owners of motor vehicles upon their application for same, showing county, receipt or certificate number, name and address of owner, amount of fee, make, year, model, license number, serial and motor numbers of vehicle, and assessor-
collector's signature. Arr. chron. by receipt no. No index. Hdw. pr.
fm. 50 pp. 10 x 8 x 1. T.a.c. off.

382. (INDEX TO CAR OWNERS), 1937-38. 2,000 cards in 2 f.d.
      Discontinued.
Card index to owners of motor vehicles registered in the county, used
for reference to automobile license receipts and license numbers, for
making duplicates of lost receipts, or for determining ownership of

stolen or abandoned automobiles, showing name and address of owner, year
date, license number, and make and model of vehicle. Arr. alph. by owner's name. Typed. 5 x 16 x 16. T.a.c. off.

383. DRIVER'S LICENSE, Feb. 25, 1936-Oct. 1, 1937. 3,000 licenses
       in 2 f.d. Discontinued as county record; licenses now issued
       by State Department of Public Safety.
Copies of licenses issued to operators of motor vehicles by assessor-collector for State Department of Public Safety, showing license number,
date issued and expiration date, name and address of person to whom issued, age, sex, height, weight, race, and color of eyes and hair; and
assessor-collector's signature. Arr. alph. by first letter of licensee's
surname, and thereunder chron. by date issued. No index. Hdw. pr. fm.
4 x 6 x 18. T.a.c. off.

Occupation Tax

384. STATE DEPARTMENTS, LIQUOR CONTROL HIGHWAY AND PUBLIC SAFETY,
       Aug. 27, 1931--. 300 papers in 2 f.d. Title varies:
       Highway, Aug. 27, 1931-Dec. 11, 1937, 1 f.d.
Copies of certificates from county judge authorizing issuance of beer and
wine licenses. Also contains: Correspondence between State and county
officials on subjects of liquor control, highways, and public safety. Arr.
by subject matter. No index. Certificates typed pr. fm.; correspondence
typed. 12 x 12 x 24. T.a.c. off.

385. (OCCUPATION TAX COLLECTIONS), Apr. 1, 1925-Sept. 16, 1933. 1 vol.
Ledger account of occupation taxes collected, showing name and address of
licensee, kind of license, date of collection, license number, amount to
State, and amount to county. Arr. alph. by licensee's name, and chron. thereunder. No index. Hdw. pr. hd. 200 pp. 10 x 14 x 3. T.a.c. va.

Reports

386. COLLECTORS COPY GENERAL STATEMENT, 1903-17, 1925--. 18 vols.
Copies of tax reports made annually by assessor-collector to State Comptroller:
       i. Form 16, lists of delinquent or insolvent taxpayers assessed
             on the rolls and advertised and reported, submitted to
             commissioners court and State Comptroller for credit as
             uncollected taxes, showing county, year date of report,
             year, page, and line of roll on which assessed, name of tax-
             payer, amounts of State ad valorem and poll taxes and county
             ad valorem, special, poll, and district taxes, total taxes
             due, and column totals; recapitulation, showing page numbers,
             amounts from each page, and total for year; assessor-collec-
             tor's certificate subscribed to before clerk, with clerk's
             attest; commissioners court certificate that lists have been
             examined in open court and that persons listed have no prop-
             erty "out of which to make the taxes assessed against them

          or have moved from county," and schedule of credits allowed, date of certificate, and clerk's attest.

   ii. Form 17, reports of errors found on tax rolls and of taxes uncollected thereon to be credited against totals charged on tax rolls, showing State and county, name of assessor-collector, year, page, and line of roll where assessment appears, name of owner, abstract or lot number, certificate, tract, or block number, survey, division, or outlot, original grantee or city or town, subdivision or addition, number of acres assessed in error, value of property, State ad valorem and poll taxes, county ad valorem, poll, and district taxes, and character of error (such as, does not own, over age, deceased, homestead, &c) assessor-collector's certificate, commissioners court certificate to examination of report, and clerk's attest. For county clerk's copies, <u>see</u> entry 21.

Also contains: Form F, supplemental rolls, 1925--, entry 358; form 18 reports of delinquents, 1925--, entry 387; form 93, redemptions, 1925--, entry 393. Arr. in sections by form nos. and thereunder alph. by taxpayer's name. No index. Hdw. and typed pr. hd. 100 pp. 16 x 24 x 1. 2 vols., 1903-17, t.a.c. va.; 16 vols., 1925--, t.a.c. off.

     387. DELINQUENT LAND SALES AND LOTS ASSESSED TO STATE (Form 18), 1884-1923. 15 vols. Untitled, 1922, 1923, 1 vol. 1925-- in Collectors Copy General Statement, entry 386.

Copies of annual reports (form 18) to State Comptroller by tax assessor-collector, of lands and lots returned delinquent for year, or reported sold to State, showing county, year, name of assessor-collector, page and line numbers of report, year, page, and line of roll on which assessed, name of owner, abstract or lot number, survey, division, or outlot, original grantee or city or town, subdivision or addition to city or town, number of acres reported sold or delinquent, amounts of State ad valorem and poll taxes, amounts of county ad valorem, poll, road, and school district taxes; and if redeemed, date and number of assessor-collector's redemption receipt, and Comptroller's certificate number; assessor-collector's certificate; and commissioners court certificate of approval. Arr. alph. by owner's name. No index. Hdw. and typed pr. fm. 150 pp. 16 x 14 x 2. 4 vols., 1884-1921, annex va.; 9 vols., 1902-21, t.a.c. va.; 2 vols., 1919-23, t.a.c. off.

   For county clerk's copies, <u>see</u> entry 22.

     388. ORANGE <u>LEADER</u>, 1908, Apr. 24, 1912, Aug. 14, 1924, June 16, 1925, June 15, 1926, June 14, 1927, May 16, 1928, July 3, 1929. 9 vols.

Issues of the daily newspaper containing delinquent tax lists as ordered published by the commissioners court, once a week for 3 weeks. Arr. chron. by publication date. No index. Pr. 100 pp. 18 x 24 x 1. T.a.c. off.

389. DELINQUENT ROLL, 1885-1938. 25 vols.
Cumulative record (form DTR) of lands and lots returned delinquent or reported sold to State and not redeemed for years covered by compilation
(made every 2 years), showing items of information as in entry 387. Arr.
chron. by years and thereunder alph. by owner's name. No index, 1885-
1938, 23 vols.; for index 1885-1912 (to 2 vols.), see entry 390. 250 pp.
18 x 24 x 2. 2 vols., 1885-1912, t.a.c.; 23 vols., 1885-1938, t.a.c. off.
    For county clerk's copies, see entry 23.

390. DELINQUENT TAX RECORD INDEX, 1885-1912. 2 vols. (1, 2).
Index by name of owner to Delinquent Roll (2 vols. in vault), entry 389,
showing name of owner, and page and line reference. Arr. alph. by name
of owner. Hdw. 30 pp. 14 x 8 x 1. T.a.c. va.

391. DELINQUENT TAX FILE, Aug. 14, 1931-Dec. 22, 1936. 30 lists in
        1 f.d.
Lists of delinquent taxpayers compiled by assessor-collector for conven-
ient reference, showing name and address of taxpayer, abstract number, to
whom assessed, kinds and amounts of taxes, and assessor-collector's signature. Arr. alph. by owner's name. No index. Hdw. pr. fm. 12 x 12 x 24.
T.a.c. va.

392. (DELINQUENT TAX NOTICES), 1924--. 16 vols.
Copies of delinquent tax notices, showing date and place issued, name and
address of person to whom mailed, name of person against whom assessment
made, page and line of roll and of delinquent tax record, years sold or
delinquent, amounts of State, county, road district, and district school
taxes, costs, total amount due, description of acreage or city lots; and
recapitulation of taxes due, showing amount of State, county road district, and other district taxes, redemption costs, and grand total; and
assessor-collector's certificate. Arr. alph. by name of owner. No index.
Hdw. pr. fm. 250 pp. 14 x 16 x 2. T.a.c. va.

393. REDEMPTIONS (Form 93), Apr. 20, 1903-23. 4 vols. 1925-- in
        Collectors Copy General Statement, entry 386.
Copies of annual reports of lands and town lots redeemed (form 93) compiled from stubs of redemption receipts, showing county, year of report,
name of assessor-collector, years redeemed, in whose name assessed, by
whom redeemed; abstract or lot number; certificate, tract, or block number; survey, division or outlot; original grantee or city or town, subdivision or addition; number of acres redeemed, State ad valorem and poll
taxes, penalty and interest; county ad valorem; district taxes, penalty
and interest; total State and county taxes, penalty and interest; total
costs; date of redemption, assessor-collector's redemption receipt number, and State Comptroller's certificate number; assessor-collector's
certificate sworn to before county clerk, and clerk's attest; commissioners court certificate to examination of report in open court and approval,
showing year of report, date of approval, schedule of taxes, and clerk's
attest. Arr. chron. by date of report and thereunder chron. by date of
redemption. No index. Hdw. pr. fm. 100 pp. 18 x 24 x 1. T.a.c. off.
    For county clerk's copies, see entry 20-ii.

394. COLLECTORS MONTHLY REPORTS, Dec. 1902--. 37 vols. and 32 un-
        bound reports. Untitled, 1936--, 1 vol. and 32 reports.
Copies of assessor-collector's sworn monthly reports to State Comptroller,
examined and verified by county clerk:

    i. Form 113, State and county taxes collected from regular rolls,
shows current year collections of ad valorem, poll taxes
collected where voting poll tax not issued, penalties, and
interest.

    ii. Form 113C (used Oct.-Jan. only), voting poll tax receipts as-
sessed on tax roll, issued, and collected (separate page for
military poll collections); shows number and date of receipt,
amount paid, name, age, race, occupation, and address of voter.

    iii. Form 113D (used Oct.-Jan. only), voting poll tax receipts as-
sessed, issued, and collected, which were not assessed on tax
rolls, shows information as in subentry ii.

    iv. Form 113E (used Oct.-Jan. only), exemption certificates issued,
shows number and date of certificate, name, age, race, occupation, and address of voter, and reason for exemption.

    v. Form 113F (used Oct.-Jan. only), total number of voting poll
tax receipts and exemptions issued, and amounts of fees due
collector by State and county; also covers alien receipts reported on forms 113G, subentry vi, and 113H, subentry vii.

    vi. Form 113G (used Oct.-Jan. only), alien polls collected from tax
rolls, shows information as in subentry iii.

    vii. Form 113H (used Oct.-Jan. only), alien polls assessed and col-
lected, shows information as in subentry ii.

    viii. Form 114, delinquent taxes collected from insolvent lists, shows
receipt number and date of receipt, name of taxpayer, kinds
and classes of taxes with amounts of each, year for which collected, penalties, interest, and grand total.

    ix. Form 115, redemptions, shows number and date of receipt, name
of person redeeming, kind of taxes with amounts of each,
penalties, interest, and grand total.

    x. Form 116, occupation taxes collected, shows month covered by
report, date, number, and series of receipt, name of person
to whom issued, nature of occupation, term of license and
amount of tax.

    xi. Form 110, State taxes collected and disposition thereof, show-
ing name and county of assessor-collector, month of report,
amount of ad valorem and poll taxes collected from September
1 to end of preceding month, collections for present month,
and total; as debit entries, amounts of collections as shown
on monthly report forms above, and total debits; as credit
entries, disposition - including commissions for collecting,
fees for issuing receipts &c, weekly remittances to State
Treasurer - and total credits; number of voting poll tax receipts and certificates of exemption issued; assessor-collector's affidavit and clerk's attest.

    xii. Form 117, summary of taxes collected during month, shows State
totals and county totals as shown on forms 113-116.

Arr. chron. by date of report. No index. Hdw. and typed pr. fm. Vols.
aver. 200 pp. 18 x 12 x 1. 36 vols., 1902-36, t.a.c. va.; 1 vol. and 32
reports, 1936--, t.a.c. off.
    For county clerk's copies, see entry 27.

395. TAX ASSESSOR-COLLECTORS WEEKLY REPORT, Dec. 11, 1926--. 4
        vols. and 4 packages. Title varies: Highway Summary, Dec.
        11, 1926-Dec. 21, 1936, 1 package; Highway Reports, Mar. 31,
        1930-Dec. 31, 1936, 3 packages; untitled, Feb. 6, 1937--,
        3 vols.
Assessor-collector's copies of reports (form 158) made each Monday to
State Highway Department, of motor vehicle license fee collections for
county road and bridge fund and for State Highway Department, showing
week ending date of report, name of assessor-collector, county license
receipt form numbers, including passenger vehicles (form 1), commercial
(form 2) farm truck (form 2A), motor busses (form 3), &c, number of vehicles of each class, inclusive receipt numbers of each class and amount
received from each, amount due county from each and amount due State; deductions for refunds and assessor-collector's commissions; net remittances
to county and to State Highway Department; assessor-collector's affidavit,
and clerk's attest. Arr. chron. by date of report. No index. Hdw. pr.
fm. 75 to 350 pp. 18 x 12 x 1. 4 packages, 1926-36, t.a.c. va.; 4 vols.,
1936--. T.a.c. off.

                                Accounts

396. RECORD OF FEES, 1929-33. 2 vols. (1, 1). Title varies: Tax
        Collector's General Fee Book, 1929-32, 1 vol. Discontinued.
Tax collector's accounts of fees earned and of office expenses, kept for
the purpose of making annual reports to State Auditor, showing explanation and amount of fee, and total for various services including assessments, collections, issuance of licenses, receipts, and certified copies,
and making highway reports, total fees earned, and fees not collected;
disbursements show amounts paid for postage, deputies' salaries, and various other deductible expenditures. Arr. chron. by date of accrual. No
index. Hdw. pr. hd. 116 pp. 18 x 14 x 1. T.a.c. va.

397. LEDGER (Tax Collector's Accounts), Mar. 31, 1921. 1 vol.
Statement of annual account with county, showing name of fund, total a-
mounts charged against assessor-collector from tax rolls, total debits;
amounts of credits (insolvents, errors, delinquents, commissions), and
total credits. Arr. in sections by funds. No index. 284 pp. 14 x 10 x
2. T.a.c. va.

398. BANK STATEMENTS, June 1930-June 30, 1932, 1939--. 62 state-
        ments in 2 packages and 1 f.d. Title varies: Bank Statements
        Highway Accounts, Jan. 1-Dec. 31, 1931, 1 package.
Bank statements issued by county depository, showing name of account, date
and amount of deposit, date and amount of withdrawal, and balance; with

canceled checks attached. Arr. chron. by date of statement. No index.
Typed pr. fm. F.d. 12 x 12 x 24; package 4 x 10 x 4. T.a.c. va.

Maps

399. ORANGE COUNTY, undated. 1 map.
Ownership map of Orange County, showing county boundaries, original pat-
entees or grantees of tracts of land, number of acres in each tract, abstract numbers, names of tract owners, location of roads, railroads, and
canals. Drawn by Cecil Coale. Pen and ink. 1 inch = 3,000 feet. 48 x
36. T.a.c. off.

400. JEFFERSON COUNTY TEXAS, Oct. 1923. 1 map.
Political map of Jefferson County, showing boundaries, streams, drainage
ditches, irrigation canals, highways, railroads, commissioners' justice,
and voting precincts, and school districts, and names of surveyor and
engineer. Drawn by Geo. W. White. Pen and ink. 1 inch = 2,000 feet.
48 x 48. T.a.c. off.

401. COUNTY OF ORANGE CEMETERY PLOT, Dec. 5, 1932. 1 map.
Ownership map of cemetery plot located on portion of the A. C. Lyons 30-
acre tract of the Anthony Harris survey, showing tract owners, number of
acres, and boundaries. L. F. Daniell, C. E. Black and white. 1 inch =
300 feet. 12 x 10. T.a.c. off.

402. CITY OF ORANGE MAP, June 15, 1931. 1 map.
Ownership map of city of Orange, showing survey number, block and lot
numbers, boundaries of additions, roads, railroads, bayous. C. R.
Goodman, C. E. Pen and ink. 1 inch = 400 feet. 60 x 40. T.a.c. off.

Acknowledgments

403. RECORD OF ACKNOWLEDGMENTS, Oct. 10, 1936--. 1 vol.
Record of instruments notarized by assessor-collector or deputies, showing date, kind of instrument, names and identification of grantor and
grantee, and signature of assessor-collector or deputy. Arr. chron. by
date of acknowledgment. Indexed alph., by first letter of grantor's surname and by first letter of grantee's, and chron. thereunder. Hdw. pr.
fm. 50 pp. 8 x 10 x 1. T.a.c. off.

XI. BOARD OF EQUALIZATION

Since 1876 the commissioners court has served ex officio as a board of tax equalization in Texas counties.[1] For the purpose of equalizing the valuations of taxable property the court sits as a board in May of each year. At this time it examines the assessment rolls to "see that every person has rendered his property at a fair market value" and, when necessary, revalues assessed property. The assessor-collector and the taxpayers are given opportunity to be heard and present evidence as to values.[2] The assessor-collector may not proceed with the collection of taxes until the rolls have been equalized and approved by the board.[3]

All of the records of this board are in the county clerk's vault unless otherwise indicated in the entries.

404. MINUTES BOARD OF EQUALIZATION, June 29, 1909---. 7 vols. (A-G). 1883-1908 in Commissioners Court Minutes, entry 1. Minutes of commissioners court sitting as a board of equalization to determine the value of property assessed for taxes, showing court term, names of members present, name of property owner, abstract or certificate number, number of acres, original grantee, lot or block number; assessed value, value increased or decreased, final valuation, owner's post office address, date notified, and names of board members not concurring. Arr. chron. by date of meeting and thereunder alph. by name of property owner. No index. Hdw. pr. hd. 350 pp. 18 x 14 x 2.

405. MINUTES OF OATHS BOARD OF EQUALIZATION, May 10, 1937---. 1 vol. Recorded copies of oaths of office taken by members of the commissioners court upon assuming duties as members of the board of equalization, showing State and county, name of member, obligations, date of oath, certification of county clerk, and filing date; and special oaths made by assessor-collector that he will inspect all taxable property, make true assessment and valuation, and submit report to the board. Arr. chron. by filing date. No index. Typed. 160 pp. 18 x 14 x 1.

406. EQUALIZATION PROTESTS, Oct. 9, 1938---. 10 letters in 1 f.d. Correspondence from property owners objecting to the valuation to which their property was raised by the board of equalization, showing date, brief description of property, value at which rendered, value to which raised, reason for protest, and property owner's signature. Arr. chron. by filing date. No index. Typed. 11 x 5 x 14.

---

1. Const. 1876, art. VIII, sec. 18.
2. Vernon's Texas St. 1936, RCS, art. 7206.
3. Ibid., arts. 7219, 7253.

407. CO. CLERK'S COPY TAX ROLL, Mar. 11, 1899-1901, 1903--. 48
            vols. Title varies slightly.
Copies of annual assessment rolls of real and personal property, filed
with the county clerk for the inspection of the public until withdrawn
for the next assessment, showing information as in entry 357. Rolls
bound by years and thereunder sometimes arr. alph. by owner's name, sometimes in sections in accordance with character of owner as individual or
corporation, and thereunder alph. by owner's name. No index. Hdw. and
typed pr. fm. 150 pp. 18 x 24 x 2. 43 vols., 1899-1901, 1903-35, annex
va.; 5 vols., 1935--, c.c. va.

408. NAVIGATION TAX ROLL 1922, 1909-13, 1922. 5 vols.
Copies of annual assessment rolls of real and personal property for navigation district, showing items of information as in entry 357. Arr. alph.
by taxpayer's name. No index. Typed pr. fm. 150 pp. 18 x 24 x 2. Annex va.

XII. COUNTY TREASURER

The office of county treasurer has been an elective one since 1850;[1]
prior to that time the treasurer was the appointee of the governing
court.[2] A treasurer was among the officers chosen at the election for
the organization of Orange County in 1852.[3]

The treasurer is elected at each biennial general election by the
qualified voters of the county.[4] He receives and disburses county funds
under the directions of the commissioners court.[5]

Accounts

General

409. CASH RECEIPTS AND DISBURSEMENTS BOOK, Feb. 1878-Dec. 22, 1892,
            1894-1921, 1938--. 16 vols. Title varies: County Treasurers
            Cash Book, 1878-82, 1890-92, 1 vol.; Co. Treas. Account Book,
            1883-92, 1 vol.; Treasurer's Account Book, 1894-1912, 4 vols.;
            untitled, Nov. 1, 1910-Jan. 31, 1913, Jan. 31, 1916-Nov. 30,
            1920, 1938, 4 vols.; Available Road Fund, 1921, 1 vol.; Treas-
            urer's Record, 1939, 1 vol.
Debit and credit accounts of all county funds, showing name of fund, date
of entry, name of person making deposit or receiving payment, warrant

---

1. Acts 1850, Gam. Laws, III, 521; and see Collins et al. v. Tracy, 36
        Tex. 546 (1872).
2. Acts 1840, Gam. Laws, II, 200.
3. Comr's. Ct. (1852-60), vol. A, pp. 12, 15, in Commissioners Court
        Minutes, see entry 1.
4. Const. 1876, art. XVI, sec. 44; Vernon's Texas St. 1936, RCS, art.
        1703.
5. Ibid., art. 1709.

number if disbursement, total amount received and distribution thereof as
to taxes, fees, and licenses; total disbursement and distribution as to
salaries, election expenses, repairs, &c; total receipts; and total disbursements. Also contains: Accounts with permanent and available school
funds, 1890-92, entry 416. Arr. chron. by date of receipt, 1878-92, 1894-
1912; arr. one section for each fund and thereunder chron. by date of entry, 1913-21, 1938--. Indexed alph. by name of fund, 1878-92, 1894-1913,
1916-20; no index, 1913-19, 1921, 1938--. Hdw. pr. hd. 135 to 225 pp.
14 x 8 x 1 to 16 x 14 x 2. 6 vols., 1878-92, 1894-1912, annex va.; 1
vol., 1910-13, bsmt.; 4 vols., 1913-19, 1921, 2d fl. witness rm.; 2 vols.,
1916-20, c.c. va.; 3 vols., 1938--, treas. off.

410. (RECONCILEMENTS), Dec. 1, 1934--. 1 vol.
Monthly reconcilements of accounts, kept to check balances, showing a-
mounts on hand as per bank statements to credit of each fund, total deposits for all funds, total amount of floating drafts, and proof balances;
and list of floating drafts, showing warrant number, amount, and name of
fund chargeable. Arr. chron. by months. No index. Hdw. pr. fm. 200
pp. 12 x 12 x 2. Treas. off.

411. (SINKING FUND ACCOUNTS), June 30, 1922-Apr. 10, 1934. 1 vol.
        1939-- in Outstanding Bonds Sinking Fund Bonds Sinking Fund
        Cash, entry 425.
Debit and credit accounts of sinking funds to retire county bond issues,
showing name, date, and amount of bond issue and rate of interest; as
debits, dates and amounts of taxes collected, and interest paid by county
depository; as credits, date and amount of payment; and cash balance on
hand. Arr. in separate sections for each bond issue and thereunder chron.
by date of entry. No index. Hdw. pr. hd. 500 pp. 14 x 10 x 4. 2d fl.
witness rm.

Road & Bridge

412. AVAILABLE ROAD FUND, 1915-21. 3 vols. (1 vol. unlabeled; 1,
        1).
Debit and credit accounts of county road and bridge fund, showing, as
debits, date and amount of receipt, from whom received, on what account,
and total debits; as credits, date and amount of disbursement, to whom
paid, by what authority, voucher number, and total credits; and balances.
No obvious arr. No index. Hdw. pr. hd. 16 x 14 x 3. 2 vols., 1915-21,
2d fl. witness rm.; 1 vol., 1919, c.c. va.

413. AVAILABLE ROAD FUND (Special Projects), 1919-21. 1 vol.
Debit and credit accounts with county road projects 1, 2, 4, 6-9, 11-13,
financed by available road fund, showing amount of cash on hand, amount
received from sale of bonds by road bond districts, amount expended to
retire old bonds and other expenses incidental to bond issue, amounts
transferred to road and bridge fund, other expenditures of project, date
and number of warrant, purpose of payment, and project number. Arr.
numer. by warrant no. No index. Hdw. pr. hd. 252 dbl. pp. (40 used)
18 x 18 x 2. 2d fl. witness rm.

414. (Road and Bridge) PROJECT (Expenditures), 1920. 6 vols. (la-
          beled by contained project nos.).
Accounts of expenditures by county road projects 6-8, 11-13, from available road fund, showing project number, name of road, warrant number, a-
mount and purpose of expenditure, and page totals. Arr. numer. by warrant number, amount and purpose of expenditure, and page totals. Arr.
numer. by warrant no. No index. Hdw. pr. hd. 150 dbl. pp. (aver. 25
used) 16 x 14 x 2. 2d fl. witness rm.

415. (SPECIAL ROAD FUND EXPENDITURES), Apr. 1, 1912-Jan. 31, 1913.
          1 vol.
Temporary accounts of expenditures from special road and bridge fund,
showing class of expenditure (advertising, lumber, culverts, surveying,
machinery, and supplies), date, number, and amount of voucher, and total
expenditures. Arr. in sections by class of expenditure and thereunder
chron. by date of voucher. Indexed alph. by first letter of first word
of class of expenditure. Hdw. 137 pp. 16 x 8 x 1. 2d fl. witness rm.

School

416. CO. TREASURER'S RECORD BOOK SCHOOL FUND, 1882-1909. 6 vols.
          1890-92 in Cash Receipts and Disbursements Book, entry 409.
Accounts with available and permanent school funds, 1882-88, 1892-1906,
showing name of fund; as debits, date, source, and amount of receipt,
and total debits; as credits, date, item, and amount of disbursement to
school district, and total credits. Also contains:
   i. Accounts with school districts, 1892-1909, and with school
           communities, 1882-93, 1906-9, showing district or communi-
           ty number; as debits, date, amount, and source of receipt,
           and total debits; as credits, date, item, and amount of
           expenditure, and total credits.
   ii. Paid school vouchers, register of, 1893-98, showing registra-
           tion date, voucher number, to whom issued, on what account,
           for what month, to whom paid, school district number, amount
           paid, and date of payment.
Arr. in sections (fund, district or community, and voucher) and thereunder chron. by date of entry. Indexed alph. by first letter in name of
fund or community and chron. thereunder, 1882-93, 1 vol.; no index, 1887-
1909, 5 vols. Hdw. pr. hd. 151 to 300 pp. 10 x 9 x 2 to 20 x 14 x 2.
4 vols., 1882-98, annex va.; 1 vol., 1894-1906, c.c. va.; 1 vol., 1906-9,
bsmt.

Conservation & Reclamation

417. (CONSERVATION AND RECLAMATION DISTRICT BOND ACCOUNT), Dec. 30,
          1931-Dec. 28, 1937. 1 vol.
Account of tax money received for payment on principal and interest of
conservation and reclamation district bonds, showing date, source, and
amount of receipt, and total debits; date, purpose, and amount of payment,
and total credits; and cash balances. No obvious arr. No index. Hdw.
279 pp. 14 x 8 x 2. Treas. off.

418.   CONSERVATION & RECLAMATION BOND & SINKING FUND, Dec. 1931--.
          1 f.d.
Miscellaneous papers relative to conservation and reclamation district
bonds and sinking funds, including bank statements, canceled bonds, coupons, and vouchers. Arr. chron. by filing date. No index. Typed pr. fm.
12 x 12 x 24. Treas. off.

Claims

419.   (TREASURER'S CLAIM REGISTER), Dec. 6, 1886-Dec. 31, 1887.
          1 vol.
Register of claims against the county, showing claim number, date of registration, classification of claim, name of payee, date and amount of
claim, by what authority issued, for what purpose, date of payment, and
remarks. Arr. numer. by claim no. Indexed alph. by name of claimant.
Hdw. pr. hd. 240 pp. 16 x 14 x 4. Bsmt.

420.   BILL BOOK, Jan. 13, 1936--. 2 vols.
Lists of claims against the county allowed and ordered paid by commissioners court, compiled by county clerk from orders in Commissioners
Court Minutes, entry 1, and used by treasurer in issuing warrants, showing date allowed, claim number, name of claimant, name of fund chargeable,
and amount allowed. Arr. chron. by date allowed, with claims numbered
consecutively. No index. Hdw. 150 pp. 12 x 8 x 1. Treas. off.

421.   UNPAID BILLS R & B (Commissioners' Precincts) #1, 2, 3, & 4,
          Jan. 1, 1939--. 75 bills in 1 f.d.
Invoices of materials and supplies presented as claims against the county,
showing county, name of creditor, date, invoice number, and articles purchased with price of each; also, lists of laborers, showing number of days
worked, amount of wages due. Arr. numer. by precinct no. No index. Typed
pr. fm. 12 x 12 x 24. Treas. off.

422.   SCHOOL FUND REGISTER, Oct. 3, 1887-Aug. 31, 1893. 1 vol. (1).
Register of claims against school communities paid by county treasurer,
showing claim number, date of registration, name of payee, for what service, date of claim, by whom registered, community number, date of payment,
amount of claim, and to whom paid. Arr. chron. by registration date. No
index. Hdw. pr. hd. 159 pp. 14 x 10 x 2. Annex va.

Warrants

423.   TREASURER'S WARRANT RECORD, Jan. 5. 1898-Feb. 12, 1904, Oct.
          1, 1921--. 7 vols. (2 vols. unlabeled; 3-5; 2 vols. unlabeled).
Register of county warrants issued, showing date, number, and amount of
warrant, name of payee, for what purpose issued, and on what fund drawn.
Arr. numer. by warrant no. No index. Hdw. pr. hd. 240 to 500 pp. 12 x
18 x 3 to 16 x 24 x 3. 1 vol., 1898-1904, annex va.; 2 vols., 1921-29,
1932-35, 2d fl. witness rm.; 4 vols., 1929-32, 1935--, treas. off.

424. (PAID WARRANTS), 1919--. 187 f.d. and 16 vols.
Original and duplicate county warrants (the caneled original being filed
with treasurer's duplicate when returned from county depository), showing
number, date and amount of warrant, name of payee, name of fund from
which paid, list material or labor covered by warrant with amount for
each item, and signatures of county judge, county clerk or deputy, treasurer, payee, and other endorsers. All warrants issued in payment for labor are accompanied by original time sheet, showing name of employee,
days worked, rate per day, total amount due, and signature of county commissioner. Arr. numer. by warrant no. No index. Hdw. and typed pr. fm.
F.d 11 x 5 x 14 to 12 x 12 x 24; vols. 600 pp. 8 x 10 x 6. 165 f.d.,
1919-32, and 16 vols., 1921-25, bsmt.; 21 f.d., 1932-39, 2d fl. witness
rm.; 1 f.d., 1940--, treas. off.

Bond Issues

425. OUTSTANDING BONDS SINKING FUND BONDS SINKING FUND CASH, June
      12, 1902-Mar. 1, 1913, Aug. 15, 1917-Apr. 15, 1924, Jan. 1,
      1939--. 5 vols. (1, 2; 3 vols. unlabeled).
Register of bonds and time warrants issued against the faith and credit
of the county; 1902-13, 1917-24 shows number of bond, date issued, date
due, coupon number, amount of bond, rate of interest, amount received
from sale of bond, to whom paid, amount of coupon, for what purpose bond
issued, date caneled, where payable, date registered, and to whom sold;
1939-- shows name, denomination, and inclusive serial numbers, rate of
interest, dates of annual or semi-annual interest payments, where payable,
reference to volume and page of recording in Commissioners Court Minutes,
entry 1, percentage of State participation in principal and interest,
bond or warrant serial numbers, total amount of annual principal and interest for each bond, due dates and dates of payment by treasurer, a-
mounts outstanding at end of year, and numerical list of coupons giving
coupon number and date of payment. Also contains: Debit and credit accounts of sinking funds to retire county bond issues, 1939--, entry 411.
Arr. in separate sections for each bond issue. No index. Hdw. pr. hd.
450 to 585 pp. 16 x 12 x 3 to 18 x 12 x 4. 4 vols., 1902-13, 1917-24,
bsmt.; 1 vol., 1939--, treas. off.

426. (BONDS OWNED BY COUNTY), Apr. 10, 1903-Aug. 1, 1939. 2 vols.
Register of bonds owned by county or by county funds, showing name of
bond, date issued, date due, from whom purchased, denomination, by whom
issued, name of county fund owning bond, date purchased, serial number,
maturity date, and dates and amounts of coupons. Arr. one page for each
class of bond. No index. Hdw. pr. hd. 200 pp. 14 x 16 x 2. 2d fl.
witness rm.

Reports

427. ANNUAL BOND REPORT, June 13, 1890-May 15, 1919. 1 vol.
Copies of treasurer's annual reports to commissioners court of outstanding bonded indebtedness of the county, showing kind of bond or warrant,
date issued, amount of indebtedness, rate of interest, maturity date,

rate of tax levy, tax levy in force for sinking fund, amounts to credit
of sinking fund and interest, amount of receipts and disbursements, from
and to what source, amount of bonds redeemed since last report, amount
outstanding, clerk's certificate, and signatures of county clerk and treasurer. Arr. by date of report. No index. Hdw. pr. hd. 20 pp. 24 x 18 x
1. Bsmt.

428. (SPECIAL AUDITOR'S REPORTS), 1926-39. 6 reports in 1 f.d.
Copies of special auditor's reports on Orange County courthouse and office building at Vidor used by county commissioner and justice of peace,
on road funds, sinking funds, outstanding bonded indebtedness, &c. No
obvious arr. No index. Typed. 12 x 12 x 24. Treas. off.

Exhibits

429. TREASURER'S RECEIPTS, Aug. 5, 1911-Oct. 1, 1914, Nov. 6, 1919-
          Nov. 30, 1920, May 28, 1925--. 55 vols. and 4 packages.
Stubs and duplicates of receipts issued to county officers by county
treasurer for money deposited, and of receipts issued for money received
in payment of county bonds, showing number, date, and amount of receipt,
name of fund and amount deposited for it, total amount of deposits, name
of depositor, date of deposit, and signature of treasurer. Arr. numer.
by receipt no. No index. Hdw. pr. fm. 40 to 750 pp. 8 x 8 x 1 to 8 x
10 x 4. 2 vols., 1911-14, 1919-20, c.c. va.; 30 vols., 1925-32, bsmt.;
23 vols., 1932--, 2d fl. witness rm.

430. CONSERVATION & RECLAMATION DISTRICT RECEIPTS, Dec. 22, 1933--.
          4 vols. Title varies: Navigation Bond, Dec. 22, 1933-Dec.
          30, 1936, 1 vol.; Navigation Book Receipts, Jan. 14-Mar. 6,
          1937, 1 vol.; Receipt Book General Fund, Sept. 18, 1937-Sept.
          14, 1939, 1 vol.
Duplicates of receipts issued by treasurer to tax collector upon deposit
of tax money from navigation, and conservation and reclamation districts,
from sale of bonds, and other sources, also, duplicates of receipts issued to county depository for interest on money on deposit, showing date,
number, and amount of receipt, to whom issued, nature of payment, to which
fund debited, and signature of treasurer. Arr. numer. by receipt no. No
index. Hdw. pr. fm. 50 pp. 14 x 6 x 1. Treas. off.

431. DUPLICATE DEPOSIT TICKETS, Sept. 5, 1923-Nov. 17, 1938.
          30 vols.
Duplicates of bank deposit slips issued to treasurer by county depository, showing name and address of bank, name of depositor, date deposited, deposit slip number, amounts of cash and checks, total deposits,
and initials of bank teller. Arr. chron. by date of deposit. No index.
Hdw. pr. fm. 50 pp. 8 x 4 x 1. 18 vols., 1923-38, treas. off.; 12 vols.,
1929-32, bsmt.

432. CHECK STUBS, Feb. 23, 1932--. 2 vols.
Stubs of checks drawn by treasurer against navigation bond account, Feb.
23, 1932--, and against conservation & reclamation general fund, Jan. 4,

1939--, showing name of depository, number, date, and amount of check, to whom issued, and district to which charged. Arr. numer. by check no. No index. Hdw. pr. fm. Torn, faded. 50 pp. 10 x 14 x 1. Treas. off.

433. BANK STATEMENTS (& Lists of Warrants), Mar. 1-Aug. 28, 1924, Aug. 31, 1932-Jan. 31, 1933, Jan. 1, 1937--. 4 f.d.

Bank statements and lists of general fund warrants. Statements show name of bank, name of account or fund, date, balance brought forward, date and amount of deposits, date and amount of withdrawals, number of checks, and new balance; lists of general fund warrants show, date, number, and amount of warrant, name of payee, and remarks. Statements arr. chron. by date issued; warrant lists arr. chron. by date paid. No index. Statements typed pr. hd.; lists typed. 11 x 5 x 14. 1 f.d., 1924, 1932-33, bsmt.; 3 f.d., 1937--, treas. off.

434. NAVIGATION BANK STATEMENTS (and Commissioners Court Orders), Mar. 31, 1927-Feb. 19, 1932. 60 bank statements and 7 orders in 1 f.d.

Bank statements of navigation funds on deposit issued by county depository, showing name and address of bank, name of fund, date of account, checks listed in detail, balance brought forward, date and amount of deposit, date and amount of new balance, number of vouchers returned, and amount and to whom paid. Also contains: Copies of commissioners court orders approving treasurer's quarterly reports, showing name and address of treasurer, date of court term, amount of receipts and disbursements in various funds, balances, date of order, date filed, and signatures of county judge and commissioners (for original orders, see entry 15-iii). Arr. chron. by date of statement or order. No index. Hdw. and typed pr. fm. 11 x 5 x 14. Bsmt.

XIII. COUNTY AUDITOR

In Orange County the office of county auditor was discontinued May 30, 1925,[1] but was reestablished December 1, 1940, when an auditor was appointed.[2] The auditor not only examines and audits the books and accounts of such county, district, and State officers as handle county funds,[3] but also prescribes the system of accounting used by the county,[4] assists in the preparation of budgets, and performs other acts essential in the orderly planning of county expenditures.[5] The auditor of Orange County is

---

1. Minutes District Court, vol. O, p. 84, in Civil Minutes Dist. Court, see entry 187.
2. Information obtained from County Judge, Orange County, Feb. 1941.
3. Vernon's Texas St. 1936, RCS, art., 1651.
4. Ibid., art. 1656.
5. Ibid., arts. 689a-9, 1652-1655, 1657-1666.

the appointee of the judge of the 1st judicial district, in which the
county is situate, and his term of office is 2 years.[6]

Since the field work on the inventory was done while the office of
county auditor was vacant, no current records are shown. All of the records shown are in the county clerk's vault except as otherwise indicated
in the entries.

435. (AUDITOR'S ACCOUNT OF DISBURSEMENTS), Oct. 17, 1919-Apr. 11,
1921. 1 vol.
Accounts of disbursements from county funds, including road district,
building, jury, general, road and bridge, sinking, and tick eradication
funds, showing name of fund, number and date of warrant, purpose and a-
mount of payment, and total disbursements. Arr. in sections by funds
and thereunder chron. by date of warrant. No index. Hdw. 150 pp. 14 x
18 x 2.

436. (PAID CLAIMS), Nov. 17, 1917-June 4, 1921. 2 vols.
Register of claims against county paid, showing date of entry, name of
claimant, purpose and amount of disbursement, name of fund from which
paid, and claim number and amount. Arr. chron. by registration date.
No index. Hdw. 112 pp. 16 x 14 x 1.

437. AUDITORS WARRANT REGISTER, Jan. 1, 1923-Apr. 28, 1924. 1 vol.
Register of county warrants issued, showing date, warrant number, to
whom paid, explanation of expenditure, and on which fund drawn. Arr.
numer. by warrant number. No index. Typed. 640 pp. 18 x 14 x 4. 2d
fl. witness rm.

438. LEDGER (General), Apr. 30-July 31, 1916. 1 vol.
Accounts of quarterly payments made by county officers to various county
funds, showing name and title of officer, name of fund, date of entry,
months covered by payment, and total for quarter. Arr. one official to
each page and thereunder chron. by date of entry. Indexed alph. by first
letter of official's surname and chron. thereunder. Hdw. 180 pp. 16 x
10 x 1.

6. Vernon's Texas St. 1936, RCS, arts. 1646, 1647.

XIV. COUNTY BOARD OF SCHOOL TRUSTEES

In 1845 management of the county schools became the responsibility of the county governing court,[1] and so remained until it passed to a separate board of school directors in 1873.[2] The board of directors was abolished in 1876, and from that time until 1911 duties involved in the supervision of county schools were divided between the county judge and the commissioners court.[3]

The present central board of school trustees was created in 1911.[4] The board is a corporate body[5] and has general control of the schools of the county.[6] There are five county school trustees, one elected from the county at large and the other four from their respective commissioners' precincts; their term of office is 2 years.[7] The county school superintendent is secretary of the board.[8]

439. MINUTES OF COUNTY SCHOOL BOARD, Oct. 8, 1917--. 2 vols. (1, 2). Minutes of meetings of the county board of school trustees, showing date of meeting, names of members present, nature of business transacted, determinative orders, president's approval, and secretary's attest. Arr. chron. by date of meeting. No index. Typed. 600 pp. 14 x 12 x 4. S.s. off.

XV. COUNTY SCHOOL SUPERINTENDENT

The office of county school superintendent was first provided for in 1873; the president of the board of school directors served ex officio as superintendent.[9] When the board was abolished in 1876 the county judge became ex-officio school superintendent.[10] By an act of 1887 the commissioners courts were authorized to provide for the election of a full-time school superintendent when they might deem it advisable,[11] and

---

1. Acts 1845, Gam. Laws, II, 1156, transferring powers conferred by Acts 1840, Gam. Laws, II, 320; Acts 1854, Gam. Laws, III, 1461; Acts 1866, Gam. Laws, V, 1088.
2. Acts 1873, Gam. Laws, VII, 540.
3. Acts 1876, Gam. Laws, VIII, 1035; Revised Statutes of Texas, 1895, RCS, arts. 3929a, 3930, 3938, 3938a; Revised Civil Statutes of the State of Texas, 1911, arts. 2763, 2815, 2827, 2837.
4. Acts 1911, 32d Leg., p. 34.
5. Vernon's Texas St. 1936, RCS, art. 2683.
6. Ibid., arts. 2676, 2681, 2741.
7. Ibid., art. 2676.
8. Ibid., art. 2681.
9. Acts 1873, Gam. Laws, VII, 540.
10. Acts 1876, Gam. Laws, VIII, 1035.
11. Acts 1887, Gam. Laws, IX, 924.

since 1907 each county having a scholastic population of 3,000 or more
has been required to elect a full-time superintendent.[12]

Orange County elected its first full-time superintendent at the general election of November 7, 1916.[13] The superintendent is elected from
the county at large for a term of 4 years.[14]

440. (SCHOOL ACCOUNTS), 1904-15, 1927--.   5 vols.
Accounts with school districts, showing name and number of district, inclusive dates, net number of scholastics including transfers to and from
other districts, assessed property valuation, tax rate for local maintenance, local tax collectible, amount of rural aid granted district, net
amount due, current State available fund, amount due local maintenance
fund, amount due transfers (independent, county-line, and common districts, and other counties), total State and county available fund, date
received, date of voucher, voucher number, from what source, to whom
payable, and date paid, State and county available fund (debit, credit,
and balance); local maintenance fund (debit, credit, and balance); and
rural aid fund (debit, credit, and balance). Arr. numer. by school district no. and thereunder chron. by date of entry. No index. Hdw. pr. hd.
600 pp. 16 x 24 x 4. 1 vol., 1904-15, bsmt.; 4 vols., 1927--, s.s. off.

441. BUDGETS ORANGE COUNTY SCHOOL, 1932--.   100 budgets in 1 f.d.
Budgets of common school districts, made by county school superintendent
as budget officer, showing information as in entry 8. Arr. alph. by
first letter of name of school district and thereunder chron. by date of
budget. No index. Hdw. pr. fm. 12 x 12 x 24. S.s. off.

442. CONSOLIDATED CENSUS ROLLS & APPLICATIONS FOR TRANSFER, 1931--.
        1,000 papers in 2 f.d.
Applications for transfers of school pupils, showing names and numbers of
districts involved, name of child, age, grade, sex, reason for transfer,
county, certificate of parents or guardian, date of application, and date
of approval by county school superintendent. Also contains: Census
rolls, entry 443. Applications arr. chron. by date of transfer; rolls
arr. by school districts and thereunder alph. by surname of child. No
index. Typed pr. fm. 1931-38; hdw. pr. fm. 1936--. 11 x 5 x 14 to
12 x 12 x 24. 1 f.d., 1931-38, c.c. va.; 1 f.d., 1936--, s.s. off.

443. SCHOLASTIC CENSUS ROLL, 1920--. 2 vols. 1931-- also in
        Consolidated Census Rolls & Applications for Transfer, entry
        442.
Consolidated census rolls, showing year of census, name, age, sex, and
address of child, district number, and name of person rendering child;
accompanied by summarization of census rolls and census of defective

12. Acts 1907, 30th Leg., p. 210; Vernon's Texas St. 1936, RCS, art. 2688.
13. Record of Election Returns, vol. B, p. 22, see entry 72.
14. Vernon's Texas St. 1936, RCS, arts. 2688, 2688a.

children not eligible for census. Arr. by school districts and thereunder alph. by child's surname. No index. Typed pr. fm. 600 pp. 14 x 12 x 2. S.s. off.

444. FAMILY CENSUS BLANKS, 1931--. 10,000 blanks in 20 bdls. Family census forms, showing whether common or independent district, district number, name, birthplace, age, sex, and defects of child, name of county in which family resided on first day of April preceding census, length of residence of family in district, name and nativity of each parent, signature and address of person rendering child, and date subscribed and sworn to before census trustee. Arr. numer. by district no. and thereunder alph. by first letter of parents' surname. No index. Hdw. pr. fm. 6 x 10 x 4. S.s. off.

445. ANNUAL TEXT BOOK REPORT AND REQUISITION, 1938--. 500 papers in 1 f.d.
Common school district head teachers' annual reports on textbooks needed, and requisitions for free State textbooks made by county school superintendent (one copy retained by superintendent and one sent to State textbook division), showing title of book, grade in which used, number of books on hand and their condition, enrollment, number of books needed, school district name and number, and signature of county school superintendent. Arr. alph. by first letter of name of school district and chron. thereunder. No index. Hdw. pr. fm. 12 x 12 x 24. S.s. off.

446. CO. SUPT. TERM REPORTS & TERM REPORTS TO CO. SUPT., 1931--. 300 reports in 1 f.d.
Contains:
    i.   Principals' reports to county school superintendent at the end of each school term, showing list of pupils enrolled, giving age, sex, and grade of each; distribution of boys and girls as to subjects taken; training of teacher; value of school property; and principal's signature.
   ii.   Teachers' and superintendents' reports made monthly to State Superintendent of Public Instruction, showing name and number of school district, date of report, amount of teacher's salary, number of days taught during month, number of pupils entering school, number of losses, total membership, aggregate attendance, aggregate absence, aggregate days of membership, average daily attendance, percentage of attendance, number of times tardy, number of pupils between ages of 6 and 17 and number between 7 and 15; name and residence of teacher, filing date of report, amount of voucher in payment of salary, name of fund on which drawn, and county school superintendent's signature.
Arr. alph. by first letter of name of school district and chron. thereunder. No index. Typed pr. fm. 12 x 12 x 24. S.s. off.

(447)

XVI. COUNTY HEALTH OFFICER

The county health officer, first provided for in 1909,[1] is the appointee of the commissioners court and is appointed for a term of 2 years.[2] Besides duties discharged in caring for county prisoners and indigents, and in connection with county quarantines, he performs many others required of him from time to time by the commissioners court, other officers of the county, and by the rules and regulations of the State health authorities.[3]

The county health officer keeps no public records.

XVII. COUNTY SURVEYOR

The office of county surveyor was created in 1837,[4] and was made elective in 1840.[5] The surveyor is elected from the county at large at each biennial general election.[6] He is the official land surveyor of the county.[7] He plays an important part in establishing boundaries,[8] including county boundaries,[9] and in the laying out of roads and highways.[10] His records are often essential in the deraignment of land titles.[11]

The surveyor's records are in the county clerk's vault.

447. SURVEYOR'S RECORD OF APPLICATION, Apr. 3, 1855---. 3 vols. (A-C).
Title varies: Surveyors Record of Certificates, Apr. 3, 1855-
Feb. 19, 1901, 1934, 1 vol.
Recorded copies of applications for surveys, applications for purchase or lease from State of mineral rights on public school lands, and applications to prospect for oil and gas on public lands, showing county, date of application, filing date, name and address of applicant, description of land, applicant's signature, notarization, and county surveyor's recording certificate. First applications are by persons owning land certificates issued by boards of land commissioners. Also contains: Surveyor's field notes, 1922--, entry 448. Arr. chron. by date of application. Indexed alph. by first letter

1. Acts 1909, 31st Leg., 1st C.S., p. 340.
2. Vernon's Texas St. 1936, RCS, art. 4423.
3. Ibid., art. 4427.
4. Acts 1837, Gam. Laws, I, 1406.
5. Acts 1840, Gam. Laws, II, 437.
6. Const. 1876, art. XVI, sec. 44; Vernon's Texas St. 1936, RCS, art. 5283.
7. Ibid., arts. 5277, 5280, 5290, 5291, 5293, 6706.
8. Ibid., arts. 5290, 5291.
9. Ibid., art. 5293.
10. Ibid., art. 6706.
11. Ibid., arts. 5277, 5280.

of applicant's surname and chron. thereunder. Hdw. pr. hd. 1855-1901, 1934; hdw. 1901--. Faded and torn, 1855-1901, 1934, 1 vol. 251 pp. 18 x 14 x 2.

448. SURVEYOR'S RECORD OF SUBDIVISIONS, 1838-1934. 3 vols. (A, A, B). Title varies: Surveyor's Field Notes, 1838-1922, 1 vol. 1922-- also in Surveyor's Record of Application, entry 447. Recorded copies of field notes of land surveys (those prior to 1852 made in other counties), showing name of applicant for survey, survey number, number of acres, reference to authority under which survey made (certificate of board of land commissioners, scrip from General Land Office, &c), location of land with reference to miles distant from county seat, description of boundaries of survey, date of survey, and signatures of chain carriers and surveyor. First volume A, containing field notes of surveys made 1838-1922, appears to be a transcription although no date of transcription or recording is shown. Arr. chron. by date of survey. Indexed alph. by first letter of name of survey and chron. thereunder. Hdw. pr. fm. 1838-1922, 1 vol.; hdw. 1854-1934, 2 vols. 295 pp. 18 x 14 x 2.

449. APPLICATIONS AND AFFIDAVITS FOR PRE-EMPTION, Feb. 9, 1891-Dec. 3, 1897. 1 vol. (A). Recorded copies of applications for public land claimed by actual settlers under preemption law, showing reference to act, name of applicant, metes and bounds of tract applied for, statement of facts upon which claim is based, applicant's signature; applicant's affidavit attested by county clerk; and county surveyor's recording certificate. Arr. chron. by date of application. Indexed alph. by first letter of applicant's surname and chron. thereunder. Hdw. pr. fm. Faded. 214 pp. 18 x 14 x 1.

450. RAILROAD AND SCHOOL LAND SURVEYS, Sept. 19, 1871-Feb. 11, 1901. 1 vol. (A). Recorded copies of field notes of surveys of land owned by railroads and by owners or purchasers of public school lands, showing county, survey number, location and description of land, date of survey, field notes, and signatures of surveyor and chain carriers. Arr. chron. by date of survey. Indexed alph. by first letter of name of survey and chron. thereunder. Hdw. Torn and faded. 136 pp. 18 x 14 x 2.

XVIII. BOARD OF LAND COMMISSIONERS (Defunct)

At the time of the organization of Orange County, the chief justice of the county, the two associate justices, and the county clerk were the members of a board of land commissioners, whose duty it was to investigate claims to lands from the public domain and pass upon their validity, and to issue land certificates in certain cases.[1] These boards continued to function until 1856, when they were finally abolished.[2]

---

1. Acts 1839, Gam. Laws, II, 112.
2. Acts 1853, Gam. Laws, III, 1324; Acts 1854, Gam. Laws, III, 1563.

451.   (ACTUAL SETTLERS' CERTIFICATES), 1854-61. In Record Embalm-
          er's (&C), entry 154.
Copies of certificates issued to actual settlers by county officers (chief
justice, county clerk, justice of peace, county judge) to prove preemption
claims with Commissioner of the General Land Office, as provided by act
of Feb. 13, 1854 (see Gam. Laws, III, 1550), showing date and number of
certificate, State and county, name of claimant, recital of fact that
claimant and two witnesses have made personal appearance before officer
and taken oath to claimant's being a bona fide settler, to his residence
upon and cultivation of the land for 3 years, and to required residence in
State, sometimes name and title of surveyor and date of survey, and officer's
attest.

452.   (UNCONDITIONAL HEADRIGHT CERTIFICATES), Feb. 1, 1853-Aug. 21,
          1857. In (Occupation Tax Register), entry 143.
Register of unconditional headright certificates issued by county court,
showing unconditional certificate number, name of grantee, number and
date of conditional certificate and name of county from which issued,
number of acres granted, names of witnesses making affidavits in proof
of applicant's residence and citizenship, and date unconditional headright certificate issued.

XIX. CORONER (Defunct)

From the time of the organization of Orange County in 1852 until
1869, the office of coroner was a separate office. It was the coroner's
duty to hold inquests in such cases of violent and sudden deaths in the
county as came to his knowledge. When there was a vacancy in the office
of sheriff, or when the sheriff was disqualified to act in a particular
case, the coroner could perform all the duties of sheriff.[1]

The office of coroner as a separate office was discontinued in
1869, when the justices of the peace became ex-officio coroners.[2]

---

1. Acts 1846, Gam. Laws, II, 1664.
2. Const. 1869, art. V, sec. 20, Gam. Laws, VII, 415; Acts 1870, Gam.
    Laws, VI, 278.

BIBLIOGRAPHY

Primary Sources

Bolton, Herbert Eugene, Athanase de Mezieres and the Louisiana-Texas Frontier, 1768-1780. Cleveland, The Arthur H. Clark Company, 1914. 2 vols.

"Boundary - United States and Mexico," Register of Debates in Congress, vol. XIV (1837), pt. 2, pp. 125-151.

Constitutions of Texas
    State, 1845, in H. P. N. Gammel, Laws of Texas, II, 1277-1302. Austin, The Gammel Book Company, 1898.
    State, 1866, in H. P. N. Gammel, Laws of Texas, V, 857-886. Austin, The Gammel Book Company, 1898.
    State, 1869, in H. P. N. Gammel, Laws of Texas, VII, 393-430. Austin, The Gammel Book Company, 1898.
    State, 1876, with amendments to date, in Vernon's Annotated Constitution of the State of Texas. Kansas City Mo., Vernon Law Book Company, 1927--. 2 pts.

Corps of Engineers, U. S. Army, The Ports of Port Arthur, Sabine, Beaumont, and Orange, Texas. Port Series No. 14, Washington, Government Printing Office, 1925. 247 pp.

Dallam, James Wilmer, comp., Opinions of the Supreme Court of Texas from 1840 to 1844 Inclusive. St. Louis, The Gilbert Book Company, 1881. 742 pp.

Gammel, H. P. N., Laws of Texas. Austin, The Gammel Book Company, 1898. 10 vols.

Hodge, Frederick Webb, Handbook of American Indians North of Mexico. Washington, Government Printing Office, 1907, 1910. 2 pts.

Jefferson County, Minutes Commissioners Court. County Clerk's office, courthouse, Beaumont.

Olmsted, Frederick Law, A Journey Through Texas. New York, Dix, Edwards & Co., 1857. 516 pp.

Texas Department of Agriculture, Insurance, Statistics, and History, Agricultural Bureau, Texas Agricultural and Statistical Report, 1888. Austin, 1889. 318 pp.

Texas Department of Agriculture, Insurance, Statistics, and History, Agricultural Bureau, Texas Agricultural and Statistical Report, 1890. Austin, 1891. 402 pp.

Bibliography

Texas General Land Office, Map of Orange County. November 1921.

U. S. Department of Commerce, Sixteenth Census of the United States,
    1940, Reports on Agriculture, Texas. Washington, Government Print-
    ing Office, 1941. 173 pp.

U. S. Geological Survey Map, Orange Quadrangle, 1926.

Vernon's Texas Statutes, Centennial Edition, 1936, and 1939 Supplement.
    Kansas City, Mo., Vernon Law Book Company, 1936, 1940. 2,576 and
    1,382 pp.

War of the Rebellion, Official Records of the Union and Confederate
    Armies. Washington, Government Printing Office, 1880-1901. 72 vols.

Winkler, E. W., ed., Journal of the Secession Convention of Texas, 1861.
    Austin, Austin Printing Company, 1912. 470 pp.

Secondary Sources

Bolton, Herbert Eugene, Texas in the Middle Eighteenth Century. Berkeley,
    Calif., University of California Press, 1915. 498 pp.

Burns, A. F., "Bob Johnson Family, Which Furnished 2 Sheriff's (sic) for
    Orange County, Came Here in Early '20's of 18th (sic) Century,"
    Orange (Tex.) Leader, May 29, 1936.

Burns, A. F., "First Train Is Brought Here in Early 70's," Orange (Tex.)
    Leader, May 29, 1936.

Burns, A. F., "Mr. and Mrs. J. C. Turner Believed To Be Oldest Native
    Born Couple Now Residing in Orange County," Orange (Tex.) Leader,
    May 29, 1936.

Burns, A. F., "News Items in First Copy of Orange Daily Tribune Give
    Interesting Facts about Early History of Town," Orange (Tex.)
    Leader, May 29, 1936.

Burns, A. F., "Oldest Church in County Is Near McLewis," Orange (Tex.)
    Leader, May 29, 1936.

Burns, A. F., "Tuning of Piano in Orange in Early 70's Resulted in Es-
    tablishment of Lumber Manufacturing Industry," Orange (Tex.)
    Leader, May 29, 1936.

"Court Held in Masonic Hall Here in 1852," Orange (Tex.) Leader, Aug.
    30, 1940.

De Cordova, Jacob, Texas: Her Resources and her Public Men. Philadel-
    phia, E. Crozet, 1858. 371 pp.

Dexter, W. W., ed., The Coast Country of Texas. Southern Pacific Passenger Department, Orange, 1903. 160 pp.

"First Public School Established in Orange in 1872," Orange (Tex.) Leader, May 29, 1936.

Fortier, Alcee, A History of Louisiana. New York, Manzi, Joyant and Company, 1904. 4 vols.

Fulmore, Z. T., The History and Geography of Texas as Told in County Names. Austin, The Steck Company, 1935. 312 pp.

Henderson, Mary Virginia, "Minor Empresario Contracts for the Colonization of Texas, 1825-1834," Southwestern Historical Quarterly, XXXI (1927-28), 295-324.

Hill, Ethel Osborn, "The Wonderland of the Sabine District," East Texas, IV (May 1930), 11-39.

"John Harmon Is First White Man to Obtain Land Grant in County," Orange (Tex.) Leader, Aug. 30, 1940.

Johnson, Frank W., and Eugene C. Barker, A History of Texas and Texans. Chicago, The American Historical Society, 1914. 5 vols.

"Life Story of W. H. Stark Is History of East Texas," Orange (Tex.) Leader, May 29, 1936.

"Local Masonic Lodge Organized in 1853 When Town Was Known as Madison; Membership Totals 192," Orange (Tex.) Leader, May 29, 1936.

"Presbyterians Organize Church Here in 1878," Orange (Tex.) Leader, May 29, 1936.

"Local Methodist Program Dates Back to 1877," Orange (Tex.) Leader, May 29, 1936.

Massengill, Fred I., Texas Towns. Terrell, Tex., Aug. 1, 1936. 224 pp.

"Memories of Old Timers Drawn Upon for Old Records," Longview (Tex.) Daily News, May 31, 1936.

"Municipal Levee Protects City from Sabine Overflow," Orange (Tex.) Leader, May 29, 1936.

"Names of Persons Living in Orange County Area in 1836 Are Found in Various Land Transaction Records," Orange (Tex.) Leader, May 29, 1936.

Orange (Tex.) Chamber of Commerce, Orange County, Where the Best Comes From. Orange, Chamber of Commerce, n. d., 20 pp.

Bibliography

"Orange County Dedicates New Courthouse," County Progress, XV (Feb. 1938), 7, 8.

"Orange County Schools Make Splendid Progress," Orange (Tex.) Leader, May 29, 1936.

"Orangefield Has Fully Accredited High School," Orange (Tex.) Leader, May 29, 1936.

Potts, Charles S., Railroad Transportation in Texas. Austin, The University of Texas, Bulletin No. 19, 1909. 214 pp.

"The Pride and Joy of Orange, Texas, Is the Wonderful Girls' School Band," Life, IX (Oct. 14, 1940), 48-50.

Russell, R. E., "History of Orange Written in 1911 Tells of Early Days," Orange (Tex.) Leader, Aug. 30, 1940.

"Saw Mill Industry Plays Major Part in Texas History," Orange (Tex.) Leader, May 29, 1936.

"School for Negroes Formed Here in 1870," Orange (Tex.) Leader, May 29, 1936.

Swinford Jerome, "A. Gilmer Pioneer in Early Saw Mill History," Orange (Tex.) Leader, May 29, 1936.

The Texas Almanac for 1857. Galveston, Richardson & Co., 1856. 159 pp.

The Texas Almanac for 1936. Dallas, A. H. Belo Corporation, 1936. 510 pp.

The Texas Almanac for 1939-40. Dallas, A. H. Belo Corporation. 512 pp.

The Texas Almanac for 1941-42. Dallas, A. H. Belo Corporation, 1940. 576 pp.

Tomlinson, Lillie Mae, "The Japanese Colony in Orange County," Texas History Teachers' Bulletin, XIV (1927), 141-145.

Woodhead, Ben S., "Orange Bengal Guards To Appear at Fat Stock Show," Houston (Tex.) Post, Feb. 2, 1941.

Wortham, Louis J., A History of Texas from Wilderness to Commonwealth. Fort Worth, Wortham-Molyneaux Company, 1924. 5 vols.

WPA Writer's' Program, comp., Beaumont. Houston, Anson Jones Press. 167 pp. (American Guide Series).

CHRONOLOGICAL INDEX

(All numbers refer to entries. A record entry number is listed
under each decade which the record covers in full or in part.
An entry number is underlined to call attention to the initial
appearance of the record; the last listing of the entry number
indicates the decade within which the record ends.)

1831-40
    448

1841-50
    164, 448

1851-60
    1, 3, 6, 47, 72, 88, 93, 94, 98, 99, 106, 108, 123, 129, 130, 134,
    135, 143, 154, 157, 172, 185, 187, 188, 214, 220, 259, 264, 266,
    267, 271, 272, 324, 356, 447, 448, 451, 452

1861-70
    1, 3, 13, 15, 37, 43, 47, 68, 72, 86, 88, 93, 94, 98, 99, 106, 108,
    123, 129, 130, 134, 135, 145, 154, 157, 172, 185, 187, 188, 191, 214,
    220, 259, 263, 264, 265, 266, 267, 271, 272, 278, 283, 284, 289, 295,
    324, 447, 448, 451.

1871-80
    3, 9, 13, 15, 37, 40, 43, 46, 47, 60, 61, 64, 68, 76-78, 86, 88, 93,
    94, 98, 99, 106, 108, 123, 126, 129, 130, 134, 135, 145, 146, 154,
    157, 172, 185, 186, 187, 188, 191, 214, 220, 251, 256, 259, 262,
    263-267, 268, 271, 272, 284, 295, 298, 324, 325, 409, 447, 448, 450

1881-90
    1, 3, 9, 13, 15, 22, 23, 37, 40, 43, 46, 47, 62, 63, 64, 68, 72, 73,
    81, 93, 94, 98, 99, 100, 108, 114, 115, 123, 126, 129, 130, 134, 135,
    144, 146, 154, 157, 164, 172, 183, 185-188, 189, 191, 214, 222, 243,
    251, 259, 264-268, 269, 271, 272, 278, 284, 286, 287, 289, 293, 298,
    318, 323, 336, 349, 351, 352, 357, 387, 389, 390, 409, 416, 419, 422,
    427, 447, 448, 450

1891-1900
    1, 2, 3, 9, 13, 14, 15, 22, 23, 36, 37, 38, 39, 40, 41, 42, 43, 45,
    46, 47, 48, 58, 62-64, 66, 68, 72, 73, 82, 87, 93, 94, 97, 98-100,
    106, 107, 108, 110-112, 114, 115, 119, 121, 122, 123, 125, 126, 130,
    133, 134, 135, 136, 146, 147-149, 154, 157, 159, 164, 172, 181, 183,
    185-189, 191, 194, 201, 206, 214, 219, 220, 222, 225, 230, 234, 237,
    243, 244, 251, 259, 262, 266-269, 271, 272, 273, 278, 281, 284, 289,
    297, 298, 304, 305, 312, 318, 323, 329, 336, 349, 351, 352, 357, 370,
    387, 389, 390, 407, 409, 416, 422, 423, 427, 447, 448, 449, 450

Chronological Index

1901-10

1-3, 9, <u>10</u>, <u>12</u>, 13-15, <u>16</u>, <u>18</u>, <u>21</u>, 22, 23, <u>24-27</u>, <u>29</u>, <u>31</u>, <u>35</u>, 36-43,
45, 48, <u>50</u>, <u>51</u>, 58, 62-64, <u>65</u>, 66, 68, <u>71</u>, 72, 73, <u>75</u>, 82, <u>83</u>, 87,
93, 94, <u>96</u>, 98-100, 106-108, 110-112, 114, 115, <u>116</u>, 119, 121-123,
<u>124</u>, 125, 126, 130, 133-136, <u>137</u>, <u>138</u>, <u>142</u>, 146, 148, 149, 154, 157,
159, <u>160</u>, 164, <u>170</u>, 172, <u>178</u>, 181, 183, 185-189, 191, 194, <u>200</u>, 201,
<u>202</u>, 206, <u>212</u>, 214, <u>218</u>, 219, 220, 225, <u>229</u>, 230, 237, <u>240</u>, 243, 244,
251, <u>252</u>, <u>254</u>, 259, 262, 266-268, 271-273, 278, 281, <u>282</u>, 284, 286,
<u>288</u>, 289, <u>290-292</u>, 293, <u>294</u>, 295, 297, 298, <u>300</u>, 304, 305, <u>307</u>, <u>309</u>,
312, <u>313</u>, <u>314</u>, 318, 323-325, <u>327</u>, 329, 336, <u>344</u>, <u>345</u>, <u>348</u>, 349, 351,
352, 357, <u>358</u>, <u>359</u>, 369, 370, <u>386</u>, 387, <u>388</u>, 389, 390, <u>393</u>, <u>394</u>, <u>404</u>,
407, <u>408</u>, 409, 416, 423, <u>425</u>, <u>426</u>, 427, <u>440</u>, 447, 448, 450

1911-20

1-3, 9, 10, 12-16, <u>17</u>, 18, 21-27, 29, <u>30</u>, 31, 35-43, <u>44</u>, 45, 48, <u>49</u>,
50, 51, <u>52-54</u>, 58, 62-66, <u>67</u>, 68, <u>69</u>, 71-73, <u>74</u>, <u>79</u>, <u>80</u>, 82, <u>85</u>, 87,
<u>91</u>, <u>92</u>, 93, 94, <u>95</u>, 96, 98, 100, <u>101</u>, <u>102</u>, <u>104</u>, <u>105</u>, 106, <u>108</u>, <u>109</u>,
110, 111, <u>113</u>, 114-116, 119, <u>120</u>, 121-126, <u>127</u>, <u>128</u>, 130, 133-138,
146, 148, 149, <u>150</u>, <u>151</u>, 154, 157, 159, 160, <u>161</u>, <u>163</u>, 164, <u>166</u>, <u>167</u>,
<u>169</u>, 170, <u>171</u>, 172, 178, <u>180</u>, 183, 185-189, <u>190</u>, 191, 194, 200-202,
<u>205</u>, 206, <u>207</u>, <u>209</u>, <u>211</u>, 214, 220, 225, 230, 234, <u>235</u>, <u>239</u>, 240, <u>242</u>,
244, <u>246</u>, <u>249</u>, 251, 254, 259, 266-268, <u>270</u>, 271-273, <u>274</u>, <u>275</u>, 278,
<u>280</u>, 281, 282, 284, 287, 289-292, 294, 295, 297, 298, <u>301-303</u>, 304,
<u>306</u>, 307, <u>308</u>, 309, <u>310</u>, <u>311</u>, 312, 314, 318, 323-325, <u>326</u>, 327, <u>330</u>,
<u>334</u>, 336, <u>342</u>, 344, 345, 349, <u>350</u>, 351, 352, 357-359, <u>362-365</u>, 369,
370, <u>377</u>, 386-390, 393, 394, 404, 407-409, <u>412-415</u>, 424, 425-427, <u>429</u>,
<u>435</u>, <u>436</u>, <u>438</u>, <u>439</u>, 440, <u>443</u>, 447, 448

1921-30

1-3, <u>11</u>, 12, 13, 15, 17, <u>19</u>, <u>20</u>, 21-24, 27, 29-31, 36, 37, 41, 44,
45, 50, 51, 53, 54, <u>56</u>, <u>57</u>, 58, 64, 67, 68, <u>70</u>, 72-74, 79, 82, <u>84</u>, 87,
91-94, 96, 98, 100-102, <u>103</u>, 104-106, 108-111, 113-116, <u>118</u>, 119-126,
128, 130, <u>131</u>, <u>132</u>, 133-138, <u>139-141</u>, 151, <u>152</u>, <u>153</u>, 154, <u>155</u>, <u>156</u>,
157, <u>158</u>, 159-161, 163, 164, <u>165</u>, 166, 167, <u>168</u>, 171, 172, <u>174</u>, <u>176</u>,
178, 180, <u>182</u>, 183, <u>184</u>, 185-191, <u>193</u>, 194, <u>197</u>, 200-202, <u>203</u>, <u>204</u>,
206, 207, <u>208</u>, 209, <u>210</u>, 211, <u>213</u>, 214, <u>217</u>, 218-220, 225, <u>228</u>, 229,
230, 234, 235, 239, <u>241</u>, 242, <u>244</u>, 246, <u>247</u>, 249, 251, 254, 259, 262,
266-268, 270-273, 275, <u>276</u>, 278, 280-282, 284, <u>285</u>, 287, 289-291,
294, 295, 297, 298, 302, 303, 306-312, 318, <u>319</u>, 323-325, 327, 330,
<u>332</u>, <u>333</u>, <u>335</u>, 336, 342, 344, 345, 349-352, <u>355</u>, 357-359, <u>360</u>, 369,
370, <u>371</u>, 377, <u>378</u>, <u>385</u>, 386-389, <u>392</u>, 393, 394, <u>395-398</u>, <u>400</u>, 404,
407-409, 411, 412, 413, 423-426, <u>428</u>, 429, <u>431</u>, <u>433</u>, <u>434</u>, 435, 436,
<u>437</u>, 439, 440, 443, 447, 448

1931-40

1-3, <u>4</u>, <u>5</u>, <u>7</u>, <u>8</u>, 12, 15, 17, 19, 20, 23, 26, 27, <u>28</u>, 29-31, <u>32-34</u>,
36-42, 45, 48, 50, <u>55</u>, 56-58, <u>59</u>, 72, 79, 87, <u>89</u>, <u>90</u>, 91-94, 100-106,
108, 114-116, <u>117</u>, 118-121, 123-126, 128, 130-135, 137-141, 151, 152,
154-161, <u>162</u>, 163, 165-167, 171, 172, <u>173</u>, 174, <u>175</u>, 176, <u>177</u>, 178,

SUBJECT INDEX

(Underscored figures refer to pages; others refer to entries)